Inclusive Literacy Lessons for Early Childhood
by Pam Schiller and Clarissa Willis

Dedication

To preschool teachers everywhere who stand up for every child's right to develop to his or her full potential on a timetable that is uniquely his or her own.

—Pam Schiller

To my mother, Jessie Clarice Hightower, who taught me both literacy lessons and life lessons.

—Clarissa Willis

Acknowledgments

Special thanks to Dr. Rebecca T. Isbell, Director of the Center of Excellence at ETSU, for her suport and encouragement throughtout this project; Sheila P. Smith, my ETSU inhouse editor; Brandy Sullivan and Leigh Perrine, my research assisstants; Michael Talley for his wonderful photographs of children; and all the children and families at the ETSU Child Study Center who graciously allowed their children to be photographed.

—Clarissa Willis

Additional Gryphon House Books Written by Pam Schiller:

And the Cow Jumped over the Moon!, with Thomas Moore

The Complete Book of Activities, Games, Stories, Props, Recipes, and Dances for Young Children, with Jackie Silberg

The Complete Book of Rhymes, Songs, Poems, Fingerplays, and Chants, with Jackie Silberg

The Complete Daily Curriculum, with Pat Phipps

The Complete Resource Book, with Kay Hastings

The Complete Resource Book for Infants

The Complete Resource Book for Toddlers and Twos

Count on Math, with Lynne Peterson

Creating Readers

Do You Know the Muffin Man?, with Thomas Moore

The Instant Curriculum, Revised, with Joan Rossano

The Infant/Toddler Photo Activity Library

The Practical Guide to Quality Child Care, with Patricia Carter Dyke

Start Smart

Starting with Stories, with Pat Phipps

The Theme Series, with Richele Bartkowiak and Patrick Brennan
  Bountiful Earth
  Bugs, Bugs, Bugs
  Critters and Company
  Fabulous Food
  Honk, Honk, Rattle, Rattle
  Me, My Family and Friends
  School Days
  Wild, Wild West

The Values Book, with Tamera Bryant

Where is Thumbkin?, with Thomas Moore

Additional Gryphon House Books by Clarissa Willis:

Teaching Young Children with Autism Spectrum Disorder

GH10357
A Gryphon House Book

Pam Schiller and Clarissa Willis

Early Childhood Education

Inclusive
LITERACY LESSONS
For Early Childhood

Illustrations: Kathy Ferrell

Gryphon House, Inc.
Beltsville, Maryland

Bulk purchase

Gryphon House books are available for special premiums and sales promotions as well as for fund-raising use. Special editions or book excerpts also can be created to specification. For details, contact the Director of Marketing at Gryphon House.

Disclaimer

Gryphon House, Inc. and the authors cannot be held responsible for damage, mishap, or injury incurred during the use of or because of activities in this book. Appropriate and reasonable caution and adult supervision of children involved in activities and corresponding to the age and capability of each child involved, is recommended at all times. Do not leave children unattended at any time. Observe safety and caution at all times.

Every effort has been made to locate copyright and permission information.

Published by Gryphon House, Inc.
PO Box 207, Beltsville, MD 20705
301.595.9500; 301.595.0051 (fax); 800.638.0928 (toll-free)

Visit us on the web at www.gryphonhouse.com

Library of Congress Cataloging-in-Publication Data

Schiller, Pam.
  Inclusive literacy lessons for early childhood / Pam Schiller and Clarissa Willis ; illustrations, Kathy Ferrell.
    p. cm.
  Includes indexes.
  ISBN 978-0-87659-299-1
  1. Language arts (Early childhood)--Activity programs. 2. Early childhood
education--Activity programs. I. Willis, Clarissa. II. Title.
  LB1139.5.L35S352 2008
  372.6--dc22

                              2007038745

 Gryphon House is a member of the Green Press Initiative, a nonprofit program dedicated to supporting publishers in their efforts to reduce their use of fiber-sourced forests. This book is printed on paper using 30% post-consumer waste. For further information, visit www.greenpressinitiative.org.

Table of Contents

Introduction

Inclusive Literacy Lessons for Early Childhood is a collection of 100 lessons designed to introduce, develop, and help children practice literacy skills and concepts. The lessons also include adaptations for children with special needs and for second language learners.

Inclusive Literacy Lessons for Early Childhood is divided into six chapters, each focusing on a different literacy element: listening, oral language, phonological awareness, letter knowledge, print awareness, and comprehension. These categories provide a full scope of literacy skills.

In the past decade, accountability expectations for preschool teachers have become an issue of great concern and debate. The emergence of neurological research several decades ago changed educational expectations drastically and with it the expectations for learning in the preschool classroom. Now, both preschool children and their teachers face greater expectations from families, public school administrators, and the federal government.

This means that preschool teachers must now be clear about the framework of their curriculum and the value of their classroom activities. Best practice in early childhood classrooms has always provided learning experiences for young children. It is now important to organize those experiences and activities and be intentional in the delivery.

The six basic literacy-building skills and concepts in this book are widely accepted among early educators and supported by reading readiness research as the foundation for ensuring that all children will be successful when formal reading instruction begins.

The purpose of *Inclusive Literacy Lessons for Early Childhood* is to provide a guide for content and presentation of literacy lessons for a variety of learners. Use the lessons for a while and you will soon be creating lessons of your own. Intention and purpose are the order of the day. It's not difficult—it's just a matter of practice.

How Literacy Develops

Children develop literacy skills in much the same way they develop speaking skills. Babies arrive without the ability to communicate anything other than their own discomfort through crying. After a few short weeks of listening intently, babies begin to babble and coo. This is the beginning of word formation. They will continue to play with the sounds of language as the babble and coo in a pattern—you talk, they listen, they babble and coo and then stop and wait for you to talk again. Already they begin to understand that communication is a two-part process. Around six months, babies begin to put the babble sounds together to form syllables, *ma-ma-ma-ma* and *da-da-da-da*. By the end of the first year, those syllables become babies' first words, which are often *mama, dada,* and *bye-bye.* At this point, babies begin to use language in a meaningful way. They say, "Mama" with hands stretched out to their mothers. They say, "Dada" when their daddies walk into the room.

During the second year, oral language really grows. By the time a baby reaches 18 months of age he or she has a vocabulary of over 200 words, if the baby has been exposed to someone who talks with him or her freely. If the baby is not exposed to someone who talks to him or her, the baby will have 181 fewer words than his peer who did have the exposure.

During the second and third years of life, toddlers begin to put words together to make short sentences and will grow in their understanding of how language is used. They will still make mistakes with the placement of "s" and the changing of verb tenses.

It is not unusual to hear toddlers say, "Look at all the peoples" or "He goed to the store."

Basically, speaking begins with listening and playing with language, which is followed by the development of oral language (vocabulary and syntax). The mastering of vocabulary and sentence structure promotes comprehension (the ability to put things in one's own words). Literacy also begins with listening (developing attention span and learning to pay attention to details) and playing with language (rhyme, alliteration, segmentation, and onomatopoeia). As children develop and practice their listening skills and explore the sounds of language (rhyme, alliteration, segmentation, and onomatopoeia), they continue to build their vocabularies. A sizeable vocabulary enhances their comprehension. The more words children have in their "tool boxes," the simpler the task of retelling stories in their own words.

When children are able to comprehend a story, it is the perfect time to begin more formal literacy instruction, such as letter knowledge and print awareness.

Listening

Listening is the foundation for all literacy development: Until children are able to listen, they cannot develop vocabulary or build comprehension.

Listening begins in the womb. During the fifth month of pregnancy, the baby's hearing is developed enough to begin to hear sounds from outside the womb. The more children are spoken to and listened to, the better listening skills they have.

Attention span is a large part of listening skills and develops with maturity. The general rule of thumb is one minute of attention for each year of development, up to the age of five, when the child picks up an additional minute. Children, like adults, utilize their attention spans for three rounds, before they are so exhausted that listening becomes too

difficult to continue. This means that a four-year-old can listen for about 12 minutes before losing attention, and a five-year-old can listen for 18 minutes before losing attention.

Attention span must be practiced to maximize its potential. With a little practice, children are able to listen for the full length of their capability. Children also must learn to listen for details, including learning to prioritize the information they hear. Children's attention spans grow as they follow directions, listen to stories, and participate in conversations.

Children with special needs also need to learn how to listen. In fact, depending on the type of special need, listening for cues may be vital for the child to understand what is happening. For example, a child with significant vision loss will learn to depend on his or her listening skills as a way to function within a preschool classroom. A child who has cognitive challenges must learn to listen for a completely different reason. For this child, listening may serve as a cue to help him or her function in the world. On the other hand, a child with a hearing loss may need to use his or her residual (leftover) hearing abilities to listen to what is said.

Oral Language Development

After listening, vocabulary is the next building block in the foundation of literacy. The components of oral language are vocabulary and accurate grammar, with the ultimate goal of fluent speech.

The size of a child's vocabulary is one of the most accurate predictors of how successful that child will be when he or she encounters formal reading instruction. The most fertile time for vocabulary development is from birth to age five. A five-year-old will typically have acquired 60% of his or her lifetime vocabulary. The more vocabulary-building opportunities children encounter, the more likely they are to increase their vocabularies. And, the more vocabulary they have, the more they acquire.

We naturally use more vocabulary with children who seem more articulate. The more we use, the more they pick up. That is why it is particularly important to spend extra time working on the vocabulary development of a child with a speech and/or language delay. Often, because of these delays, these children do not have the same opportunities to develop their language skills as their peers.

Opportunities for building vocabulary occur throughout the day in the classroom—during group discussions, while singing, or while listening to a story. It takes an in-tune teacher to capitalize on these opportunities. Staying attuned to the children is a big part of becoming more intentional and purposeful in our teaching.

Modeling sentence structure and grammar and encouraging children to make adaptations help them develop their grammar skills. When children hear the correct use of grammar, they eventually modify their own use of grammar. Your role is to coach them gently by restating their questions and responses without embarrassing them or making too much fuss about their errors. Children with cognitive delays or severe language delays need even more help. Unlike their peers, they have difficulty learning from modeling and watching what others do. Instead, they need specific and direct instruction on how to use language, and they also need extra practice. For these children, it is important to break down new information or instructions into smaller steps and practice each step with the child before moving to the next step.

Vocabulary and grammar each play a role in a child's ability to comprehend. The more vocabulary a child has, the greater his or her ability to fully understand the plot and details of a story.

Phonological Awareness

Phonological awareness is sensitivity to sound. For preschool children, sound discrimination activities include recognizing same and different sounds, playing with onomatopoeic words, matching rhyming word pairs, and identifying the repetitive sound in an alliterative phrase or sentence.

The foundation for sound discrimination is wired in the brain during the first year of life, as a neuron is assigned to every sound in a baby's native language (44 phonemes in English). The more the child is spoken to, sung to, and read to, the more discriminate the neurons become. The brain is so fertile to sound during the first year of life that it is capable of wiring sounds for as many different languages as it experiences.

Opportunities to develop phonological awareness include focusing on alliteration; onomatopoeic words; and rhyming word patterns in songs, books, and activities. Watch for opportunities and turn those sound experiences into lessons. Become more intentional and purposeful in your instruction.

Often, children with special needs do not develop awareness of the sounds they hear. Sometimes, they are unable to develop a phonological system that helps them decode words. For example, a child who is deaf will not learn how to sound things out and combine sounds to read words. Instead, it is important that the child learns how to use words in context rather than in isolation. Children with language delays need extra practice to develop their phonological awareness. It is, however, very important that these children develop this skill, as there is a direct relationship between phonological awareness and future success with reading. This is also true for children with cognitive deficits as well. Research has shown that breaking down a task into small steps and allowing the child extra time to practice each step can help him or her learn the skills necessary to build phonological awareness.

Definitions for phonological awareness components are as follows:

- **Alliteration**—The repetition of a consonant sound in a series of words, such as, "Peter Piper picked a peck of pickled peppers." Children are able to hear the repetition of the /p/ sound, but do not necessarily need to identify that the sound is made by the letter "p."

- **Onomatopoeia**—Words that sound like what they describe, for example, *pitter-patter, moo, quack, beep,* and so on.
- **Rhyming words**—Words with the same ending sound.
- **Segmentation**—The ability to isolate sounds from a stream of speech, to hear individual words within a sentence and syllables within a word.
- **Sound discrimination**—The ability to hear differences in sounds, to determine likenesses and differences in sounds.

Letter Knowledge and Recognition

Letter knowledge and recognition is the ability to recognize all 26 letters of the alphabet in both uppercase and lowercase forms and to understand that letters are the foundation of words.

It is important to teach the alphabet to children in such a way that they understand that it is flexible and moveable. This concept is often hampered by the fact that children learn the alphabet song early in life and sing it over and over again. The initial wiring for letter knowledge gets connected and reinforced in a low-functioning part of the brain, far away from the place where it will be needed in rational thought. When children continually say and sing the alphabet starting with "a" and ending with "z," they tend to think of the alphabet as linear—that it always must start with "a" and end with "z." This creates a challenge when they begin to move from letters into words.

Children need to sing the alphabet song forward and backward. They need to sort letters by type of line used to make the letter. They need to see letters as independent components that have many ways to be organized. This is especially true for children with special needs, who often do not generalize information well. In other words, although a child might be able to participate in singing the alphabet

song, he or she may not understand that letters are combined to make individual words.

For children who cannot see letters, it is important that they learn what letters look like by other means, such as touching letter cutouts. It is also imperative that children with special needs learn new concepts in context. So, learning letters in isolation may have little meaning for a child with cognitive challenges, while learning the letters in his or her name and the sound that each letter makes is a very important functional (lifelong) skill that will be of benefit.

Print Awareness

Print awareness is the knowledge that printed words move from left to right and from top to bottom. It is also the awareness that print has many functions—labeling items, creating lists, conveying information in newspapers, telling stories in books, identifying exits and entrances, and so on.

Look for opportunities to use print in the classroom.

Print awareness begins when children start to identify their favorite eating spot by its logo or sign or point out that a stop sign means stop. This is referred to as environmental print.

Some children will begin to combine letters to make words, usually starting with their own names. Others will actually pretend to write a message by making pretend letters (using letter approximations) (see Appendix—Writing Continuum on page 286).

Research has shown that children with special needs require more visual cues to help them learn to recognize print in the environment, such as pictures. Children with special needs need additional opportunities to practice print awareness, and often group lessons may need to be repeated and expanded. It is important that children with special needs have multiple opportunities to practice what they learn in a variety of settings.

Comprehension

Comprehension is the internalization of story. It develops when children have an opportunity to retell stories in their own words, act out stories, and listen to stories that are not accompanied by illustrations. It is through comprehension skills that children are able to make the story their own.

Comprehension is enhanced when children use higher-level thinking skills, make applications, conduct analyses, experiment with synthesis, and make evaluations.

Children who understand the concepts authors use to create stories will use story language to predict story events, cognitively organize story ideas, and involve themselves in the storyline while listening to stories. This strengthens their comprehension of stories while listening. In addition, understanding how authors describe settings, develop characters, and organize the storyline helps young children craft their own stories.

Because children with special needs may not have the same internalization skills as their peers, it is important to look for ways to help them involve themselves in the storyline. Short attention spans often interfere with developing critical listening skills. In addition, a child with limited language repertoire will need implicit instructions and will need multiple opportunities to understand what words mean and how they are used in context. Because comprehension involves both seeing pictures and words and hearing words, it is especially important that children with vision or hearing loss receive specialized instruction. Stories and activities should be adapted in a way that these children can understand, so that they have the same opportunities to learn comprehension.

General Guidelines for Children with Special Needs

Just like typically developing children, children with special needs have strengths and weaknesses. Some children may have a recognizable syndrome, for example, a child with Down syndrome or a child who wears a hearing aid. Other children may exhibit delays, but may not have been diagnosed with a specific condition or syndrome. With time and practice of skills, many seemingly delayed children will ultimately catch up in their development. Young children might be diagnosed as having a developmental delay because it is unknown if the child's condition will be ongoing or he or she will eventually develop at the same rate as his or her peers. In other cases, children may be at risk for a special need because of their environment or a chronic health condition, such as ear infections or a depressed immune system.

Regardless of the challenges children may face, all children can learn and all children should be allowed to participate in everyday routines and activities to the best of their capabilities. Special adaptations may be necessary. Sometimes, a child is only able to participate partially. Research tells us that children learn best in natural environments with typically developing peers.

Each child is unique. The following list is intended to be a guide for when working with children with special needs. Depending on the type and severity of the special need, a child may exhibit one or more of these characteristics. When working with children with special needs please keep in the mind the following:

1. **Make the child a valued member of your classroom community:**
   - Children in your classroom look to you as a role model. They watch what you say, what you do, and how you act. It is important that the other children in your class see that you view all children, especially children with special needs, as valuable class members who are not only important to you but important to each other.
   - Always use **people-first language.** Refer to the child first and the special need last. Try to avoid using words such as "disability" or "handicapped" because they imply the child has a deficit. For example, Sara is a child with autism—she is not the autistic child in your class. Bill is a child with a hearing loss—he is not a deaf child.
   - Answer children's questions about a child with a special need honestly and openly. Provide enough information to help the typically developing child see that his or her classmate is like him or her but learns differently or needs help doing some things.

2. **To encourage acceptance of children with special needs by their peers, try the following:**
   - Plan activities that include the child. Look for ways to help the child with delays participate in everyday activities and routines. If the child cannot fully participate and do everything just like his or her peers,

look for ways to adapt an activity so the child can partially participate.
   - Read stories that feature people with special needs as members of a community.
   - Teach all the children in your classroom that everyone has strengths and everyone has weaknesses.
   - Adopt a zero-tolerance policy for bullying, teasing, and laughing at others, regardless of their abilities.
   - Remember, all children can learn, some children just take more time and practice.
   - Children with special needs need to feel successful. Give the child a task he or she can do before introducing something he or she is just learning to do.

3. **Work with the child's family:**
   - Unless you have a child with special needs, you can never truly understand the perspective of parents who do. You can sympathize and try to appreciate how parents might feel, but you can never really know the day-to-day realities of living with and caring for a child with special needs.
   - For parents of a child with special needs, their child is not just a disabled child. He or she is special and is a valued member of the family. Try to work under the belief that parents of a child with special needs are doing the best they can with the resources they have at the time.
   - Be respectful of their opinions. Parents often agree that the one thing that a teacher can do to understand their perspective is to be respectful of their opinions and treat them as valued contributors.

Categories of Special Needs

This book organizes special needs into broad general categories representing the major types of special needs more commonly seen in preschool settings. These categories are not meant to be all inclusive, rather they are guidelines to help teachers plan for children with special needs in their classrooms. Children within each category may have only a few of the characteristics mentioned below while others may have many more. Some children may have a specific condition that falls into more than one category, such as a child with cerebral palsy who may have issues with both motor skills and communication or speech. It is always important that you treat each child as an individual and help him or her grow and learn as much as possible.

The six categories are as follows:
- Visual Impairments
- Hearing Impairments
- Motor Delays
- Cognitive Challenges
- Speech and Language Delays
- Behavior/Emotional Issues

Children with Visual Impairments

The term *visual impairment* is used to describe the functional loss of vision, not the specific eye disorder itself that causes the problem. Eye disorders that can lead to visual impairments include retinal degeneration, albinism, cataracts, glaucoma, muscular problems that result in visual disturbances, disorders of the cornea, diabetic retinopathy, congenital disorders, and infection. Children with visual impairments may be diagnosed as partially sighted, having low vision, legally blind, or totally blind. This diagnosis will usually come from a developmental pediatrician working with an ophthalmologist (doctor who specializes in treatment of eye conditions).

- **Partially sighted** indicates that there is some type of visual problem that results in a need for special education or special adaptations.
- **Low vision** generally refers to a visual impairment that is more severe and not necessarily limited to distance vision. Low vision applies to all individuals with sight who are unable to read a book at a normal viewing distance, even with the aid of eyeglasses or contact lenses. They use a combination of vision and other senses to learn, although they may require adaptations in lighting or the size of print, and, sometimes, Braille.
- **Legally blind** indicates that a person has less than 20/200 vision in the better eye or a very limited field of vision (20 degrees at its widest point).
- **Totally blind** children learn via Braille or other non-visual media and have very little, if any, residual vision.

Children with visual impairments:
1. Learn best through their other senses and will learn faster when something is presented with touch or sound.
2. Need to be able to hear what is being said or described, because this is the sense they depend on most.
3. Often use touch to learn about someone. Teach peers to use "soft touches" and to let the child get to know them by gently touching their face.

Suggestions for the classroom:
- Provide the child with time to experience new concepts by touch or sound.
- Help the child orient to new concepts by giving him or her a frame of reference, such as, "Yesterday, we talked about things we eat for breakfast. Today, we will to talk about things we eat for lunch."
- If the child has some vision, line drawings with a minimum of background clutter work best. For example, use a simple line drawing of a cow, rather than a farm scene with a barn and many animals. Books containing photos of real objects, people, and places should be provided.
- Preferential seating is important. If the child has *peripheral vision,* make sure he or she is seated so that his or her peripheral vision is optimized. Lighting should be appropriate and not cause a "glare" effect.

What the teacher can do to help:

1. **Learn as much as possible about the child:**
   As the child's teacher, it is important to find out as much about his or her visual limitations as possible. The child may have an orientation and mobility specialist or teacher of the visually impaired who can help plan activities best suited for him or her. The purpose of any program for a child who has visual challenges includes:
   - Working with the child and his or her family to help him or her make the best use of the vision that he or she has (residual vision).
   - Providing multiple opportunities to explore, experience, and feel safe in the daily environment.

2. **Plan activities based on the child's residual vision:**
   - Stimulate the child's vision. If the child is not used to being asked to use his or her functional or residual vision, he or she may need a lot of help and encouragement.
   - Residual vision can often be optimized through training and effort. However, the child's overall visual acuity or field of vision will not change.
   - Look for ways to change the environment, such as lighting, and low vision devices, such as magnifiers.
   - You can often make an object more easily seen by enlarging it or placing it closer to the child.
   - Contact a professional, such as an *orientation and mobility specialist* (person who is specially trained for program planning and training the visually impaired), to help determine what the child can do.
   - Try to make vision training part of the everyday schedule.
   - Provide variety, so the child does not get bored with the same daily activities.
   - Remember to train his or her other senses as well. Ultimately, the child may come to depend on his or her other senses or sensory clues.

- Use a dark pen for writing and provide markers, pens, and paper using contrasting or bold colors.
- When the child gets tired, quit. If he or she becomes too upset or frustrated, he or she may be less willing to try new activities.

3. **General suggestions to consider when making adaptations for a child with visual impairments:**
   - Usually, but not always, a child with a visual impairment learns to depend on other senses to help him or her. Listening is often an asset for a child with visual impairments.
   - A child with visual challenges may not build his or her vocabulary in the same way as typically developing peers. To help him or her learn new words, try to find real objects that he or she can learn with.
   - If the child has some vision, be sure to print words large enough for him or her to see. When you print words for him or her, use thick markers, such as a thick-line black marker.
   - It is important for a child with visual challenges to know what will happen next and the boundary of where to stand or sit.
   - Remember that children with visual challenges may be hesitant to put their hands into something unfamiliar (such as the paper bag containing letters). Tell the child that you will do it with him or her. Place your hand on top of the child's while he or she puts his or her hand in the bag.
   - Children who are visually challenged need concrete experiences to make the connection between an object and its name or use.
   - When standing in a circle, encourage the child to put his or her hand on the shoulder of the child in front of him or her.
   - Select books that have print that is large enough for the child to see or give the child a copy of the book to place in front of him or her. Use a book light or adaptive

magnification device if it will help the child see the book more easily.

- If the child has residual vision (usable vision), make sure he or she can see each item and that he or she is not seated where glare from the window or other lighting will affect his vision.

Guiding a Child Who Is Blind or Visually Challenged

1. Approach the child and call him or her by name.
2. Hold out your arm and invite the child to hold your wrist.
3. Walk a little in front of the child.
4. Remember to talk about where you are going.
5. If you are walking the child over to a chair, take his or her hand and place it on the back of the chair.
6. If you are going down steps, pause and say "step up" or "step down." When you reach level ground, take a step, then pause to give the child time to complete the last step. Remind the child that you will stop at the edge of each step so the child can step down before you go to the next step.

Children with Hearing Impairments

Types of Hearing Loss

Generally speaking, a child with a hearing loss will be diagnosed based on the type of hearing loss and the degree or severity of the hearing loss. The type of hearing loss is determined by the part of the auditory systems that is damaged. They include conductive, sensorineural, and mixed.

- **Conductive hearing loss**—This type of loss happens when sound is not conducted properly through the ear. A child with this type of loss will have difficulty hearing faint sounds. In many cases, conductive hearing loss can be corrected with medication or surgery.

- **Sensorineural hearing loss**—This type of loss occurs when there is inner ear damage or damage to the nerve pathways to the brain. A sensorineural loss cannot be corrected with surgery or medication. Children with this type of loss will have difficulty understanding speech and hearing sounds clearly.
- **Mixed hearing loss**—Sometimes, a child may have a combination of a conductive hearing loss and a sensorineural loss.

The degree of hearing loss is used to describe the severity of the loss. The severity is determined by the softest level at which the child can hear a sound. Losses are classified as mild, moderate, severe, and profound.

- **Mild loss**—Difficulty hearing speech in crowded or loud environments, can manage in quiet environments and when able to see the teacher.
- **Moderate loss**—Difficulty understanding conversational speech; requires very loud volume on an audio player or television.
- **Severe loss**—Significant difficulty with speech, usually needs extra information, such as pictures or prompts to understand what is said.
- **Profound loss**—Cannot hear most conversations, the child would be considered deaf and would need to learn other methods to understand what the speaker is saying, such as reading lips and/or using sign language.

How well a child can function with a hearing loss is determined by such factors as whether the loss is unilateral (in one ear only) or bilateral (in both ears); whether the loss will get worse as the child gets older (progressive) or whether the loss came on suddenly. Some hearing loss fluctuates, which means that, at times, it will not be as severe, or it will be more severe, such as when the child has fluid in the middle ear or an ear infection.

Children with hearing impairments:

1. Depend on vision to learn new concepts.
2. Will understand less, not more, when you exaggerate your lip movements or speak very loudly.
3. Should always be seated where they can see the teacher's face.
4. Often pretend to understand something by nodding their heads.
5. May depend on sign language as a method of communication.
6. Often watch a speaker's face or lips for clues about what the speaker is saying.

Suggestions for the classroom:

- Use visual representations to teach new concepts, such as picture cards that show what to do first, second, and so on.
- If the child has some residual hearing, ask the child questions to see if he or she understood what you said.
- Use normal vocabulary, but be prepared to restate, point to, or demonstrate new concepts.
- Use sign language to communicate or read lips for clues about what is being said.

What the teacher can do to help:

1. **Learn as much as possible about the child:**
   - Depending on the type of hearing loss a child has (see "Types of Hearing Loss" on page 17), he or she may be able to hear certain types of sounds. Some children have high-frequency loss, which means they can hear most speech sounds but not highly pitched sounds. Other children have low-frequency hearing loss, which means they have more difficulty hearing sounds that are made in the low frequencies.

Unfortunately, most speech occurs in low frequencies.
   - Work closely with the child's speech/language pathologist, audiologist, or teacher, to make sure the child has the materials he or she needs and is seated so he or she can see and hear you speak.

2. **A word about sign language:**
   - Not all children who are hearing impaired will use sign language. If it has been determined that a child in your class will use sign language to communicate, it is important that you learn some simple signs.
   - Sign language is fun and, with practice, relatively easy to learn. Involve other children in the class and teach them some functional signs, too.
   - Tips for using sign language with young children can be found at www.deafness. about.com. This website also has a link where the reader can click to watch an adult model demonstrate various signs.
   - If the child uses sign language, display the signs on your alphabet wall cards. Many wall cards are available in English, Spanish, and American Sign Language.

Signing helps children communicate their wants and needs.

3. **General suggestions to consider when making adaptations for a child with hearing impairments:**

   - If the child uses residual hearing and has some functional use of hearing, combine gestures with verbal cues.
   - Make sure the child can see your lips and face when you speak to him or her.
   - Children with hearing impairments often have very limited vocabulary. To help build new vocabulary, the child may need extra clues, such as pictures.
   - Children with hearing impairments often need extra help using descriptive words.
   - Model for the child exactly what you expect him or her to do, so he or she understands what is expected.
   - A child with hearing impairments may not fully understand the words in a rhyme.
   - Working collaboratively with a peer will be easier if the child understands exactly what he or she and the peer are expected to do.
   - Before beginning the activity, demonstrate one-on-one with the child what you will be doing.
   - Some children with hearing impairments may nod and look at you as if to say, "I understand," when in reality, they don't. Children learn early that if they pretend to hear something, adults will often leave them alone.

Children with Cognitive Challenges

The term *cognitive challenges* decribes a child with cognitive skills that are significantly below that of his or her peers. Rarely is "mental retardation" used to describe these children. Children with cognitive challenges face many more obstacles than their peers. How much they learn and how well they develop often depends on more than just the severity of their cognitive abilities. Sometimes it depends on other factors, such as how well they get along with others, how well they adjust to new surroundings, and how motivated they are to try new things. Some children with cognitive delays will have other coexisting disabilities, such as motor impairments, speech and language delays, and behavior or emotional issues. Young children with cognitive challenges will need extra help and practice to learn functional or everyday skills, such as going to the bathroom, eating, getting dressed, and washing their hands.

Children with cognitive challenges:

1. Have difficulty understanding new concepts.
2. Become upset when their routines are changed or varied.
3. Will need something presented more than once and may require that the same thing be taught repeatedly before understanding it.
4. Need new concepts and activities broken down into smaller steps.
5. Become easily frustrated and give up when they think they cannot do something as well or as quickly as others.
6. Have trouble *generalizing* information across setting and environments.

Suggestions for the classroom:

- Present new concepts in short segments and use as many of the child's senses as possible.
- Let the child know what will happen next. Tell him or her before the routine is changed.
- Plan activities that encourage opportunities to practice a new concept repeatedly.
- Use short sentences when explaining something new.
- Concentrate on what the child can do rather than what he or she cannot do.
- Help everyone who works with the child understand that he or she may not learn something in the same way or as quickly as others, but he or she can and will learn.

Note: Text in italics is explained in the Glossary on pages 245–247.

What the teacher can do to help:

1. Learn as much as possible about the child:
Generally, when we think of a child with cognitive challenges, the word mental retardation comes to mind. Children with cognitive challenges face many more obstacles than their peers. How much they learn and how well they develop often depends on more than just the severity of their cognitive abilities. Sometimes, it depends on other factors, such as how well they get along with others, how well they adjust to new surroundings, and how motivated they are to try new things.

2. Provide extra help in learning functional skills:
Life skills have been given many names—self-help skills, everyday skills, independent living skills, and *functional skills*. Life skills help children manage routine activities, such as dressing, eating, or going to the bathroom. These are skills a child needs to be independent. In terms of literacy skills, the common signs that a child must recognize in the environment are often called survival signs and include common things around them, such as restrooms, exits, and stop signs.

It is often difficult for a preschool teacher to decide which of the functional skills is the most important to teach. Always keep in mind that success often depends on both the child's readiness and the family's willingness to reinforce the skill at home. It is important to work with the child's family to help determine what life skills to teach first. If the skill is a high-priority skill for the child's family, they are more likely to work with him or her at home to learn it.

3. General suggestions to consider when making adaptations for a child with cognitive challenges:
- It is important to break any activity or direction into small steps and model each one for the child.
- Avoid doing things for the child that he or she can do. Never having to do things

independently fosters "learned helplessness," a situation in which the child deliberately pretends that he or she cannot do something because the child has learned that if he or she acts helpless someone will do it for him or her.
- Children with cognitive delays can and do learn new concepts; they just need extra time and extra practice.
- Changes in the daily routine can be very overwhelming to a child with cognitive challenges, so make one change at a time.
- Assign the child to a peer buddy who will be patient and understanding with the child.

Functional or Self-Help Skills

Functional or self-help skills are skills that will help children manage activities. These are the skills that a child needs to be independent. In terms of literacy skills, the common signs that a child will need to recognize in the environment are often called survival signs and include common things around them, such as restrooms, exits, and stop signs.

General guidelines to use when teaching a functional skill:
- The teacher and the child's family should use the same words and encourage the child to practice the skill in the same way.
- Functional skills are learned easiest in the environment in which they naturally occur. In other words, you should teach a child to brush his or her teeth in the bathroom, not at the desk.

Preschool functional skills usually fall into the following broad categories:
Feeding
Using utensils to eat
Simple table rules
Social context of mealtime

Toileting

Asking to go to the toilet

Taking care of own toilet needs

Washing hands after toileting

Handling unplanned situations

Self-help

Brushing teeth

Washing and drying face

Tolerating a bath

Dressing

Getting dressed for school

Getting dressed to go outside

Taking off clothes

Putting on shoes

Simple routines

Getting up in the morning

Arriving at school

Learning the daily school schedule

Handling transition times, such as getting ready
   to go to lunch or going outside

Getting ready to go home

Adjusting after a period of being out of school
   (after vacation, illness, and so on)

General guidelines to use when planning to teach a new functional skill:

1. Start by deciding which skill is the most important to the child and his or her family.
   - This decision should be based on the developmental level of the child and on the wishes of his or her family.
   - Carefully observe the child to make sure he or she is ready to learn the new skill. Trying to teach a life skill before the child is ready can be confusing, frustrating, and frightening for the child, and can sometimes delay his or her learning the skill.
   - Remember to include everyone who works with the child, so that they know you will be teaching the child a new skill.

2. Think about the challenges you face when introducing a new skill.
   - Look for factors that need to be addressed, such as hypersensitivity to touch, short attention span, or the child's fear of trying new things.

- Children with cognitive challenges do best with concrete terms. So, make sure you use terms that are not confusing.

3. Make a task analysis or step-by-step guide for completing the skill. A task analysis is like a recipe that you (the teacher) follow each time you teach the self-help skill.
   - Write down each step and then go over the list to see if you have left off anything important.
   - Be very detailed and describe what you want the child to do.
   - Practice the skill several times yourself, using the list you made for the child.
   - Watch yourself as you model each step. Remember, things that seem natural to you, like flushing a toilet or rinsing a toothbrush, may not be natural for the child.

4. Make another task analysis that you will use with the child.
   - This list is much less detailed and simpler than the list you made for yourself.
   - Be very specific, concise, and clear about what the child is to do.

5. Make sequence cards for each step and use clear pictures.
   - Make another set of cards to send home.
   - It is always good to make a third set of cards as a backup, in case something happens to the sequence cards.
   - Place the sequence cards in front of the child and talk about each one. Remember to use clear, concrete language.
   - Model each step for the child before asking him or her to start the task.

6. Generalization, or applying the same skill to a new setting, is often very difficult. Don't be discouraged if a skill that the child has learned at school does not immediately transfer to another environment.

7. Give the child time to practice one step of the skill before going on to the next. Expecting too much too soon can be overwhelming for both you and the child.

Children with Delayed Motor Development

Motor development is generally defined by two areas: *fine motor skills* and *gross motor skills*. Fine motor skills include using muscles necessary for such activities as holding a fork, buttoning clothes, drawing, or painting. Gross motor skills involve using muscles for such activities as riding a tricycle, jumping, walking, and running. Young children with mild motor delays may benefit from using utensils with special handles and puzzles with large knobs on each piece. Children with more severe motor delays may depend on a wheelchair or adaptive walker to move around the classroom. It is very important to know as much as possible about a child with motor delays before the child comes into your classroom. If the child uses a wheelchair or other adaptive equipment, it may be necessary to rearrange the room so that the child will have space to move around the room.

Children with delayed motor development:
1. Require proper positioning to be physically comfortable enough to learn new concepts. If the child is uncomfortable, he or she will not be able to concentrate.
2. May fatigue more quickly because it takes more effort to accomplish a motor task.
3. Are not slow or mentally challenged. Don't assume that a motor impairment means that the child has a mental impairment as well.
4. Can usually *partially participate* in most activities, with simple adaptations.

Note: Text in italics is explained in the Glossary on pages 245–247.

Partial participation is like job sharing; children work together to complete a task.

Suggestions for the classroom:
- Consult with the physical therapist (PT) or occupational therapist (OT) and learn what simple adaptive devices, such as pencil grips or clothespins used to help turn pages, will help the child.
- Change the child's position often, so he or she does not become uncomfortable.
- Allow time for the child to rest if he or she becomes tired or fatigued by a new activity.

What the teacher can do to help:
1. Learn as much as possible about the child:
Work with the PT or OT so that you know how to position the child so he or she is comfortable. It is very hard for the child to attend and participate in classroom activities if he or she is positioned incorrectly.

2. **Look for simple adaptations you can make to help the child participate:**

   ■ Make page-turners, so the child can turn the pages of a book independently. Examples include a wooden clothespin on each page that gives the child a handle to hold when turning the pages, a dot of hot glue on the upper right or left hand corner of each page (wait for each dot to dry/cool before applying to the next page), or a metal paper clip at the upper left hand corner of each page to provide something for the child to grasp. (Stagger the placement of the clips so the pages are easy to turn.)

Placing a white board at an angle makes it easier for the child to write or draw.

   ■ Use simple switch adaptations, such as a single button switch that can be used to interrupt the battery and allow a child to turn a battery-operated device, like a tape recorder or toy, on or off by pressing the switch (see Appendix—Adaptive Switches on page 250).

3. **General suggestions to consider when making adaptations for a child with delayed motor development:**

   ■ Seat or position children with motor delays in a way that is comfortable and allows them access to what is happening.

   ■ Allow the child to participate partially, even if he or she cannot complete the activity in the same manner as his or her peers.

   ■ For a child with severe motor delays, such as those seen in some forms of cerebral palsy, it may be necessary to use a communication board to teach the child.

   ■ Remember that children with motor delays do not necessarily have cognitive delays. With simple adaptations, they can participate and learn the same way as their typically developing peers.

   ■ A child with motor delays, especially a child who is in a wheelchair, will need new objects or labels presented at his or her eye level.

Children with Speech or Language Delays

Speech and *language delays* are the most commonly seen special need in preschool settings. Children with speech delays generally have difficulty with the way they say words or sounds. It is important to know the sequence of normal speech development in order to determine if the child has a delay that is not within that sequence. Some children will enter preschool with speech that is immature (such as baby talk). Others will have significant delays in speech development, making their words unintelligible or unable to be understood even with careful listening. When a word or sound that should have already developed is said incorrectly, a child may be diagnosed with an *articulation disorder.* A language disorder is defined as a deficit in using language, vocabulary development, understanding language and *pragmatic language.* Children with autism and cognitive challenges often have pragmatic language delays. Pragmatic language involves using language in a social setting. For example, knowing what is appropriate to say, when to say it, and the general give-and-take nature of a friendly conversation.

Children with speech or language delays:

1. Often do not understand what is being said, especially if you use long sentences.
2. Need help in naming common objects and/or activities.
3. Sometimes require an alternative method of communication, such as a communication board.
4. Do not understand simple directions.
5. Become frustrated if their speech is not understood by others.
6. Will sometimes resort to tantrums out of a frustration to be noticed and understood.
7. Will not participate at all because they do not understand how to respond or what is required.

Suggestions for the classroom:

- Use simple sentences and ask the child to repeat what you say.
- Describe what is happening in the classroom.
- Use pictures as clues to what you are saying.
- If you do not understand what the child is saying, do not look away or act frustrated. This only makes the child more anxious.
- When the child gets frustrated and cries and/or throws objects, assess the situation and try to verbalize what he or she may be feeling, "Austin, you are upset because you did not want to stop building with the blocks."

What the teacher can do to help:

1. **Learn as much as possible about the child:**
Work with the speech language pathologist and try to find out as much about the child's speech and language as possible. The child may have difficulty with certain sounds. The speech pathologist can help you recognize the sounds that the child should be saying correctly by age four or five and the sounds that develop when the child is older. It is very important that the child not be pressured early to make sounds that develop later when he or she has better control of the muscles in his or her mouth.

2. **Look for ways to help the child feel more comfortable:**
   - Use picture schedules to help the child know what is going to happen next.
   - Ask the child questions about things that interest him.
   - Encourage the child to use descriptive words about color, size, and so on.
   - Do not assume the child knows the name of something or its use, such as a paintbrush or toy.
   - Try *slotting,* a technique where you start a sentence and leave a blank for the child to fill in.
   - Sometimes, deliberately call an object by another name. For example, point to the book and say, "Jacob, hand me the puzzle." Wait and see if the child will correct you.
   - For many children, learning simple sign language does not keep them from developing later verbal skills. Instead, it bridges the communication gap between nonverbal language (signs) and verbal or spoken words.

3. **General suggestions to consider when making adaptations for a child with speech or language delays:**
   - Children with language delays learn best when directions are brief and concise.
   - Describe each step of the activity as you do it.

- Sometimes children with speech delays need to see how to make a certain sound.
- Make sure directions are simple and clear.
- Remember that a child with a speech or language delay may not have the vocabulary necessary to describe what he or she sees.
- When teaching new words to a child with limited language, select words that are more concrete, such as simple nouns or verbs.

Children with Behavioral or Social-Emotional Issues

Children with emotional or behavioral problems may be diagnosed with a particular disorder, such as autism spectrum disorder, or they may not have a diagnosis at all. Sometimes children with extreme emotional behavior will be classified as having a pervasive developmental delay. It is rare to see a child in preschool diagnosed with a severe psychiatric disorder, such as childhood schizophrenia, although according to the research it is becoming more common.

Children with behavioral or social-emotional issues:
1. May find new activities overwhelming and react with a violent outburst.
2. Have trouble concentrating when information is presented in large chunks.
3. May be unable to finish a task that requires intense concentration.
4. Feel that they are too stupid to learn new things, so they will not try, rather than experience failure.

Suggestions for the classroom:
- Present new information in short segments and break it down into manageable steps for the child.
- Praise the child often when he or she accomplishes something new or stays on task for a given period.

- If you see that the child is getting frustrated or upset by an activity, "redirect" him or her to something that is less stressful.
- Teach the child to accept natural consequences for his or her actions. If a child tears up the artwork he or she has started, then the child doesn't get to work in the art area for a while.

What the teacher can do to help:

1. **Learn as much as possible about the child:** Some behaviors are related to a specific condition, such as autism, while others may be the result of a circumstance, such as a change at home or the loss of a grandparent. If the child hurts others with his or her outbursts, it important for the teacher to keep both the child and his or her classmates safe. If the child hurts himself, it may be a sign that the child has serious issues and a behavioral specialist may need to be contacted.

2. **Create an environment that is proactive: It is much easier to prevent a tantrum or outburst than to deal with one. Consider the following:**
   - **Placement**—Look at appropriate placement options. Sometimes, an environment or situation can be too stressful for a child.
   - **Curriculum**—The unwritten curriculum involves the consistent use of appropriate social skills. A child with poor social skills will not be easily accepted by his or her peers.
   - **Materials**—Select materials that encourage interaction and lessen the possibility of the child's reacting in a negative manner.
   - **Rules**—Keep rules simple and remember to review them often.
   - **Consequences**—Make consequences natural and be consistent!

3. **General suggestions to consider when making adaptations for a child with behavioral or social-emotional issues:**
   - The most important key to getting a child with emotional/behavior issues to try a new activity is to let him or her know what will happen next.

- Sometimes, children with behavior issues get so caught up in the activity that they forget there are other children present, causing the child to accidentally run into a peer or push him or her down.
- Children with emotional issues have a great deal of difficulty waiting for a turn.
- A child with severe behavior issues may have great difficulty with being blindfolded.
- Children with behavior issues, especially those with autism spectrum disorder, may be hesitant to move into an unfamiliar environment.
- A child with cognitive challenges needs encouragement to learn new words and also to use the words he or she already knows.
- Children with behavior issues tend to get frustrated very easily and often do not attend well in group activities.
- Children with emotional issues may find it very difficult to answer questions.
- A therapy ball or a beanbag chair will make sitting in a large group easier for a child with emotional issues.
- Many children with behavior issues relate better to real objects than to pictures.
- Some children are very sensitive to touch and do not enjoy singing songs with movements.
- Remember that children with emotional issues may have trouble attending and staying engaged in an activity.
- Working with a partner can be very frustrating for a child with behavior issues.
- Some children become overstimulated by lots of movement.
- Children with emotional issues often respond well to music.
- Following directions is often difficult for a child with emotional issues.

Autism Spectrum Disorder

Adaptations specifically for children with autism are included under emotional/behavior headings throughout the book. However, because a child with autism may have difficulty with behavior, communication, functional skills, and sometimes motor skills, you will find many of the adaptations in this book from those categories apply to children with autism as well. Autism is a very complex developmental disability that typically appears during the first three years of life and continues throughout adulthood. It is called a spectrum disorder because a child may have characteristics that range from mild to quite severe. While each child with autism is unique, it is generally agreed that all children with autism spectrum disorders have difficulty in varying levels of:

- language and communication;
- social relationships;
- response to sensory stimuli; and
- will usually display behaviors that are not typical of their peers.

In a preschool setting, a child's specific strengths usually center on the activities he or she enjoys most. That is because most typically developing children spend more time doing the things that are fun for them and less time doing things that are difficult. Children with autism are the same as other children in that they also have individual preferences and styles. However, their preferences are often expressed in different ways. For example, a child with autism may move, play with toys, or relate to objects differently than her peers. While a typically developing child may take turns rolling a car back and forth with a friend, a child with autism may play only with red cars and instead of rolling the car along the floor, he or she will turn it over and spin one wheel repeatedly. Children with autism often have difficulty controlling their responses to the environment and are upset when something in their daily routine changes, and may have tantrums or outbursts when routines change. Most children with autism also have trouble with sensory integration. However, it is important to note that a child can have a sensory integration disorder without having autism.

Sensory Integration Disorders

Sensory integration (SI) is a process that occurs in the brain. It allows us to take in information through our senses, organize it, and respond to the environment accordingly.

The terms Sensory Integration Dysfunction, Sensory Integration Disorder, and Sensory Modulation Disorder are terms used to describe a child who is unable to analyze and respond appropriately to the information received from his or her senses. A child with Sensory Integration Dysfunction has problems adapting to the everyday sensations that others take for granted. Many children with autism spectrum disorder have a Sensory Integration Disorder. However, it is possible to have one without having the other.

How Do I Know If a Child Is Oversensitive or Undersensitive?

Sense	Oversensitive	Undersensitive
Vision (sight)	■ Covers his or her eyes when the lights are too bright ■ Is overwhelmed by too many colors and items in the classroom ■ Rubs his or her eyes or squints his or her eyes frequently	■ Does not respond to light ■ Holds items close to his or her face as if he or she can't see them ■ Stares at flickering fluorescent lights
Sound	■ Covers his or her ears ■ Responds to sounds other children ignore ■ Will act as if he or she can't hear when you call his or her name, but then responds when a child drops a toy ■ Yells with fingers in ears	■ Speaks loudly ■ Turns the volume up on the TV or computer ■ Sings loudly ■ Always plays with toys that make loud noises
Smell	■ Holds his or her nose at common odors ■ Sniffs the air or sniffs other people	■ Ignores bad odors ■ May sniff people or toys
Touch (tactile)	■ Gets upset when someone touches him ■ Is very sensitive to textures and materials ■ Is opposed to getting dirty or touching certain toys ■ Scratches at his or her skin or startles when something touches him	■ Bumps into people ■ Chews on items frequently ■ Is unaware of temperature changes ■ Is seemingly unable to tell when he or she is in pain or hurt ■ Does not cry when he or she falls down
Taste	■ Gags when he or she eats ■ Only eats food of a certain texture ■ Is sensitive to hot or cold foods	■ Wants only spicy food ■ Adds a lot of pepper or salt to his or her food ■ Licks objects or toys
Movement	■ Does not like to move, dance, climb, or hop ■ Sways ■ Seems to walk "off balance"	■ Does not get dizzy when he or she whirls or turns around ■ Loves to move fast ■ In constant motion ■ Rocking ■ Moves his or her body all the time

What Can I Do to Help a Child with Sensory Integration (SI) Disorder?

Children with sensory integration (SI) disorders sometimes respond well to items that enable them to calm down so that they can better organize all the input they receive through their senses. Some examples of such calming objects (calmers) and organizers include: things to chew on (chewies), toys that vibrate, weighted vests, soft things that they can squeeze, beanbag chairs or therapy balls to sit on, and stretchy material, such as latex, that they can use for a body cocoon.

The most common calmers and organizers include the following:

- **Chewies:** For a child with issues relating to touch, chewing on something soft can be very relaxing. Chewies can be purchased from companies who specialize in sensory integration materials or inexpensively made from the tubing used in ice makers.
- **Vibrating toys:** Vibration can be very calming to the proprioceptive system. Examples of vibrating items include pens, toothbrushes, toys, pillows, and cell phones.
- **Weighted objects:** A weighted object might be used to help a child who has difficulty with balance or with his or her proprioceptive system. A weighted vest, backpack, fanny pack, or blanket can help the child feel more grounded and less concerned about his or her sense of movement. Deep pressure helps children calm down.
- **Oral motor activities:** These activities are designed to help the child with issues related to his or her mouth and to touch. Blowing bubbles, eating crunchy foods, biting on a washcloth, and blowing a cotton ball across the table with a straw can help the child satisfy the need for oral stimulation and movement.

What Can I Do to Make Sure That a Child with Sensory Integration Disorder Does Not Go into Sensory Overload?

One of the most important things you can do is make sure the light in the classroom is not too bright. Fluorescent lights can be especially distracting for children with sensory integration disorders and with autism spectrum disorders. Look for ways to use indirect lighting (lamps, for example) or, at least, nonfluorescent overhead lights.

Regulate noise in the classroom so that it is not so loud that a child is unable to function. Watch for signs that the child is being overwhelmed by noise. This may be indicated if he or she begins to nervously look around the room, begins fidgeting, or covers his or her ears with his or her hands. Provide a quiet place for the child to go to desensitize and get away from the noise. There are, of course, times when noise is unavoidable.

Using a familiar object, like a rolling pin, encourages a child to try something new, like multicolored goop.

Consider the texture of the materials in your learning centers, and provide items with textures that you know the child might enjoy. If experience has shown that he or she seems to do better with soft textures, provide a softer surface for him or her to play on, such as a mat or craft foam. Using something as simple as a foam hair curler as a pencil grip can make all the difference in whether a child learns to write or avoids it altogether. A child who can never sit on a carpet square during circle time may be more content sitting on a beanbag chair or balancing himself on a large therapy ball.

Working with a peer buddy helps a child participate in a new activity.

Be aware of the smells in your classroom. To you, the sweet smell of rose-scented air fresher might be pleasing and enhance your classroom. However, it could interfere with the ability of a child with sensory integration to learn. If you use scents in the classroom, use natural ones, and then, only after you have determined that the child with autism can tolerate them. For example, you may try peppermint, lavender, or vanilla, instead of sweet flowery scents.

Peer Buddy

Using a peer buddy is a good method to help a child learn a new or developing skill while interacting with a peer. The peer buddy should be trained in his or her role. Explain to the peer that you are inviting him or her to be a peer buddy for _____ (use the child's name), and that, if he or she accepts your invitation, he or she is only the peer buddy for this activity. Tell the child how pleased you are that he or she has decided to help you.

Basic guidelines include:

1. Pair children carefully: Consider maturity level and communication skills.

2. Introduce buddies to the behavior and communication skills of the child with special needs. If the child has specific issues, such as behavior outbursts or severe speech delays, explain this to the peer buddy in simple concrete language.

3. Use the **Stay, Play, Talk** method:
    Stay: Buddies stay close to their friends. They greet their friends by name.
    Play: While following their partners around, buddies should join in—even a very young child can learn partial participation.
    Talk: Buddies talk about what is going on and describe things to their peer buddies.

4. Practice in class, and remember that it may be necessary to model for both buddies what you want them to do.

5. Start buddy sessions during snack time and/or free choice time. Start with four to six minutes and work your way up.

6. Encourage the relationship through positive support.

7. Keep in mind that relationships take time, and the goal of this activity is to help both children learn to be friends.

8. When enjoyable interactions between children are happening, expand to a more structured activity and higher skill development.

9. As the children become more comfortable with each other, you will need to remind them less frequently about the rules for social interaction.

10. If one peer buddy does not work out, don't give up; keep trying.

References

Bloodgood, J.W. 1999. What's in a name? Children name writing and literacy acquisition. *Reading Research Quarterly,* 34(3), 342-367.

Burgess, S. R. 2006. The development of phonological sensitivity. In D. K. Dickinson & S. B. Neuman (Eds.), *Handbook of Early Literacy Research* (Vol. 2). New York: The Guilford Press.

Dickinson, D.K. & Neuman, Susan B. (Eds.). 2006., *Handbook of Early Literacy Research* (Vol. 2). New York: The Guilford Press.

Dickinson, D. K. & Tabors, P. O. 2001. B*eginning literacy with language.* Baltimore, MD: Paul Brookes Publishing Co.

Dickinson, D. K., McCabe, A., & Essex, M. J. 2006. A window of opportunity we must open to all: The case for pre-school with high quality support for language and literacy. In D. K. Dickinson & S. B. Neuman (Eds.), *Handbook of Early Literacy Research (Vol. 2).* New York: The Guilford Press.

Gargiulo, R. M. & Kilgo, J. 2000. *Young children with special needs.* Albany, NY: Delmar Thomson Learning.

Gunning, T. G. 2003. *Creating literacy instruction for all children.* Boston, MA: Pearson Education, Inc.

Hoff, E. 2006. Environmental support for language acquisition. In D. K. Dickinson & S. B. Neuman (Eds.), *Handbook of Early Literacy Research (Vol. 2).* New York: The Guilford Press.

Isbell, R. 2002. Telling and retelling stories: Learning language and literacy. *Young Children,* 57(2), 26-30.

Juel, C. 2006. The impact of early school experiences on initial reading. In D. Dickinson & S. B. Neuman (Eds.). *Handbook of Early Literacy Research (Vol. 2).* New York: The Guilford Press.

McCardle, P. & Chhabra, V. 2004. *The voice of evidence in reading and research.* Baltimore, MD: Paul Brookes Publishing Co.

McGee, L. M., & Richgels, D. J. 2003. *Designing early literacy programs: Strategies for preschool and kindergarten children.* New York: Guilford Press.

Pogrund, R. L. & Fazzi, D. L., Eds. 2002. *Early focus: Working with young children who are blind or visually impaired and their families. Second Edition.* New York: American Federation for the Blind.

Sandall, S.R. & Schwartz, I. S. 2002. *Building blocks for teaching preschoolers with special needs.* Baltimore, MD: Paul Brookes Publishing Co.

Sandall, S., Hemmeter, M. L., Smith, B. J., & McClean, M. 2005. *DEC Recommended Practices—-A comprehensive guide for practical application in early intervention/early childhood special education.* Missoula, MT: Division of Early Childhood of the Council for Exceptional Children.

Singer, D., Golinkoff, R. M., & Hirsh-Pasek, K. (Eds.). 2006. *Play=learning: How play motivates and enhances children's cognitive and social emotional growth.* New York: Oxford University Press.

Stichter, J. P. & Conroy, M. A. 2006. *How to teach social skills and plan for peer social interactions.* Austin, TX: Pro-Ed.

Willis, C. 2006. *Teaching young children with autism spectrum disorder.* Beltsville, MD: Gryphon House.

Inclusive Literacy Lessons for Early Childhood

Chapter 1

Listening

Overview

Listening is the foundation for all literacy development—until children are able to listen, they cannot develop vocabulary or build comprehension.

Listening begins in the womb. During the fifth month of pregnancy, the baby's hearing is developed enough to begin to hear sounds from outside the womb. Children are especially curious about the sounds of language, right from birth. The more they are spoken to and listened to, the better concept they have about listening.

Attention span is a large part of listening skills and is developed with maturity. The general rule of thumb is one minute of attention for each year of development, up to the age of five, when the child picks up an additional minute. This rule continues up to the adult attention span, which is 20 minutes. Because children and adults can use their attention spans for three rounds before they are too exhausted to listen attentively, an adult can listen for an hour before losing the ability to stay focused. This means that a four-year-old can listen for about 12 minutes before losing his or her attention. A five-year-old can listen for 18 minutes before losing attention.

Attention span must be exercised to maximize its potential. With a little practice, children will be able to listen for the full length of their capability. Children also need to learn to listen for details, which require learning to prioritize the information that is heard. Children exercise their attention spans as they practice following directions, listen to stories, and participate in conversations.

Children with special needs also need to learn how to listen. In fact, depending on the type of special need that the child has, listening for cues from the outside world may be vital for the child to understand what is happening. For example, a child with significant vision loss will learn to depend on his listening skills as a way to function within a preschool classroom, whereas a child who is not cognitively intact must learn to listen for a completely different reason. For this child, listening may serve as a cue to help him function in the world. On the other hand, a child with a hearing loss may need to use his residual (leftover) hearing abilities to listen to what is said.

Stop, Look, and Listen!

Children will:

- listen with purpose.

Vocabulary

dance
go
listen
look
stop

Materials

music with a variety of tempos
art paper
book and recording
crayons
rhythm band instruments

Introducing and Developing the Lesson

- ❏ Ask the children to show you their ears.
- ❏ Engage them in a discussion about listening and how they use their ears to listen.
- ❏ Play Stop, Look, and Listen! Tell the children that you are going to play a song and that while the song is playing they should dance and move creatively. When the music stops, tell the children they must
  1. Stop.
  2. Look at you.
  3. Listen for what you ask them to do. (Jump one time, stand on one foot, shake hands with a friend, and so on).
- ❏ Practice the game several times. It may be necessary to remind the group what to do when the music stops.
- ❏ Invite one of the children to be the "leader" in the game.
- ❏ After a few rounds of the game, stop and ask the children some questions, such as, "How did you know when to dance and when to stop?"

Practicing the Lesson

- ❏ Provide rhythm band instruments in the Music Center for the children to play Freeze. Suggest that one child play an instrument, while other children dance to the sound of the instrument and stop when the sound of the instrument stops.
- ❏ Provide a book and listening tape or CD in the Listening Center. Have the children listen for the sound of the ringing bell to know when to turn the page of the book.

Reflecting on the Lesson

Ask the children:

- ❏ *Could you play the game with a blindfold on?*
- ❏ *Do you need your ears to play the game? How do you use your ears?*

Special Needs Adaptations

Special Need	Adaptation
Visual Impairments	■ To help the child learn when to stop, guide him through acouple of practice sessions. Place your hand on his shoulder when the music stops and explain to him that when the music stops he should also stop. Children with significant visual impairments will want to explore the area where they will be dancing, so they can orient themselves to the space. This activity will work best if there are some natural boundaries, such as a wall or chair, designating where the child is to dance.
Hearing Impairments	■ Depending on the severity and type of hearing loss the child has (see Types of Hearing Loss on page 17), it may be necessary to hold up a stop sign to show him when it is time to stop. If the child has a severe-profound loss, place him near the music so he can feel the vibrations.
Cognitive Challenges	■ Break the activity into small steps and model each one for the child. After you model a step, invite the child to do that step with you. If the child is hesitant, gently take his hands and do the activity with him. Start and stop the music frequently, so he has extra practice time. Use verbal encouragement. For example, you might say, "You stopped exactly when the music stopped!"
Motor Delays	■ Seat or position children with motor delays in a way that is comfortable and allows them access to what is happening. If the child cannot walk or dance around, encourage him to move his body to the music or give him a colorful scarf to wave in time to the music.
Speech/ Language Delays	■ Keep the directions brief and concise. Use simple words to describe stopping or hold your hand up, with the palm facing the child, to cue the child to stop. Point to yourself, so the child will look at you, and model how to stop. ■ If the child is having difficulty knowing what to do next, hold up picture cards to help him understand what to do. A touch on the shoulder can be a cue to remind him not to start moving until the music starts.
Emotional/ Behavior Issues	■ Let the child know what will happen next. Fear of the unknown causes unnecessary anxiety and often causes the child to respond negatively when new activities are presented. Set boundaries, showing the child where he can move and provide ample space for the activity. Sometimes, children with behavior issues get so caught up in the activity that they forget there are other children present and accidentally run into a peer or push them down.

Listening

Loud and Soft

Introducing and Developing the Lesson

- ❑ In a whisper, say, "Today we will be talking about loud and soft sounds."
- ❑ Ask the children to demonstrate making soft and loud sounds.
- ❑ Play Loud-and-Soft Hide-and-Seek. Select a child to be "IT." Tell IT that you will be hiding a beanbag somewhere within the circle area.
- ❑ Explain that when IT returns to the room, the class will sing a song and use their voices to guide IT to the beanbag. When the class sings loudly, it means that IT is close to the beanbag. When the class sings softly, it means that IT is not close to the beanbag.
- ❑ Practice the game one time, to show the group how to play it.
- ❑ While IT is out of the room, hide the beanbag.
- ❑ After IT finds the beanbag, discuss the game by asking "Was it easy to follow the sound clues? How did IT know when he was close to the beanbag?"

Children will:
- ■ distinguish differences in sounds.

Vocabulary
loud
sing
soft
sound

Materials
beanbag
cookie sheet
film or pill canisters or potato chip cans
shoes with soft and hard soles
small items (paper clips, gravel, Styrofoam packing chips, washers)
variety of objects (washers, cotton balls, sponges, stringing beads)

Practicing the Lesson

- ❑ Provide a variety of objects (washers, cotton balls, sponges, stringing beads, and so on) and a cookie sheet to make a "dropping spot" in the Science Center. Invite the children to determine whether an object makes a loud or a soft sound when hitting the cookie sheet by dropping the objects onto the cookie sheet.
- ❑ In the Dramatic Play Center, provide several different types of shoes with soft and hard soles. Have the children use each pair of shoes to walk on a hard surface and determine whether the shoes create a loud or soft sound.
- ❑ Make Sound Shakers. Place small items (paper clips, gravel, Styrofoam packing chips, washers, and so on) inside film canisters or inside potato chip cans. Place these Sound Shakers in the Discovery Center. Encourage the children to shake the shakers and determine whether the resulting sound is soft or loud.

Reflecting on the Lesson

Ask the children:
- ❑ *Which things in your home make soft sounds? Which things make loud sounds?*
- ❑ *When you are happy about something, you usually clap your hands. When do you clap the loudest?*

Special Needs Adaptations

Special Need	Adaptation
Visual Impairments	■ Allow the child to hold the object you are going to hide and to feel it, so he knows what he will look for. Assign a peer buddy to help him when it is his time to be "IT." (See page 29 in the Introduction for notes about Peer Buddies.)
Hearing Impairments	■ Teach the children that waving your hands in the air and wiggling your fingers is a form of clapping in sign language. Fast waving and wiggling means "loud clapping" and slow wiggling and waving means "soft clapping." Use "hand wiggling," rather than singing, so IT will know he is getting close to finding the item.
Cognitive Challenges	■ Sing a song that is familiar to him so he will feel comfortable participating in the activity. Hide the object in a place where the child will find it easily. Encourage the child not to give up if he becomes frustrated and cannot find the object. ■ Model each step of the game. Then, ask the child to show you what to do. Avoid doing the activity for the child as it could foster "learned helplessness," a situation in which the child deliberately pretends that he cannot do something because he has learned that if he acts helpless someone will do it for him. *If the child does not know what to do, you may need to assist him.*
Motor Delays	■ If the child is in a wheelchair, encourage classmates to drop items on the tray of his chair to determine if they make "loud" or "soft" sounds. ■ If the child is mobile, make sure the environment is clear of any large obstacles that could cause the child to fall.
Speech/ Language Delays	■ Model the concepts of "loud" and "soft" before beginning the activity. Practice saying something loudly, then softly, and invite the child to join you. ■ Describe each step of the activity as you do it. For example, say, "Gabrielle is leaving the room," "I am hiding the beanbag behind the blocks," and so forth. Modeling is an important tool that will help a child with language delays learn new concepts.
Emotional/ Behavior Issues	■ Children with emotional delays have a great deal of difficulty waiting. When introducing a new concept that involves turn-taking, give him a turn early in the game so he does not become frustrated while "waiting."

Listening Story Response

Introducing and Developing the Lesson

❑ Purr like a cat. Then, discuss the sounds that cats make—meow, hiss, and purr. Hiss like a cat and invite the child to hiss, too.

❑ Tell the children you are going to tell them a special story about a cat whose name is Abby, the Tabby! Explain that they will need to use their ears to listen carefully, because they will be making cat sounds throughout the story. Direct the children to purr when they hear that Abby is happy and to hiss with they hear that Abby is unhappy.

❑ Read the listening story, "Abby, the Tabby!" (see page 266 in the Appendix), to the children.

❑ Ask questions about the story and the sounds Abby makes. *What things make Abby purr? What things make her hiss?*

Practicing the Lesson

❑ In the Discovery Center, provide a cookie sheet and several items that will provide loud and soft sounds when they are dropped onto the cookie sheet. Have the children drop the items, one at a time. Instruct them to purr when items make a soft sound and hiss when items make a loud sound.

❑ In the Art Center, provide paper, crayons, and a tambourine. Select one child to be the tambourine player. Instruct children to color while the tambourine is being played and to stop coloring when the tambourine stops.

❑ Make a recording of the "Abby, the Tabby!" story and place it in the Listening Center. Encourage the children to continue to make the sounds that accompany the story.

Reflecting on the Lesson

Ask the children:

❑ *Cats purr when they are happy and content. What sounds do you make when you are happy?*

❑ *How well were you able to remember to make the sounds as you heard the words* happy *and* unhappy? *Did you get better toward the end of the story?*

Children will:
- listen intently.
- listen with purpose.

Vocabulary

actions

ears

hear

listen

response

story

Materials

cookie sheet

crayons

paper

recording device

recording media

tambourine

variety of objects (washers, cotton balls, sponges, stringing beads)

Special Needs Adaptations

Special Need	Adaptation
Visual Impairments	■ Residual vision is the vision that a child with visual impairments can use. For children with significant vision impairments (loss), use a stuffed cat and invite the child to feel the cat and hold it while you tell the story.
Hearing Impairments	■ Invite the child to place his hand on your throat while you make the purring noise, and to place his palm a few inches away from your mouth as you make the hissing noise.
Cognitive Challenges	■ Tell the child that you will be talking with the large group about a cat. Show the child a picture of a cat. Practice making "purring" and "hissing" noises with the child.
Motor Delays	■ If the child has significant motor delays and cannot make a hissing noise or a purring noise, suggest that he substitute with a sound that he can make.
Speech/ Language Delays	■ Sometimes, children with speech delays need to see how a sound is made. Show the child that you place your tongue just behind your lower front teeth when making a "hissing" sound and at the roof of your mouth when you "purr."
Emotional/ Behavior Issues	■ This lesson is an opportunity to talk about how to treat animals, such as using "soft touches." Explain that sometimes, a cat may hiss or try to scratch if it is upset, but that even when an animal is upset with us, it is important not to kick, hit, or hurt the animal in any way.

Whispering

Children will:
- listen intently.
- develop phonemic awareness.

Vocabulary

game	speak
hear	throat
listen	whisper

Materials
blindfold
recording device
recording media

Whispering to a friend can be fun and challenging.

Introducing and Developing the Lesson

- ❏ After demonstrating how to whisper, ask the children to place their hands on their throats while whispering their name and then while saying their names.
- ❏ Ask a child to describe what he feels. Does it feel the same, or different? How is whispering different from speaking?
- ❏ Tell the children that they are going to play a whispering game.
- ❏ Show the children the gestures you will use to signal the start and finish of each round of the game.
- ❏ Sit the children in a circle. Ask for a volunteer to be the "listener." Take the volunteer aside and select a name he is to listen for.
- ❏ Blindfold the volunteer and walk him back to the circle. Have the children begin to whisper their names. Have the volunteer clap when he hears the classmate whose name he was told to listen for.
- ❏ Continue the game with a new "listener."

Practicing the Lesson

- ❏ Record children whispering their names, one at a time. Ask the children to listen to the tape and clap when they hear their name.
- ❏ Suggest that the children whisper when they are talking with their friends during Center Time. *Is it easier or more difficult to listen when listening to someone who is whispering?*
- ❏ Sing songs in a whisper. Is the song more or less interesting when sung in a whisper?

Reflecting on the Lesson

Ask the children:
- ❏ *When do people whisper?*
- ❏ *Does whispering make you listen more closely? Why?*

Special Needs Adaptations

Special Need	Adaptation
Visual Impairments	■ Children with visual impairments are usually very good listeners. Use this lesson as an opportunity to focus on the strengths of this child. Invite him to be the first "listener."
Hearing Impairments	■ While children with hearing impairments may be unable to be a "listener," they could participate in other ways. For example, invite the child with hearing impairments to be the "listener's helper." Because the listener is blindfolded, this child could guide him as he walks around the circle.
Cognitive Challenges	■ For a child who has trouble understanding what he is expected to do, start by modeling the activity for him. Play the game with him two or three times, one-on-one. If he forgets what to do, gently remind him. It will be much easier when the large group plays the game if the child with cognitive challenges has already played it before and knows what to expect.
Motor Delays	■ A child with motor delays may have difficulty walking around and may not understand about being blindfolded. Play the game in a small group with this child. Invite three or four people to sit facing the child. Blindfold the child, tap one child on the shoulder, and invite him to whisper his name. The child with motor delays can then lean toward or point to the child saying his name.
Speech/ Language Delays	■ Make sure the directions are simple and clear. Before beginning the large group activity, demonstrate for the child what will happen, one step at a time. Wait a moment and invite the child to imitate what you just said or demonstrated.
Emotional/ Behavior Issues	■ Blindfolding may be difficult for a child with severe behavior issues. To avoid a tantrum or upsetting the child, invite him to close his eyes or turn his back to the group instead of being blindfolded.

What Did I Hear? (Gossip)

Children will:
- listen intently.
- remember what they hear.

Vocabulary

hear
listen
repeat
whisper

Materials

masking tape
nail or ice pick (adult only)
paper towel tubes
string (1 piece–8' long)
metal cans (2)

Introducing and Developing the Lesson

- ❑ Review how to whisper with the children.
- ❑ Whisper the directions for the game.
- ❑ Seat the children in a circle and tell them you are going to play a game with them called "What did I hear?"
- ❑ Whisper a short phrase to the child on your left and have that child repeat the phrase in a whisper to the child on his left.
- ❑ Continue around the circle until the last child repeats the phrase out loud to you. *Is the phrase the same as when you started it?*
- ❑ Continue playing the game until the children tire of it. Alternate the children who start the word or phrase that begins a new round of the game.

Practicing the Lesson

- ❑ During the day, whisper directions. For example, directions for learning centers, directions for going outside, and so on.
- ❑ Provide empty paper towel tubes. Have the children use the tubes to deliver whispered messages to friends. Do their friends get the messages?
- ❑ Make can telephones. First punch a hole with a nail or an ice pick in the bottom of two metal cans (an adult-only step). Help the children with the remaining steps: place masking tape around the mouth of the open end of each can; cut a piece of string 8' long; run one end of the string through the hole from the bottom in one can and tie it off; and run the other end of the string through the hole in the other can and tie it off. Stretch the string between the two cans and show the children how to use them to talk. Suggest that children try delivering a message to their partner in a whisper. *Can your partner repeat your message?*

Reflecting on the Lesson

Ask the children:

- ❑ *Do you think the phrase would have made it around the circle if we had spoken it instead of whispered it?*
- ❑ *Has anyone ever tried to tell someone something for you and did it incorrectly? How did you feel? What did you do?*

Special Needs Adaptations

Special Need	Adaptation
Visual Impairments	▪ The child with visual impairments may need to place his hand on the shoulder of his peer as he whispers into his ear. Remind the class that this child uses his hands to give him clues to things that he cannot see with his eyes.
Hearing Impairments	▪ Understanding what is being said when someone whispers could be very difficult for a child with hearing impairments. Adapt the activity by encouraging the child to be the person who picks the phrase that the others will whisper.
Cognitive Challenges	▪ Unless the child is sitting beside you, you may need to whisper gently in his ear the "phrase" he is to repeat. The goal for this child may be different than the goal for other children; the goal may be just to follow a two-step direction rather than to repeat exactly what he hears.
Motor Delays	▪ The concept of partial participation means that the child participates in an activity, even if he cannot complete the activity in the same manner as his peers. A child with motor delays may need to work with a friend: The child who is the whisperer says the phrase to each of them, but the friend is the one who whispers the phrase to the next person.
Speech/ Language Delays	▪ A child with a speech delay may not be easily understood by others. In order for him to participate, it may be necessary for you to suggest a message for him to use (select one that he can say easily).
Emotional/ Behavior Issues	▪ Children with behavior issues may have difficulty waiting their turn. For this child, the large group activity can lead to an outburst. Play the game first with a small group of three or four children before playing it as a large group.

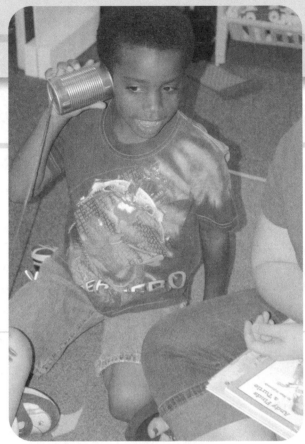

Tin can telephones encourage communication.

Listening Walk

Children will:

- listen with purpose in a new environment.

Vocabulary

hear
list
listen
nature

Materials

basket of items that make sounds
   (for example, a whistle, a bird
   whistle, a bell, rhythm sticks)
paper
pencil

Introducing and Developing the Lesson

- ❑ Engage the children in a discussion about the sounds that occur in nature, such as birds chirping, wind blowing, branches snapping when stepped on, and so on.
- ❑ Encourage the children to brainstorm a list of the sounds that occur outdoors.
- ❑ Take the children on a listening walk outdoors.
- ❑ Bring the list of nature sounds with you. Place a check mark beside the sounds the children hear on their walk.

Practicing the Lesson

- ❑ Provide a basket of sound makers, such as a whistle, a cheerleader's pompom, a bird whistle, rhythm sticks, a bell, and so on. Invite the children to use the items to recreate the sounds they heard on their nature walk.
- ❑ Invite the children to participate in *A Weather Story* (see page 266 in the Appendix). Discuss the items used to recreate nature sounds. Are they close to the real thing?
- ❑ Show the children how to make a rain sound by patting their hands on their thighs. Show them how to make a wind sound by blowing air through their curled tongue. *What other nature sounds can you make using your body?*

Reflecting on the Lesson

Ask the children:

- ❑ *What would it be like if there were no sounds in nature? How would you know it was raining if you were inside? Would you be able to see a bird if you did not hear it first?*
- ❑ *Can you make a rain sound with your body? Show me. Can you make a wind sound with your mouth? Let's hear it.*

Special Needs Adaptations

Special Need	Adaptation
Visual Impairments	■ Children with visual impairments can participate in the nature walk, but they will need to be guided. See page 17 in the Introduction for information on how to correctly guide a child who is visually impaired.
Hearing Impairments	■ During the nature walk, when a child hears something, like a bird, point to the bird so that the child with hearing impairments understands you are listening to the bird.
Cognitive Challenges	■ Children with cognitive challenges need extra help when going outside with a group. To provide the child as much independence as possible, teach him that when you hold your hand up and make the stop gesture (hand up with palm facing the child), it means it is time to stop what he is doing. Practice using this gesture with him throughout the day.
Motor Delays	■ Select a "path" for the nature walk that includes areas that are accessible for a child who uses a walker or wheelchair.
Speech/ Language Delays	■ When a child identifies a sound on the nature walk, point out the source. For example, if a child hears a bird, point to the bird and say, "Listen. That blue bird is singing." Wait. If the child does not respond, gently take his hand and help him point to the bird. Invite him to say the word "bird" as he points.
Emotional/ Behavior Issues	■ Children with behavior issues, especially those with autism spectrum disorder, may be hesitant to move into an unfamiliar environment. Prior to the nature walk, tell the child where you are going and what you will be doing. Knowing what will happen next can minimize the child's anxiety and fears about the unknown.

Sound Hunt

Children will:

- listen with purpose.

Vocabulary

find
hear
hunt
listen
sound

Materials

beanbag
bell

Introducing and Developing the Lesson

- ❑ Talk with the children about finding things that are hidden. If necessary, remind them about playing Hide and Seek, looking for Easter eggs, and going on treasure hunts.
- ❑ Ask them questions about how they locate hidden items. Many of their responses will mention using their eyes.
- ❑ Tell the children that they are going to go on a hunt for which they will need to use their ears instead of their eyes.
- ❑ Play Hot and Cold Hide and Seek: Select a child to be "IT." Tell IT that you will be hiding a beanbag somewhere in the room. Ask IT to step outside the room, explaining that, when he returns to the room, you will sing a song and use your voices to guide him to the beanbag. When you sing loud, it means that he is close to the beanbag. When you sing softly, it means that he is not close to the beanbag.
- ❑ While IT is out of the room, hide the beanbag.
- ❑ Bring IT back into the room and play the game.

Practicing the Lesson

- ❑ Play Ring-a-Ling Hide and Seek. Ask for a volunteer to be IT. Give IT a bell. All the children hide their eyes while IT finds a hiding place. Tell IT to ring the bell every so often to provide a clue about where to find him. When IT is found, allow him to select a new child to be IT.
- ❑ Take a walk outdoors. Listen for a sound and then try to find the origin of the sound.

Reflecting on the Lesson

Ask the children:

- ❑ *How is using your ears to find someone or something different from using your eyes? Is it more difficult? Why?*
- ❑ *Name some things that you might locate using your ears in place of your eyes, such as a cricket, a bee, a barking dog, and so on.*
- ❑ *Name some things that you might use both your ears and your eyes to find, such as an ambulance, a cuckoo clock, a water fountain, and so on.*

Special Needs Adaptations

Special Need	Adaptation
Visual Impairments	■ Adapt this activity for a child with visual impairments by hiding an object in a specific place, such as in the Block Center or in the Home Living Center, and telling the child in which general area the object is hidden.
Hearing Impairments	■ Help this child participate by giving him some cues, such as pointing toward the general area where the object is hidden or before the activity, showing him in which areas you will hide the object. For example, walk to the Home Living and the Literacy Centers and point to those two learning centers.
Cognitive Challenges	■ You may have different goals for a child with cognitive challenges. He may practice listening by following step-by-step directions until he finds the object. For example, you may tell him where the object is hidden to see if he can locate that particular place in the classroom; you could say, "The bells are hidden in the stove in the Home Living Center."
Motor Delays	■ Hide the object in a space that will be easier for the child to access, such as the Sand and Water Table.
Speech/ Language Delays	■ Review the following vocabulary words and demonstrate the meaning of each one for the child: *find, hear, hunt, listen,* and *sound.*
Emotional/ Behavior Issues	■ Play the listening game one time with the child one-on-one. Children with emotional issues often do not respond well to group games. If the child knows how to play the game, he may be more willing to participate.

Sound Sequence

Children will:

- hear and repeat a sequence of sounds.

Vocabulary

hear
listening
order
sequence
sound

Materials

music recordings
rhythm band instruments

Introducing and Developing the Lesson

- ❏ Show the children the rhythm band instruments and encourage them to explore the sounds that each instrument makes.
- ❏ Explain how the children can play a game called Sound Match with the instruments.
- ❏ Tell the children to close their eyes. Play three instruments in a sequence, and then tell the children to open their eyes.
- ❏ Ask for a volunteer to repeat your sequence.
- ❏ Tell the children to close their eyes again while the volunteer creates a new sequence of three sounds using the instruments.
- ❏ To make the game more difficult, try making a series of sounds with the same instrument. For example, ring the bells once, then twice, and then once again.
- ❏ Continue playing the game until children tire of it. Change the game slightly by creating a sequence of sounds that use one of the instruments more than once.

Practicing the Lesson

- ❏ Play music and invite the children to use rhythm instruments to accompany the music. After the music has ended, invite each child to demonstrate the sound his instrument made.
- ❏ Invite the children to create a clapping pattern. For example, a child might clap once and then two times quickly. The other children listen and then repeat the sequence of claps.

Reflecting on the Lesson

Ask the children:

- ❏ *Is it easier to hear a series of sounds made with different instruments than it is to hear a series of sounds made with the same instrument? Why?*
- ❏ *Name things in your home that make several sounds in a row (telephone, alarm clock, doorbell).*

Special Needs Adaptations

Invite children to play instruments to accompany the music.

Special Need	Adaptation
Visual Impairments	■ Invite the child with visual impairments to select the instrument he would like to play. Use three trays or box lids, and place a different instrument in each. Suggest that the child touch and examine each instrument before selecting the one he wants to use.
Hearing Impairments	■ A child with severe hearing loss will need extra help to learn how to identify sounds that are associated with the instruments used in this lesson. Hold up an instrument, such as a bell, and let the child see the instrument as you play it. Then, let the child touch the instrument and feel the vibrations as you play it.
Cognitive Challenges	■ Rather than closing his eyes, allow the child with cognitive challenges to keep his eyes open when you play the instruments. A realistic goal for him might be to identify or point to the instrument as you play it.
Motor Delays	■ If the child is able to move a muscle voluntarily, he can play along. For example, a child with cerebral palsy may be unable to use his hands, but may be able to use his feet to play a drum. If the child has extremely limited motor skills, adapt the activity by attaching a battery interrupter switch (see page 250 in the Appendix—Adaptive Switches) to a recording device. Record an instrument being played. The child can use his arm or hand to press the switch and activate the recording.
Speech/ Language Delays	■ To develop the child's vocabulary, give him a chance to interact with each instrument before asking him to select one. Show him an instrument, say its name, and play it. Invite the child to do the same. Look for intentional behavior, even if you are not sure what the child wants. For example, hold up the bells and cymbals and say, "Do you want to play the bells (jingle them) or the cymbals (clang them)?" The child may not be able to select one or point to the instrument he wants to play. However, if he moves his body or looks toward one instrument, treat that movement as an intentional choice. Say, "Oh you looked at the bells." Hand the bells to the child. Honoring the child's choices and treating this gesture as an intentional form of communication will help him begin to understand that communication is intentional.
Emotional/ Behavior Issues	■ Children with emotional issues often respond well to music. Select a song that the child enjoys and invite him to play along. If the child is overwhelmed with too many choices, offer him two instruments and let him choose which one to play.

Sounds Within Sounds

Children will:
- listen intently.
- discriminate between sounds.

Vocabulary

blend
hear
listen
music
sounds
voice
where

Materials

recording device
recording media
rhythm band instruments

Introducing and Developing the Lesson

- ❑ Tell the children that they are going to sing "The Calliope Song."
- ❑ Divide children into four groups. Instruct group one to make sound 1. Group two will make sound 2. Group three will make sound 3. Group four will make sound 4.

  Sound 1: Um pa pa, um pa pa…

  Sound 2: Um tweedli-dee, um tweedli-dee…

  Sound 3: Um shhh, um shhh…

  Sound 4: Hum the circus song (the song generally heard on a merry-go-round)

- ❑ Talk about the combination of sounds. Ask the children if what they heard seemed to be one sound or many different sounds. Sing the song again and ask the children to attempt to hear each sound separately. Point out that, in the song, the sounds blend together and are unified by rhythm (beat and meter).

Practicing the Lesson

- ❑ Tell the children to close their eyes while you make three sounds simultaneously using rhythm band instruments or other objects. Ask the children to identify the three instruments you played. Suggest that each child select a partner and continue playing the game with their partners.
- ❑ Explain to the children that it is often hard to hear individual sounds when many different sounds are present. Discuss the sounds that occur on the playground. *Is it easy to hear your name when someone calls you on the playground?* Talk about the cafeteria. *Is it easy to hear a conversation while so many people are talking?*

Reflecting on the Lesson

Ask the children:
- ❑ *Why is it more difficult to hear a specific sound when several sounds occur at the same time?*
- ❑ *What makes musical instruments sound pleasant when they are all playing at the same time?*

Special Needs Adaptations

Special Need	Adaptation
Visual Impairments	■ Because a child with a visual impairment learns to depend on other senses to help him, his listening skills are often well developed. Use this activity as an opportunity to let the child excel and demonstrate his ability for his classmates.
Hearing Impairments	■ Depending on the severity of the impairment, the child may be unable to participate in some games. Look for ways to adapt an activity that focuses on what the child sees rather than what he hears. For example, invite the child to leave his eyes open as the instruments are played.
Cognitive Challenges	■ Instead of playing three sounds, adapt this activity by playing only one sound. The same adaptation can be made when the child is playing with a partner.
Motor Delays	■ A child with motor delays, especially a child with significant delays, may not be able to speak. Look for ways he can participate, such as inviting him to point to a picture of an instrument after you play it. Remember to make sure the child is positioned in his wheelchair in a comfortable position. When introducing an activity or a new object, bring it to his eye level, so he can see it.
Speech/ Language Delays	■ Demonstrate each rhythm band instrument for the child. Encourage him to watch you as you play a sound, and then close his eyes and see if he can identify the sound you played. Remember to tell the child the name of the instrument when you play it.
Emotional/ Behavior Issues	■ For a child with emotional issues, you may find it best to assign him a peer partner who is patient. If possible, let him pick his partner, allowing him to feel more in control. The child with significant issues, such as autism, may benefit from a gradual introduction to a new activity. Give him the option not to participate if he prefers to watch. Decide ahead of time which goal is more important—his participation without a tantrum or outburst, or forcing him to comply and risking an outburst. Look for signs that he is frustrated or upset and allow him to leave the group if he gets agitated. However, if he gets upset and begins a tantrum, it may be necessary to insist that he continue or finish the activity after the outburst. This demonstrates to the child that his outbursts will not result in his being able to get out of an activity. It is very important for children with behavior issues to understand that there are some activities where they have control and can choose to participate and other activities where their participation is required.

Listening

Listening for Directions

Children will:
- follow simple directions.

Vocabulary
direction
follow
hear
listen

Materials
book from the library
box (construction paper must be
    able to fit inside)
construction paper
cup of paint
marble
recording device
recording media
spoon

Introducing and Developing the Lesson

- ❑ Ask for a volunteer and then tell that child to get a specific book from the library.
- ❑ Give the child directions, telling him three specific things. For example, "Gabrielle, will you go to the Library Center and bring me the book with the dinosaur on the front and the red letters?"
- ❑ When the volunteer returns with the book, discuss the three things he had to listen for—*dinosaur, front of the book,* and *red letters.* What would have happened if he had not listened to all three parts of the directions?
- ❑ Invite the children to follow the directions in "Teddy Bear, Teddy Bear" (see page 265 in the Appendix).
- ❑ Invite the children to make up new lines to the chant.

Practicing the Lesson

- ❑ Play Simon Says: Select a child to be Simon. Have Simon stand in front of the other children. When Simon prefaces an instruction with "Simon Says," as in "Simon says, 'Stand up,'" the children should do it, and when Simon does not say "Simon Says," as in "Stand up," they should not do it. Encourage Simon to use two- and three-part directions. For example, "Simon says, 'Touch your ear and turn around.'"
- ❑ Record directions for an art project. Have the children listen to the directions prior to doing the art project. For example, the directions for marble painting might be: 1) Select a sheet of construction paper; 2) Place your paper into the box provided; 3) Use the spoon to remove a marble from a cup of paint and place it into the box; and 4) Move the box back and forth to roll the marble across your paper and create a design.

Reflecting on the Lesson

Ask the children:
- ❑ *Have you ever made a mistake because you didn't listen to the directions? When?*
- ❑ *Do you need to follow directions when you brush your teeth? Play a game?*

Special Needs Adaptations

Special Need	Adaptation
Visual Impairments	■ Start with two verses and give him the opportunity to practice those before adding more verses.
Hearing Impairments	■ If the child uses sign language, start with one-step directions and build up to two- and three-step directions. If the child uses residual hearing and has some functional use of hearing, combine gestures with verbal cues. Remember to make sure he can see your lips and face when speaking to him.
Cognitive Challenges	■ Make directions simple and direct. For example, say, "Go to the Block Center." When the child goes to the Block Center, give him the next instruction, "Pick up a block." Wait a moment and say, "Bring it to me." If the child does not understand what you are asking him to do, you may need to model it for him.
Motor Delays	■ Adapt the verses of "Teddy Bear, Teddy Bear" so they include movements that the child can do. For example, instead of "Teddy Bear, Teddy Bear, turn around" you might say, "Teddy Bear, Teddy Bear, blink at the sound/Teddy Bear, Teddy Bear, look at the ground."
Speech/ Language Delays	■ Combine directions with simple tasks you want the child to learn, such as, "Turn on the light" or "Turn off the light." Play a game with a box and an object. Practice giving directions that reinforce learning functional opposite pairs. For example, "Put the ball on the box" or "Put the ball under the box." Look for opportunities to expand learning, so the child can learn to follow two-step directions.
Emotional/ Behavior Issues	■ A child with behavior issues may have great waiting for his turn to follow directions, so allow him to go second or third. Make sure you give him a directive that he can and will be able to accomplish. Follow up his turn by smiling at him and telling him he did well. Thank him for sitting quietly while others take their turns.

Listening

Back-to-Back Listening

Children will
- listen intently.

Vocabulary
directions
follow
hear
listen

Materials
color tiles for each child (one each of red, green, yellow, and blue)
light source
sheet

Back-to-back listening with a friend makes listening more fun.

Introducing and Developing the Lesson

- Begin Circle or Group Time with your back to the children. Start with the usual greeting and activities. Turn around and then engage the children in a discussion about the difference between listening to directions when facing someone and listening to directions when you can't see the speaker's eyes and mouth. *Why is it easier to follow directions when you are looking at the speaker?* Tell the children that today they are going to learn about listening carefully.

- Give each child four color tiles—one red, one green, one yellow, and one blue. Direct the children to stack their tiles in a specific order. For example, place the yellow tile on the bottom, the blue next, followed by the red tile, and then the green tile.

- Ask the children to find a partner. The partners decide which child will be the speaker and which child will be the listener. Then, have the children sit back-to-back. The speakers tell the listeners how to stack the color tiles. The speaker stacks his own tiles as he tells the listener how to stack his tiles. Then the partners compare their tile towers.

Practicing the Lesson

- Invite the children to build towers while sitting back-to-back with a partner as they did during the lesson.

- Hang a sheet and place a light source behind it. Have a volunteer stand behind the sheet. Ask for a volunteer and give that child directions for different movements. For example, you might say, "Jump up and down and clap your hands." Continue giving directions that get progressively more difficult until the child is no longer able to follow the directions. Select another listener and try the activity again. Discuss this activity when you are finished.

Reflecting on the Lesson

Ask the children:

- *Do you think you would get better at building color towers back-to-back with a partner if you practiced more?*

- *What did you have to do to get the tower right when you couldn't see the tower your partner was making?*

Special Needs Adaptations

Special Need	Adaptation
Visual Impairments	■ For a child with visual impairments, adapt the lesson by giving him tiles that are slightly different in size and/or shape. Change the directions so he can participate with his classmates. Or, you may direct the other children to stack their tiles in a specific order while you direct the child with visual impairments to stack his according to size. For example, place the small square tile on the bottom and the round tile on top of it.
Hearing Impairments	■ Because a child with hearing impairments must see the speaker at all times, place him where he can see you, even if the other children in the classroom cannot see you. Explain to them that he gets to see you because it is the only way he can understand what you say.
Cognitive Challenges	■ Give the child with cognitive challenges fewer tiles and make the directions simple. For example, instead of four tiles, give him two tiles. Make sure he can tell you the color of each tile before asking him to participate in the activity.
Motor Delays	■ A child with motor delays may have difficulty picking up tiles. Adapt the activity for him by having him stack objects that are easily picked up, such as plastic cups (preferably the ones with two handles) or four blocks of four different colors with knobs glued to the side for easy handling (see page 251 in the Appendix—Adaptive Handles).
Speech/ Language Delays	■ All of the activities in this lesson will be easier if the child knows and understands the directions. Demonstrate what he will be expected to do (stack tiles, build with a partner, and sit back to back). Model each step for him. Because the child may have limited language, it is important for him to see you demonstrate what is expected.
Emotional/ Behavior Issues	■ Start with instructions that you know he can do, and gradually make them more difficult. If he returns to his seat without getting upset, be sure to praise him. You might say something like, "You followed the rules very well."

Echo Songs

Children will:
■ listen and repeat what is heard.

Vocabulary
echo
hear
listen
repeat

Materials
deep aluminum pan
Little Beaver and the Echo by Amy
    MacDonald
paper-towel tubes

Introducing and Developing the Lesson

❑ Talk about what an echo is: An echo happens when sound bounces off things. The sound has to be loud and a fair distance from what it bounces off (wall, mountainside, and so on). An echo occurs a second or two after the original sound is made.

❑ If possible, take the children into an area in the school where they can hear an echo. Bathrooms sometimes produce an echo. Rooms with smooth walls, little furniture to absorb sound, and a high ceiling work best.

❑ Like a sound echo, echo songs are songs that have repeated lines. Sing the echo song, "I Met a Bear" (see page 257 in the Appendix). Remind the children to listen closely to what you sing so they will be able to repeat the lines accurately.

❑ After singing the song, talk with the children about listening carefully and the importance of repeating exactly what they hear.

Practicing the Lesson

❑ Give the children a deep aluminum pan. Have each child attempt to create an echo by putting his face inside the pan and speaking. Try using empty paper-towel tubes to direct the sound into the pan. Sound normally scatters; a tube will help keep the sound more concentrated.

❑ Read *Little Beaver and the Echo* by Amy MacDonald. Read the story a second time and invite the children to be the echo.

Reflecting on the Lesson

Ask the children:
❑ *What do you have to do to be able to repeat a sentence back to someone exactly as they say it?*
❑ *What is an echo?*

Special Needs Adaptations

Special Need	Adaptation
Visual Impairments	■ To help the child understand the concept of echo, he may need a visual representation. Get a tennis ball and bounce it off a surface that makes a noise. Place the child's hand on the ball and gently guide the ball with the child holding it down to the surface and back up. Explain that sound, although invisible, bounces off objects in the same way as the ball.
Hearing Impairments	■ Because the child may have difficulty hearing all the words, practice singing "I Met a Bear" with him several times before introducing it to the rest of the class.
Cognitive Challenges	■ Give the child with cognitive challenges fewer verses of "I Met a Bear" to learn. If the child cannot sing all the words, encourage him to hum along as the others sing.
Motor Delays	■ If the child cannot control his movements, as you sing each repeating verse of "I Met a Bear," provide a loop tape and a single button switch so the child can play the repeating verse.
Speech/ Language Delays	■ To help the child increase his vocabulary, provide a picture of each item mentioned in "I Met a Bear." Invite the child to hold up the picture when you say the name of it. Later, when you are working one on one with him or in a small group, invite him to use each word in a sentence.
Emotional/ Behavior Issues	■ Because "I Met a Bear" has so many verses, the child may become frustrated and yell out "I can't!" or "No!" in the middle of the song. Before starting the chant, remind him that he can stop at any time. While not all activities can be optional, it is important for the child to learn that participation without an outburst is sometimes more important than completing every activity.

Books That Support Listening

All Cats have Asperger Syndrome by Kathy
    Hoopmann *

Anansi and the Talking Melon retold by Eric A.
    Kimmel

Do Your Ears Hang Low? by Caroline Jayne Church

Epossumondas by Coleen Salley

Evan Early by Rebecca Hogue Wojahn *

Leo the Late Bloomer by Robert Kraus *

Little Beaver and the Echo by Amy MacDonald

Listen to the Rain by Bill Martin, Jr.

My Friend Isabelle by Elizabeth Woloson

The Listening Walk by Paul Showers

Moses Goes to a Concert by Isaac Millman *

Polar Bear, Polar Bear, What Do You Hear? by Bill
    Martin, Jr. and Eric Carle

Rolling Along: The Story of Taylor and His Wheelchair
    by Jamee Riggio Heelan *

The Very Quiet Cricket by Eric Carle

We Can Do It by Laura Dwight*

We'll Paint the Octopus Red by Stephanie Stuve-
    Bodeen *

*Why Mosquitoes Buzz in People's Ears: A West African
    Tale* by Verna Aardema

* Denotes books about children with special needs

Chapter 2

Oral Language Development

Overview

Oral language development refers to the building of vocabulary and the perfecting of the accuracy of grammar. The ultimate goal is to produce fluency of speaking.

An infant with a talkative caretaker will have about 181 more words in her vocabulary than a child with a caretaker who is not as talkative. By the age of two, the gap has grown to 294 more words. This information alone provides a strong case for talking, as much as possible, to young children.

The size of a child's vocabulary is one of the most accurate predictors of how successful that child will be when formal reading instruction is introduced. The most fertile time for vocabulary development is from birth to age five. A five-year-old will typically have acquired 60% of her lifetime vocabulary. The more vocabulary building opportunities children encounter, the greater the chance their vocabularies will grow. The more vocabulary they have, the more they acquire. It is natural to use more vocabularies with children who seem to be more articulate. The more you use, the more they pick up. That is why it is particularly important to spend extra time working on the vocabulary development of a child with a speech and/or language delay. Often, because of these delays, they do not have the same

opportunities their peers have to develop their language skills.

Opportunities for developing children's vocabulary occur throughout the day in the classroom. There are vocabulary opportunities during group discussions and when children sing or listen to a story. However, you must be in tune to these opportunities to capitalize on them. Staying in tune is a big part of becoming more intentional and purposeful in your teaching.

Children develop the correct usage of sentence structure and grammar when they hear you model it and when you encourage children to make adaptations. When children hear the correct use of grammar, they modify their use. Your role is to coach them gently by restating children's questions and responding without embarrassing them or making too much fuss about their errors. Children with cognitive challenges or severe language delays need even more help. Unlike their peers, they have difficulty learning from modeling and watching what others do. Instead, they need specific and direct instruction on how to use language, and they also need extra practice. For these children, it will be important to break down new information into small bits and directions into small steps. Practice each step with the child before going to the next step.

Vocabulary and, to a lesser degree, grammar each play a role in children's ability to comprehend what they hear. For example, the more vocabulary a child has, the greater her ability to understand fully the plot and details of a story. After listening, vocabulary is the next building block in the foundation of literacy.

What's in the Box?

Children will:
- use descriptive language.
- listen intently.

Vocabulary
clues
guess
hard
heavy
light
loud
questions
quiet
soft

Materials
box
decorative paper and bow
toy

Preparation
Find a special (or a familiar) toy. Wrap it in a box with decorative paper and bow.

Introducing and Developing the Lesson

- ❏ Show the children the box with the toy inside.
- ❏ Tell the children that they will learn how to listen closely to clues and ask questions to determine what is inside a box.
- ❏ Say, "Okay! Are you ready to find out what's inside? I will give you some clues and let you guess what is inside."
- ❏ Ask for a volunteer and allow that child to pick up the box, shake it, and determine if the item inside is heavy or light.

Encourage children to guess what is in the wrapped box.

- ❏ Allow another volunteer to shake the box to see if the item makes a loud or soft sound.
- ❏ Give the children clues, until someone guesses what's in the box. For example, if the item is a blue crayon from the Art Center, you might say, "It is blue. It is from the Art Center, and it is round."

Practicing the Lesson

- ❏ Find a box with a lid. Suggest that one child put a toy in the box and play "What's in the box?" with a friend.

Reflecting on the Lesson

Ask the children:
- ❏ *How can you find out what is inside a box when you don't know what is in it and you can't open the box?*
- ❏ *What is a clue?*

Special Needs Adaptations

Special Need	Adaptation
Visual Impairments	■ Allow the child to examine the box independent of the rest of the class. Encourage her to touch the bow, the sides, and the bottom. Try to use an item that makes a noise, so when she shakes the box she will hear the noise. When you are exploring the box with the rest of the class, let her examine it with her hands after you complete each step of unwrapping it.
Hearing Impairments	■ If the child has some residual hearing, make sure she understands what you are doing. Be sure to use words such as first, second, next, and so on as each clue is given and as the gift is unwrapped.
Cognitive Challenges	■ Show the child three items and ask her to tell you the name of each. Tell her that one of the three items you showed her will be wrapped in the box. This will make it easier for her to name the item when the box is opened.
Motor Delays	■ If the child's motor skills are such that she cannot participate in unwrapping an item, use a colorful gift bag instead of a box.
Speech/ Language Delays	■ Use the same procedure described under cognitive challenges. Remember to use only three or four objects and to show each of them to the child before selecting one to put in the gift box. Help the child describe each item to you as she looks at it. Encourage her to use words that describe the item, such as color, size, shape, and so on.
Emotional/ Behavior Issues	■ To help the child stay engaged, select an object for the gift box that is a preferred item. Make sure it is made of a material that the child will touch. Remember that some children have tactile sensitivity, which means there may be some textures or materials that are unpleasant to them. Some children may be hesitant to reach inside and touch something unknown to them. You may need to model how to reach inside the box. Remember to smile as you reach in the box, so the child knows it is an enjoyable activity.

Vocabulary

I Spy

Children will:

- increase their descriptive vocabulary.

Vocabulary

attributes
describes
descriptive
words

Materials

attribute blocks
bag
basket
red construction paper, cut into a square
two or three items that are simple to identify by touch

Introducing and Developing the Lesson

- ❏ Sing "If You're Happy and You Know It." Instead of the usual second and third verse, use the following verses:

  If you're happy and you know it, point to something red.
  If you're happy and you know it, point to something round.

- ❏ Engage the children in a discussion about the word "attributes." Explain that attributes are words that describe something.
- ❏ Hold up a square of red construction paper. Ask the children to describe the paper. *It is red. It is square. It is paper. It has four sides.*
- ❏ Tell the children that they are going to play a game during which they will need to pay careful attention to attributes.
- ❏ Play I Spy. Gather the children into a group and challenge them to find items in the room.
- ❏ Choose easy-to-find things using words that the children understand so children are successful finding things as they learn to play. Increase the difficulty as children become more familiar with the game.
- ❏ Discuss how to play the game. The children must listen to the description of the object (its attributes) and then look carefully at objects in the room, trying to find objects that fit the description.

Practicing the Lesson

- ❏ Provide a basket of attribute blocks. Encourage the children to sort the items by attributes and then describe the attributes that they used for their sorting criteria.
- ❏ During snack time, ask the children to describe their snacks.

Reflecting on the Lesson

Ask the children:

- ❏ *Describe one of the things that were spied while playing I Spy.*
- ❏ *How do you think someone might describe you?*

Special Needs Adaptations

Special Need	Adaptation
Visual Impairments	■ Adapt the activity by playing I Spy differently. Place five objects on a tray and ask the child who is visually impaired to examine them. Remember that she may examine them by touching, smelling, and listening to the noises they make. Typically developing peers can play along with her. Then describe an item on the tray for the child to identify. As the child becomes more adept at playing, increase the number of items on the tray.
Hearing Impairments	■ Make sure the child understands the rules of the game and why you are playing it. Play the game with fewer players and limit the area in which the object is located. If the child uses sign language, look for new words she can learn and teach them to the entire class.
Cognitive Challenges	■ Help this child understand the rules and acquire the vocabulary necessary to describe items. First, play I Spy with her one on one to help her become familiar with the rules. As you play, tell her what you are describing as you describe it for her to spy.
Motor Delays	■ Be sure to select items for I Spy that the child can see. Remember, a child in a wheelchair may have a more limited field of vision. Encourage the child to participate in the activities. Because children with special needs need extra encouragement to try something new, remember to use cues such as a nod, a smile, or a pat on the shoulder to encourage them.
Speech/ Language Delays	■ The child may not have the vocabulary necessary to describe what she sees or to understand what you are describing when you play I Spy. It may be necessary to adapt the activity by showing her how to play the game. Break down each step and ask her to do it along with you. When you are describing an item, you may need to give the child a hint, such as, "I am going to describe a book on the shelf." First, direct the child's attention to the books. Next, say, "I spy a book with a red cover." Encourage the child to play along. If possible, get her to practice her language skills by making a sentence with the object you select to spy.
Emotional/ Behavior Issues	■ Children with emotional challenges are more likely to participate when they feel they can succeed. Start by making sure the child knows exactly what you are describing. Nod when the child answers correctly. If the child seems to be enjoying the game, ask her to spy something and describe it for a small group of peers.

Make a Word Web

Children will

- develop vocabulary.
- speak in complete sentences.
- engage in conversation.

Vocabulary

describe
know
sentences
web
word

Materials

basket
books about dogs
chart paper
marker
items that relate to a dog (collar,
    can of food)
items that are not related to a dog
    (glove, doll, crayon, scissors)
masking tape
paper or plastic bone
picture of a dog

Introducing and Developing the Lesson

- ❏ Engage the children in a discussion about dogs. Ask them what they know about dogs. "Does anyone have a dog?"
- ❏ Create an information word web. Make a circle on chart paper. Print "dogs" in the center of the circle.
- ❏ As the children tell you what they know about dogs, encourage them to use complete sentences.
- ❏ Write the information they provide about dogs on lines that extend out from the circle.
- ❏ Use masking tape to make a circle on the floor with lines extending out from the circle to simulate the word web. Place a picture of a dog in the circle.
- ❏ Provide a basket full of items with some that are related to dogs (collar, bone, can of food, squeaky toy, ball, and so on) and some that are not related to dogs (glove, doll, crayon, scissors).
- ❏ Challenge the children to find the items related to dogs and place them on the lines around the circle to create a concrete word web.

Practicing the Lesson

- ❏ Fill the Library Center with books about dogs.
- ❏ Visit a pet store or kennel, or invite someone to bring a dog to class. Invite the children to help you make a list of things they notice about dogs.
- ❏ Encourage the children to draw pictures of dogs.
- ❏ Sing songs about dogs, such as "Bingo" and "Fiddle-i-Fee" (see pages 254 and 256 in the Appendix).

Reflecting on the Lesson

Ask the children:

- ❏ *What did you learn about dogs today?*
- ❏ *What information about dogs was most interesting to you?*

Special Needs Adaptations

Special Need	Adaptation
Visual Impairments	■ Instead of placing a picture of a dog in the circle, use a stuffed dog. Allow the child to examine the stuffed dog and all the items that will be placed at the end of the tape lines. Let her feel each one and tell her the name of each item if she does not already know it.
Hearing Impairments	■ The child can participate in this activity if she understands what is expected of her. Hold up a picture of a dog and explain that the class will be talking about dogs.
Cognitive Challenges	■ Adapt the concrete word web for a child with cognitive challenges by excluding items not related to dogs. Include only three or four concrete items and ask the child to name them for you. If the child is able, invite her to describe each item using more than one word.
Motor Delays	■ Provide a picture of a dog for the child to look at when she is describing what she knows about a dog. If she is unable to help place items on the concrete word web, let her participate partially by holding each item for the other children.
Speech/ Language Delays	■ If the child does not have enough vocabulary to tell you what she knows about dogs, give her some hints such as, "How big is a dog?" "What does a dog wag?" "What does a dog eat?" After you have made a list on chart paper of everything the children know about dogs, go over the list with the child and ask her to make a sentence with each word.
Emotional/ Behavior Issues	■ Use this lesson as an opportunity to stress how to use gentle touch when petting a dog and how to treat a pet kindly. It is important for a child to learn that it is never okay to hit, kick, or mistreat an animal, even if you become upset or frustrated with that animal.

A Word a Day

Children will:
■ build vocabulary.

Vocabulary
more
vocabulary
words

Materials
chart paper
crayons
index cards
Lilly's Purple Plastic Purse by
    Kevin Henkes or *My Granny's
    Purse* by P. H. Hansen
    (optional)
marker
purse
recipe box
ring

Introducing and Developing the Lesson

❑ Hold a purse in your hand and show it to the children. Ask them what you are holding. Make a list of the words they use to name it—*purse, pocketbook, handbag, change purse,* and so on. Explain that words are used to express ourselves, to describe things, and to understand others. Tell them that today they will be learning new words.

❑ Read *Lilly's Purple Plastic Purse* by Kevin Henkes, *My Granny's Purse* by P. H. Hansen, or make up your own story about a purse.

❑ Pick out key vocabulary words in the story and discuss them prior to reading the book or telling your own story. Write the new words on index cards and place them in a box like a recipe box. Tell the children that you are going to keep the new words they learn each day in this special box.

❑ Help each child build her own "Word Bank." Let each child choose her favorite new word from the words you introduce during story time. Print each child's chosen word on an index card and punch a hole in the top left corner. Place her card in a special box or on a ring clasp. Allow the children to illustrate their cards, so they will have picture clues to remind them of their new words.

Practicing the Lesson

❑ Create a cheer to use when the children use one of the day's new words. For example, say, "Hip, hip, hurray! Gabrielle used a new word today!"

❑ Encourage children to ask you to write new words they encounter during the day on additional index cards. Help them add the cards to their individual word banks.

❑ Ask the children to help label three items in the classroom. Allow them to choose the items and help make the labels. Do not label more than three items, because children will be overwhelmed if confronted with too many labels. After a few days, remove the labels and place them in a Classroom Word Bank and three new labels can be created.

Reflecting on the Lesson

Ask the children:
❑ *Which of today's words do you like best?*
❑ *Use (say one of today's words) in a sentence.*

Special Needs Adaptations

Special Need	Adaptation
Visual Impairments	■ To help this child learn new words, find objects that she can learn to name. For example, after you select a book to read to the class, identify several objects from the book that are new for the child. As you read a word, hand the object to the child so she can explore it with her hands.
Hearing Impairments	■ A child with a hearing impairment often has very limited vocabulary. To help build new vocabulary, the child may need extra support. Reinforce her learning new words by describing each new word to her in short, simple sentences. Some children with hearing impairments may nod and look at you as if to say, "I understand," when in reality, they don't. Children learn early that if they pretend to hear something, adults will often leave them alone. Don't assume the child knows a word. Encourage her to use it in a sentence and to describe the word for you.
Cognitive Challenges	■ A child with cognitive challenges needs encouragement to learn new words and to use the words she already knows. Her word bank may have fewer words than her classmates', but it is important that she is able to use the words in her box appropriately. After you identify a new word for the child to learn, look for multiple opportunities throughout the day for her to use the word. Don't forget to tell her family about her new vocabulary word and encourage them to use it as well. This fosters the child's ability to generalize and respond the same way to the same thing in different settings.
Motor Delays	■ A child with motor delays, especially a child who is in a wheelchair, will need new objects and/or words presented at her eye level.
Speech/ Language Delays	■ When teaching new words to a child with limited language, select words that are more concrete, such as simple nouns or verbs. If possible, put a picture of the word on the cards in her word bank to help her identify the word.
Emotional/ Behavior Issues	■ Children with emotional issues are more likely to participate in an activity if they know exactly what will happen next. Remember to tell or show her what will happen next. Issues Explain that her word bank is not a real bank where you put money but another word for a word list.

Some children need visual and auditory cues to learn about new objects.

Sing a Song

Children will:
- increase vocabulary.

Vocabulary
actions
describe
vocabulary
words

Materials
basket of small toys and objects that have more than one name (for example, car, automobile)
markers
paper
star template

Introducing and Developing the Lesson

❑ Ask for a volunteer to stand up. Ask the class to describe what the child is doing (standing).

❑ Whisper into the child's ear, directing her to jump. Now ask the children to describe what their friend is doing (jumping). Whisper to the volunteer to turn in circles. Ask the children to describe what their friend is doing now (turning).

❑ Explain that words are used to describe people, objects, and actions. Tell the children that they are going to practice using descriptive and action words.

❑ Sing "Twinkle, Twinkle, Little Star" (see page 260 in the Appendix). Use your voice to demonstrate what a tiny star might sound like. Sing the song a second time, using "gigantic" instead of "little." Again, use your voice to demonstrate gigantic. Sing the song another time, changing the description of the star and using your voice, if possible, to reinforce the description.

❑ Try this with other songs that the children know.

Practicing the Lesson

❑ Provide a star template, paper, and markers for the children to create a variety of different kinds of stars. With their permission, label their stars.

❑ Provide a basket of small toys and objects that have more than one name, such as a car (automobile), teddy bear (stuffed animal), penny (coin/money), and so on. Have the children describe each toy and provide as many different names as they know for each item.

Reflecting on the Lesson

Ask the children:

❑ *After singing "Itsy Bitsy Spider," can you think of a new spider to sing about? Try singing about the spiders that children suggest.*

❑ *Which type of star did you like the best?*

Special Needs Adaptations

Special Need	Adaptation
Visual Impairments	■ A child with visual impairments may not know what a star is or how it looks in the sky at night. Make a cardboard cutout of a star and invite the child to trace it with her hands. Talk about stars and how they twinkle. Remember to use concrete language, because, for a visually impaired child, the concept of twinkling may be difficult to understand.
Hearing Impairments	■ The sign for "star" (see page 252 in the Appendix) is easy to make. Teach the whole class the sign for "star" and invite all them to sign the word "star" when they hear it in the song.
Cognitive Challenges	■ Invite the child to sing along, even if she does not know all the words to the song. To help the child learn action words, play a game where you say an action word, such as "jump." Then do the action. Try additional words like "hop," "walk," "sit down," and so on. Make a list of the action words the child is learning and send it home with her. Invite her family to use the words when speaking with her. Remember, it is always a good idea to make sure the child understands and uses one word before teaching her a new one.
Motor Delays	■ Look for words that describe actions that the child can do. A child with limited mobility may be unable to turn around, but she can clap her hands or stomp her feet.
Speech/ Language Delays	■ Make a list of action words and suggest that the child do each action (jump, hop, clap, and so on). If the child does not understand, model the action for her and then ask her to join you.
Emotional/ Behavior Issues	■ If the child understands the instructions, she may be more willing to participate in the activity. For a child who is reluctant to try new activities, do not worry about whether she gets the movements correct. Remember that what is important is that she participates and has fun trying something new.

Vocabulary

Add a Word

Children will:
- practice using descriptive words.
- expand a sentence.

Vocabulary
add
description
descriptive
sentence
words

Materials
ball (optional) **Note:** Do this
    lesson using a ball as a prop, if
    you feel that the children need
    support to come up with
    descriptive words for a ball.
chart paper
crayons or pencils
index cards
markers
rebus cards
yarn

Introducing and Developing the Lesson

- Tell the children that they will learn about using descriptive words.
  Print each word of the following sentence on individual index cards: *I
  like my shoes with red stripes, rubber soles, white laces, and round toes.*
  Place the first four cards (for the words "I like my shoes") on the floor,
  reading them as each is put down.
- Tell the children that you are going to make the sentence longer by
  adding descriptions of the shoes. Add each set of descriptors—"with
  red stripes," "rubber soles," "white laces," and "and round toes"—one
  set at a time, and reread the sentence each time you add words to it.
- Place a strip of yarn along the bottom of the words of the original
  sentence, so children can see how much the sentence has grown.
  Point out how much more we know about the shoes with all the
  descriptive phrases added.
- Start a sentence and allow children to add descriptive words or phrases.
  For example, your sentence might be "I have a ball." Children can then
  add descriptors, such as *big, red, striped, rubber, bouncing,* and so on.
- Print the original sentence on chart paper and then print the new
  sentence with each descriptive word or phrase under the original
  sentence, so children can actually see the sentence grow. Discuss how
  much more you know about the ball after hearing all the descriptors.

Practicing the Lesson

- Place rebus cards for "big" and "little," colors words ("red," "blue,"
  "yellow," "green," and so on), patterns ("plaid," "stripe," "polka dot," and
  so on), "soft," "hard," "loud," and so on in the Language Center. Place rebus
  cards for objects, such as a "ball," "shoe," "doll," "book," and so on in the
  center as well. Have the children use the descriptive rebus cards to describe
  the object rebus cards. For example, if the child chooses the object book,
  she might choose the descriptive cards for "big," "soft" and "red."

Reflecting on the Lesson

Ask the children:
- *What words would you use to describe yourself?*
- *How do descriptive words help us communicate more clearly?*

Special Needs Adaptations

Special Need	Adaptation
Visual Impairments	■ After you have made the long sentence and placed a piece of yarn on it to show how long it has become, invite the child with visual impairments to feel the yarn. By feeling the length of the yarn, she has a sense of how long the sentence is.
Hearing Impairments	■ Invite the child to add to the sentence by signing a word or by selecting a word from a picture cue.
Cognitive Challenges	■ To help the child participate in developing the class sentence, help her add a word by asking a specific question. For example, if you are using the sentence, "I have a ball," ask the child a directed question such as, "What color is the ball?" The child can add *big, red, striped, rubber, bouncing,* or so on, and then print the new sentence with the child's word.
Motor Delays	■ If the child is unable to select the rebus cards she needs to describe the object she picks, look for alternative ways for her to do so. For example, attach wooden clothespins to the rebus cards to make them easier to pick up if the child has difficulty grasping flat objects.
Speech/ Language Delays	■ Before asking the child to select rebus cards to describe her sentence, make sure she knows the names on the cards. Review each one with her and help her identify color words, size words, and other words that she may not know. If she is overwhelmed by the number of cards, use fewer cards.
Emotional/ Behavior Issues	■ Children with behavior issues tend to get frustrated easily and often do not attend well in group activities. Invite the child to help you measure the sentence with the yarn or to help you place each card as you read it. Actions and movement help children with short attention spans stay focused and engaged.

Signing helps the child add new words to her vocabulary.

Opposites

Children will:

- increase vocabulary.
- use vocabulary related to opposites.

Vocabulary

big	over
describe	short
fast	slow
hard	soft
in	tall
little	under
opposites	words
out	

Materials

basket of items that represent
    opposites
chart paper
marker
playdough

Introducing and Developing the Lesson

- ❏ Tell the children that they will learn about other pairs of opposites.
- ❏ Collect a basket of items that represent opposites—a big button and a small button, a tall straw and a short straw, a soft ball and a hard ball, and so on.
- ❏ Take the pairs of items from your basket, one pair at a time. Pass the items around the circle so children can examine them.
- ❏ Ask the children to describe the items. Write their descriptions of each pair on chart paper. Point out the descriptive words that make each pair opposites.
- ❏ Sing and dance "The Hokey Pokey." Discuss the opposites *in* and *out*. Repeat the verses, using other body parts and opposite words.

Practicing the Lesson

- ❏ Have an Opposite Hunt. Take a walk around the classroom or school in search of opposites.
- ❏ Place the basket of opposite pairs in a center and invite the children to match the pairs. Talk with them as they work.
- ❏ Sing songs that focus on opposites, such as "Itsy Bitsy Spider" on page 258 or "Sing a Song of Opposites" on page 259.
- ❏ Give the children playdough. Ask them to shape large and small balls, long and short snakes, and tall and short towers.

Reflecting on the Lesson

Ask the children:

- ❏ *This is the end of our school day. What is its opposite? (start, beginning)*
- ❏ *Describe some of the opposites we have discussed today.*

Special Needs Adaptations

Special Need	Adaptation
Visual Impairments	■ This child will learn opposites more easily if she has tangible objects to see, touch, and experience. For example, objects that are soft/hard, little/big, and so on.
Hearing Impairments	■ When teaching opposite pairs, model the ones that are not tangible. For example, walk over and turn off the light and say or sign "off." Then, walk over and turn on the light and say or sign "on." Hold a book over your head and say or sign "up." Place the book on the floor and say or sign "down." (See pages 252–253 in the Appendix for the signs.)
Cognitive Challenges	■ Because children with cognitive challenges need a little more time and practice, it may may not be possible to teach them multiple opposite pairs. Select four or five opposite pairs that are functional (most useful) for them to know and concentrate on those. For example, on/off, in/out, up/down, little/big, and hot/cold. Teach one pair each day until the child has learned them all. Remember to start each day with a review of the opposite pair that the child learned the day before. Provide multiple examples for the child and use the words regularly in your everyday routines.
Motor Delays	■ If the child has severe motor limitations, adapt the activity by demonstrating opposites using objects that the child can pick up.
Speech/ Language Delays	■ Before starting this activity, make sure the child knows the names of the objects you will be using. Also, ask the child to describe how the object is used, as this will make it easier for her to identify the opposite of that object.
Emotional/ Behavior Issues	■ Any change in routine can trigger an outburst. To avoid this, tell the child what is going to happen next. Before dancing "The Hokey Pokey," tell the child exactly what she and her classmates will be doing and what will happen. This helps the child feel less anxious about a new activity.

Combining music and movement reinforces the concept of opposites.

Things That Go Together

Introducing and Developing the Lesson

- ❑ Sing "What Goes Together?" (see page 261 in the Appendix) to the tune of "Itsy Bitsy Spider."
- ❑ Talk with the children about the concept of things that go together. Point out the things mentioned in the song. Tell the children that they will be learning about things that go together.
- ❑ Collect items that go together: for example, a knife and a fork, a toothbrush and toothpaste, a cup and a saucer, and a sock and a shoe. Discuss the items with the children. Have them describe the relationship between the pairs of items.
- ❑ Explain that several items go together. Ask "What goes with…?" questions, such as:
  - What goes with bread?
  - What goes with hamburgers?
  - What goes with paper?
  - What goes with a comb?
  - What goes with a birthday party?
  - What goes with peanut butter?

Children will:

- increase vocabulary.
- recognize words that describe related things.

Vocabulary

button
coat
dog
flea
go together
pairs
words

Materials

several items that go together (for example, a toothbrush and toothpaste)

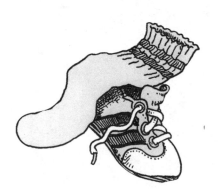

Practicing the Lesson

- ❑ Place the basket of items that go together in a center and encourage the children to match the items again.
- ❑ Invite children to draw pictures of things that go together. Help them label the items in their pictures.
- ❑ Read *Wordsong* by Bill Martin, Jr. or *This Is the House That Jack Built* by Pam Adams or Simms Taback.

Reflecting on the Lesson

Ask the children:

- ❑ *What would you say if someone asked what belongs to you?*
- ❑ *What things belong in our classroom?*

Special Needs Adaptations

Special Need	Adaptation
Visual Impairments	- Give the child time to examine the items that go together. If the child has residual vision, make sure she can see each item and that she is not seated where glare from the window or other lighting will affect her vision.
Hearing Impairments	- As you talk about each pair of items that go together, hold one item in one hand (such as a plate) and the other item in the other hand (such as a fork). As you describe how the items go together, put them together in one hand or in front of you (remember to make sure the child can see the items).
Cognitive Challenges	- As you talk about what things go together, show the child concrete examples. For example, if you ask, "What goes with a birthday party?" show her pictures of gifts, a cake, or a party hat. After you talk about what goes with an item, ask her to tell you or show you. Review what you have learned throughout the day to reinforce what you have talked about.
Motor Delays	- When asking the "What goes with…?" questions, provide pictures for a child with severe motor delays. If she cannot speak she can point or turn her head toward the picture she needs.
Speech/ Language Delays	- Reinforce vocabulary by talking with the child about how the items are used in everyday routines. If the child is unfamiliar with the item, demonstrate how it is used. It is important that children not only learn the names of items that go together but how and why the items go together.
Emotional/ Behavior Issues	- When you sing the song, explain that it is a familiar song using different words. Some children, especially those with autism, get upset when familiar things are changed or arranged differently. Before singing the song, explain that, "Today, we are going to be using a tune we know and adding new words to it."

Spatial Relationships

Children will:

- increase spatial vocabulary.
- demonstrate understanding of spatial vocabulary.

Vocabulary

around
behind
beside
down
in
in front
on
out
over
through
under
up

Materials

beanbags
blocks
box
classroom furniture
yarn

Introducing and Developing the Lesson

- ❑ Tell the children that they will be learning about position words, which are words that tell where something is located.
- ❑ Sing "Itsy Bitsy Spider" (see page 258 in the Appendix) with the children. Discuss the position words in the song—*up*, *down*, and *out*.
- ❑ Place a tower of blocks on the floor and ask a volunteer to demonstrate the spatial words of *over*, *under*, *through*, and *around* using the block.
- ❑ Practice using position words by giving the children directions to take a book to a specific location. For example, "Richele, please take this book and place it on the shelf in the Library Center" or, "Evan, please take this book and place it inside the box outside the door."
- ❑ Discuss the importance of position words. Without position words, we would not know how to find things or tell others where to put things!

Practicing the Lesson

- ❑ Place a box and beanbags in the Gross Motor Center. Have the children toss the beanbags into the box and then describe the location of the spot where their beanbags land.
- ❑ Create a maze by stretching yarn between table legs, chairs, and classroom furniture. Have the children navigate the maze. Challenge them to describe their movements through the maze. How many positional words do they use?
- ❑ Play games that focus on position words, such as "Go In and Out the Windows" (see page 262 in the Appendix).

Reflecting on the Lesson

Ask the children:

- ❑ *What position word might you might use when you are setting the table?*
- ❑ *What position word would you use to tell someone where the trash can is in our classroom?*

Special Needs Adaptations

Special Need	Adaptation
Visual Impairments	■ It is important that children with visual impairments learn about position words. Instead of giving directions about where to place a book, adapt the activity by placing the book in a specific location and walking with the child to talk about where the book is placed. Model placing the book on the shelf. Then, ask the child to place the book on the chair. Next, model placing the book under the table, and invite the child to place the book under the chair. Continue, until you have modeled several place words and given the child an opportunity to practice using each word in a functional way.
Hearing Impairments	■ Help the child learn a few simple place word signs such as the signs for "in," "out," "under," "over," and "around" (see pages 252–253 in the Appendix). Other children in the class might enjoy learning to sign a few place words as well.
Cognitive Challenges	■ Before beginning this lesson, make sure the child understands the meaning of place words. Use a few real items, such as a small box, cup, and a block. Ask the child to put the block on the box (remember that it may be necessary to show her). Then, reinforce the learning by inviting her to place the block on another item (book, chair, and so on). Continue practicing with each place word until you feel the child can demonstrate an understanding of the word. To avoid confusing the child, select three or four place words to demonstrate and practice before adding new ones.
Motor Delays	■ Because the child may not be able to move about the room easily, give her place word instructions using items that are nearby or items that are easily accessible. For example, place several items in front of her and ask her to put the book inside the box or place the marker in the cup.
Speech/ Language Delays	■ Look for opportunities throughout the day to reinforce her learning. For example, when you are going outside, you might say to her, "We are inside the room and now we will walk _____." See if the child is able to fill in the blank for you. When she is working in a center, say, "Put the book on the shelf. Now, put the book under the table." If possible, reverse the activity and put the book somewhere and invite the child to tell you where the book is.
Emotional/ Behavior Issues	■ Participating in novel activities, although exciting for most children, can cause children with emotional issues to be anxious. To avoid upsetting the child, invite her to use place words but encourage her to demonstrate her understanding by using preferred items or toys, such as placing her favorite car under the chair or on the shelf.

Colors

Children will:

- increase their descriptive vocabulary.

Vocabulary

black
blue
green
orange
purple
red
white
yellow

Materials

cellophane sheets in different colors
chart paper
construction paper in red, yellow, orange, green, blue, purple, black, and white
cups in three different colors
marker
playdough in different colors

Introducing and Developing the Lesson

- ❑ Tell the children that today they will be learning about color words and how they are used to describe things. Show the children a sheet of red construction paper. Ask them to name the color. Challenge the children to name other things in the classroom that might be that color. List their ideas on chart paper. Ask for a child to volunteer to create a sentence that uses the word "red."
- ❑ Continue with other colors of construction paper. You may need more than one day to complete this activity.
- ❑ Place three colored cups on a table. Give a direction to the children that would be better understood and easier to follow if you included a color word. For example, "Gabrielle, will you get the cup from the table and bring it to me?" When Gabrielle comes back with a cup, tell her that you wanted a different color cup. If she asks which color cup you want, tell her.
- ❑ Make a point of helping children see that the more information we give someone, the more clearly they understand us.

Practicing the Lesson

- ❑ Mix two batches of playdough. Make one batch blue and one batch yellow. Give each child a small ball of each color of playdough. Encourage them to knead the two balls of playdough together to create one ball that is a new color of playdough. What color is the new playdough?
- ❑ Give the children different sheets of cellophane in different colors. Have them take their cellophane sheets outside on a sunny day to create colorful shadows. Challenge the children to find a partner and make a shadow using each partner's cellophane. Encourage the children to describe the shadows that they make.
- ❑ Sing songs about colors, such as "The Color Song" (see page 255 in the Appendix).

Reflecting on the Lesson

Ask the children:

- ❑ *What color is your shirt (or pants, or shoes)?*
- ❑ *What is your favorite color? Why?*

Special Needs Adaptations

Special Need	Adaptation
Visual Impairments	■ Some children have difficulty distinguishing colors. Here are some hints to help: Make sure that background papers contrast highly with the materials being used. Dark colors such as black or dark blue generally work best for backgrounds; brighter, more intense colors make better foreground colors. If you use more colorful backgrounds, consider medium blues, purples, and greens. Children who have cortical visual impairments respond best to red and yellow since color vision is usually not affected in these children.
Hearing Impairments	■ Show the child a sheet of red construction paper. Ask her to name the color. ■ Adapt the activity by asking the child to show you things in the room that are red. You may need to model for her what you are asking her to do. Use pointing and gestures to help you identify what you are asking her to do.
Cognitive Challenges	■ If the child does not know the names of all the colors, use this lesson as an opportunity to provide multiple opportunities to identify the following colors: red, yellow, blue, and green. Use real objects that are functional for the child. For example, use her favorite cup, a book she enjoys, or a favorite toy. ■ Talk about the color of the object in the context of how the child uses that object. For example, say, "Find your cup." The child picks up the cup. "The cup is yellow." The child puts down the cup. "Show me the yellow cup."
Motor Delays	■ Use three colored cups with handles, such as "sippy" cups. Instead of placing them on the table and asking the child to walk and get them, place each one directly in front of the child and ask her to pick up one that is a certain color.
Speech/ Language Delays	■ Review color words with the child before beginning this activity. Many children have difficulty generalizing from object to object. In other words, the child may be able to identify a yellow cup but not a yellow ball.
Emotional/ Behavior Issues	■ Following directions is often difficult for a child with emotional issues. Shorten the directions so that the child can achieve success. Do not select this child to be the one who picks up the wrong cup. Instead, let her watch the activity and select her to be the one that picks up the correct cup.

What Do You See?

Children will:

- develop their descriptive vocabulary.

Vocabulary

attributes
describe
see
words

Materials

chart paper
crayons
orange, tangerine, or other fruit
paper
photograph or a simple
    illustration from a story book

Introducing and Developing the Lesson

- ❑ Show the children an orange. Pass the orange around the circle. Ask them to describe the orange. *What shape is the orange? What color? What size? What does the skin look like? Is it shiny? Is it rough? Is it smooth?*
- ❑ Tell the children that words that are used to describe something or someone are called *descriptive words* or *adjectives*.
- ❑ Show the children a photograph or a simple illustration from a story book. Ask for a volunteer to describe what she sees.
- ❑ Write the description, in sentence form, on a sheet of chart paper. As other children add to the description, add the adjectives to the sentence and rewrite the sentence below the original sentence. Continue to write each sentence under the previous one, so children can see that the sentence continues to grow as their adjectives are added. If necessary, ask the children questions to encourage them to add more descriptive words or adjectives. For example, if the photo is a picture of a girl eating an ice cream cone, the first sentence might be, "This is a girl eating ice cream." Additional sentences might be as follows:
  - This is a girl eating ice cream on a cone.
  - This is a girl with long hair eating ice cream on a cone.
  - This is a girl with long hair eating green ice cream on a cone.
  - This is a girl with long brown hair eating green ice cream on a cone.

Practicing the Lesson

- ❑ Invite the children to draw a self-portrait. Challenge them to describe their pictures. With permission, transcribe their descriptions onto their drawings. Ask them questions to encourage full descriptions of their self-portraits.
- ❑ Invite each child to share a toy from home. Ask the children questions about their toys to encourage them to describe their toys.

Reflecting on the Lesson

Ask the children:

- ❑ *How can we use our words to communicate with our friends more clearly?*
- ❑ *How would you describe yourself to a friend?*

Special Needs Adaptations

Special Need	Adaptation
Visual Impairments	■ Adapt the activity by using a colorful object, such as a truck or favorite toy instead of a picture. The child with visual impairments can participate, although her sentences may not be as descriptive; suggest that she describe it according to how it feels or smells.
Hearing Impairments	■ Children with hearing impairments often need extra help in using descriptive words. Encourage the child to describe the picture in terms of color or size. Encouraging the child to use color or size words helps her begin to understand the idea behind using descriptive language (adjectives).
Cognitive Challenges	■ A child with cognitive challenges will more than likely be using telegraphic speech or using one or two words to make a sentence. Ask her a question that will help her use a descriptive word. For example, if you are describing a picture of a child on a farm, she may say "farm" or "boy." Make a sentence, and ask her to repeat it after you, such as, "The boy is on the farm." Next, expand the child's learning by asking a question, such as, "What is the boy wearing?" The child may answer "jacket." Then, ask, "What color is the jacket?" and the child answers "blue." Next, invite the child to help you make a sentence, such as, "The boy on the farm is wearing a _____ (leave it blank) jacket." If the child answers "blue," you would say, "Yes, the boy on the farm is wearing a blue jacket." Invite the child to repeat the sentence after you say it. This technique is called slotting, where the child fills in the blanks. It reinforces new vocabulary.
Motor Delays	■ If the child does not have the motor skills to pick up the orange, hold it for her and give her a chance to smell it. ■ Remember, for a child with limited head control, an object needs to be at her eye level in order for her to see it.
Speech/ Language Delays	■ A child with speech and language delays can participate in this activity using the same modifications described above for children with cognitive challenges. In addition, look for ways to help the child expand her sentences.
Emotional/ Behavior Issues	■ Because the goal of the activity is to learn to use descriptive words, honor the child's preferences when selecting a picture for the child to describe. For example, if you know that a child who is given to outbursts likes kittens, select a picture that features kittens.

Questions and Answers

Children will:

■ practice asking and answering questions.

Vocabulary

answer
ask
conversation
pattern
question
reply

Materials

Brown Bear, Brown Bear, What Do You See? by Bill Martin, Jr.
chart paper
marker
simple photo, (for example, a butterfly or a cow)
white poster board

Introducing and Developing the Lesson

❑ Ask for a volunteer to demonstrate what to answer when someone asks, "What is your name?" Ask a second volunteer to demonstrate what to answer when someone asks, "How are you?"

❑ Print, "What is your name?" and "How are you?" on chart paper. Point out the question mark following each question. Tell the children that the question mark tells a reader that the words are a question that needs an answer.

❑ Tell the children that today they will be practicing asking and answering questions. Sing "Where Is Thumbkin?" (see page 261 in the Appendix) and point out the question-and-answer format of the song.

❑ Print the words to "Where Is Thumbkin?" on chart paper. Point out the question marks after "Where is Thumbkin?" and "How are you today, sir?" Point out the absence of a question mark following "Here I am" and "Very well, I thank you."

❑ Sing the song again, moving your hand under the words of the song as you sing it.

Practicing the Lesson

❑ Make What Am I? game cards (see page 274 in the Appendix).

❑ Sing other songs that have question-and-answer formats, such as "Billy Boy" and "Can You Move with Me?" (see page 254 in the Appendix).

❑ Read *Brown Bear, Brown Bear, What Do You See?* by Bill Martin, Jr. Discuss the question–response pattern of the story.

Reflecting on the Lesson

Ask the children:

❑ *Why do people ask questions?*

❑ *What question would we ask someone if we wanted to know who they played with today?*

Special Needs Adaptations

Special Need	Adaptation
Visual Impairments	■ Make sure the print is large enough for the child to see. ■ If a child has significant vision loss she may be unable to see the print or she may need to use a print magnifier.
Hearing Impairments	■ Make a question mark sign and cut it out. Invite the child with hearing impairments to hold it and talk about questions or sign questions to her. Work on questions that are considered functional for the child. A functional word, sometimes called a life-skill word, is a word or activity that the child will use throughout her life, such as saying her name when asked. Practice asking the child her name and teaching her how to respond.
Cognitive Challenges	■ It is especially important that a child with cognitive challenges learn important information such as her name, address, phone number, and her parents' names. Make the child an identification card (see page 249 in the Appendix—Identification Card) with her name, address, phone number, and parents' names printed on it. Use a different color highlighter to highlight each piece of information. For example, highlight her name in yellow, her address in pink, and so on. Begin by placing the card in front of the child. Practice pointing to her name when you say, "What is your name?" Even if the child is verbal and knows how to say her name, it is a good idea for her always to carry an identification card. If she gets lost, she is more likely to become upset and forget information she knows.
Motor Delays	■ For a child with severe motor delays, such as those seen in some forms of cerebral palsy, it may be necessary to teach the child to use a communication board. Later, as the child gets older, she may even use an electronic device. Young children traditionally start with a simple communication board. After she is familiar with some of the pictures on her board, start to ask her questions, such as, "Can you show me what we ate for lunch?"
Speech/ Language Delays	■ To help the child feel more successful, select at least one question that the child knows the answer to. Because the child may need extra help in both asking and answering a question, invite a peer to practice with her.
Emotional/ Behavior Issues	■ Children with emotional issues, especially those with autism, may find it very difficult to answer questions. To encourage them to try, start by asking them yes/no questions. If the child does not answer or refuses to respond, invite her to nod her head yes or no. It is very important that children with autism or emotional issues learn to interact with others.

Sentence development

Alphabet Posters

Children will:
- use descriptive vocabulary to complete sentences.

Vocabulary
describe
me
words

Materials
audio recorder
construction paper (several 9" x
    12" white sheets)
crayons
file folder
media for recording
photos of the children in class

Preparation
Ask the children to draw a self-portrait on the construction paper. Position the paper so that their pictures are vertical. Print the first letter of the child's name in uppercase and lowercase letters at the top right corner of the paper. Print the child's name across the bottom of the paper. Use uppercase for the first letter and lowercase for the remaining letters. Send the portraits home with a request for families to help the children write stories or some special information about them on the back of their pictures. Have the children bring their "Alphabet Posters" back to school. Make a poster for yourself.

Introducing and Developing the Lesson

- Show the children your "Alphabet Poster." Point out the first letter of your name at the top right and your name at the bottom of your portrait. Tell the children what you wrote on the back. Don't read it.
- Tell the children that everyone has a story to tell and that everyone in the class is going to tell their stories to the rest of the class.
- During Circle or Group Time throughout the day (or week), allow a few children to show their posters and tell their friends what is written on the backs of their posters. Continue until all children have had a chance to speak. Help reluctant speakers by asking questions.
- After each child finishes showing her poster and telling her story, display the photo in the classroom or in the hallway.

Practicing the Lesson

- Collect photos of the children and display them inside a file folder. Encourage each child to record something about herself on the audio recorder. Place the recording and the folder in the Listening Center. Challenge children to match the speaker on the recording with a photo in the folder.
- Read *Alicia's Happy Day* by Meg Starr, *Amazing Grace* by Mary Hoffman, *Bob* by Tracey Campbell Pearson, *Edward the Emu* by Sheena Knowles, *Imogene's Antlers* by David Small, or *Koala Lou* by Mem Fox. At the end of the story, ask the children to tell you one thing they learned about the main character in the book. Encourage them to speak in complete sentences.
- Have each child select a partner and sit facing her partner. Encourage the partners to tell each other something about what they like to do at school. Bring all the children together in a circle. Ask each child to tell the group something she learned about what her partner likes to do at school.

Reflecting on the Lesson

Ask the children:
- *Tell me something you learned about a friend today.*
- *Why might it be important for us to be able to tell others about ourselves?*

Special Needs Adaptations

Special Need	Adaptation
Visual Impairments	■ Instead of drawing a picture of herself, invite the child to bring a collection of things from home that shows what she likes to do. For example, the child may bring in a toy, an empty container of her favorite food, a favorite piece of clothing, or a book.
Hearing Impairments	■ Invite the child to watch while a peer draws a picture so the child will know what she should do.
Cognitive Challenges	■ After the child has drawn a picture of herself, ask her to point to various things on the picture. ■ Prompt her by saying, "Show me your eyes" or "Point to your mouth."
Motor Delays	■ If the child does not have the motor control to draw a picture, help her by drawing the picture for her. Be sure to ask for her input.
Speech/ Language Delays	■ Encourage the child's family to help you reinforce the concepts of this lesson at home by asking her to describe her picture for them.
Emotional/ Behavior Issues	■ Remind the child that this activity is fun. Don't forget to use your body to cue the child that it is fun and enjoyable. If the child gets upset and does not want to finish her picture, allow her to put it up and go back to it later.

Sentence development

Toy Ads

Introducing and Developing the Lesson

Children will:
- use descriptive words.

- ❏ Ask children to describe toys that they have. Ask them what they like about their toys and why they wanted to have them?
- ❏ Tell the children that they will be learning to use words that describe something in an appealing way.
- ❏ Show children a toy ad. Pick an ad that will be interesting to the children. Read the words on the ad.
- ❏ Have the children think about buying the toy that is advertised in the ad. What makes it appealing? What else might the ad say to about the item being advertised?
- ❏ Encourage children to think of a toy they would like to have or select a well-loved toy from your classroom. Help the children create an ad for the toy. Invite them to dictate the words for their ad to you to be transcribed.

Vocabulary
appealing
describe
words

Materials
crayons
paper
toy ad

Use stories as a prompt to encourage children to talk about toys they like.

Practicing the Lesson

- ❏ Provide magazines with ads for children's toys. Encourage the children to look through the magazine for a toy that they like. Ask them to describe the toy. Read the ad to the children. How many of their words are in the ad?
- ❏ Place a box of toys in the center of the circle and ask each child to take one toy. Have the children take turns describing the toy that they have chosen, using at least two words.

Reflecting on the Lesson

Ask the children;
- ❏ *What do you think an ad for a toy might say?*
- ❏ *Describe an ad for a toy that you saw in a magazine. Does it make you want the item being advertised? Why?*

Special Needs Adaptations

Special Need	Adaptation
Visual Impairments	■ Instead of making individual toy ads, make a collaborative toy ad. The child with visual impairments might describe what she would like to have in her ad and a peer can draw it for her. ■ If each child wants to make her own ad, bring in different types of materials for the child with visual impairments to feel. She can then use the materials to construct her own ad.
Hearing Impairments	■ Explain to the child that a toy ad is like an advertisement that is designed to make someone want to buy that toy. Invite the child to tell you about a toy she would like to buy. If she has difficulty selecting a toy, give her a toy from the classroom and ask her to describe it for you.
Cognitive Challenges	■ To help the child with cognitive challenges identify a toy for her ad, select two toys from the classroom and ask her to show you which one she likes best. Learning to make choices is a very important life skill for a child with cognitive challenges to learn.
Motor Delays	■ Show the child two or three toy ads. Remember to hold them at an angle that is comfortable for the child. Once she has selected one, invite a friend to cut out pictures of that toy from one of the ads. If the child has the motor skills to paste the pictures onto a poster board, she can make her poster independently or ask a friend to help.
Speech/ Language Delays	■ Make sure the child understands all the new vocabulary associated with this activity. For example, explain that an ad is used to help sell something. If the child has limited experience with print ads talk about some of the ads she may have seen or heard on television. Help the child understand what an ad is by showing her an ad and asking questions, such as, "What is this?" (Point to the toy), "What color is it?" and "Tell me what you like about this toy."
Emotional/ Behavior Issues	■ For a child with emotional issues, it is important that she understand she has options for parts of this activity and not for others. For example, it would not be a good idea to let her choose not to make an ad at all, as this would convey the message that she can choose only those activities that she prefers. This is not the case—especially as the child gets ready for other school environments, such as kindergarten and first grade. However, what helps a child with emotional issues is to provide a choice about how she completes an activity. Tell her that she can draw, cut out pictures, or dictate sentences to you about the toy she likes. This is more likely to happen if you offer a picture or a real object that is a favorite of the child.

Classroom Photos

Children will:

■ increase their descriptive vocabulary.

Vocabulary

describe
photograph
see
words

Materials

chart paper
colored tape
construction paper (several 8" x 10" white sheets)
marker
photos of the children
zipper-close plastic bags (gallon size)
stapler

Preparation

Take photos of children during Circle or Group Time and as they work in centers. Print the photos and glue them onto 8" x 10" white construction paper.

Introducing and Developing the Lesson

❑ Engage the children in a discussion about classroom activities. Ask children to talk about the things they do during Circle or Group Time and Center Time. Tell the children that they are going to practice using descriptive words.

❑ Pass the photos around the circle, one at a time. Ask the children to describe what they see in the photos. Print their descriptions on chart paper. Ask questions to encourage the children to improve the sentences by adding descriptive words. Explain that the more words they use to describe what they see, the better you understand what they are describing in the photograph.

❑ This may take more than one Circle or Group Time. Be sensitive to children's attention spans. This activity is great to do with several small groups of children.

❑ Transcribe each photo's description below the appropriate photo on the construction paper. Place the pages into gallon-size zipper-close plastic bags. Create a Classroom Photo Book by placing the bags on top of each other and stapling across the bottom to create a baggie book. Cover the staples with colored tape. Place this book in the Reading Center.

Practicing the Lesson

❑ Encourage children to draw pictures of their favorite classroom activities. When they are finished drawing, ask them to describe what is happening in their pictures. With children's permission, transcribe their descriptions onto the backs of their pictures.

❑ Talk with children as they play in centers. Ask them to describe what they are doing. Ask questions that encourage the use of descriptive words.

Reflecting on the Lesson

Ask the children:

❑ *Which activity did you enjoy most today? Why?* (Encourage the children to use descriptive words.)

❑ *Why do we use descriptive words?*

Special Needs Adaptations

Special Need	Adaptation
Visual Impairments	■ Make the print larger on her description. Use thicker markers, such as a thick-line black marker, to write the child's description.
Hearing Impairments	■ When you pass the pictures around the circle, if the child with hearing impairments is unable to describe what she sees in the picture, encourage her to sign to you.
Cognitive Challenges	■ A child with cognitive challenges may become tired with the process of describing pictures. Instead, invite her to tell you one word that describes a picture as she looks at it. ■ Ask her questions that will encourage her to use a longer description.
Motor Delays	■ If the child is not able to hold a picture or does not have the speech control to describe the picture, ask the child to point to a picture while a peer describes it for her. However, she may choose to point to that activity and invite a peer buddy to draw it for her. This can help children learn to collaborate with each other.
Speech/ Language Delays	■ If the child is not able to make a descriptive sentence, she could add a few descriptive words. For example, if a picture of a child has been described with a sentence such as, "Josh has on a new shirt." You might ask her, "What color is Josh's shirt?" as you look at the picture. When she answers "red," affirm this by saying, "Yes, Josh is wearing a red shirt." If the child remains engaged in the activity, invite her to repeat the sentence after you.
Emotional/ Behavior Issues	■ Be sure the child does not become too frustrated with this activity. If she cannot make a new sentence to describe the picture, ask her to describe something in the picture. Write down what the child says. You may decide that the goal for this child is to participate in the activity without getting upset. Later, if you have the opportunity to work one-on-one with the child, you can encourage her to use longer sentences.

Things I Like to Do

Children will:

- tell a simple personal narrative.

Vocabulary

describe
like
words

Materials

chart paper
marker
paper for drawing
photos from magazines
physical prop to go with picture
    (optional)
picture of yourself doing
    something you enjoy

Introducing and Developing the Lesson

- Tell the children that today they will be talking about things they like to do.
- Describe something you really enjoy doing. If you have a picture of yourself doing that activity or a special prop (measuring cup for cooking, book for reading, trowel for gardening, ski gloves for skiing, and so on), bring it with you to show to the children.
- Ask the children to describe something they like to do. Coach them to use two complete sentences, if possible.
- Make a list of the activities children name. Do any of the children name the same activity? Do they like the activity for the same reasons?

Practicing the Lesson

- Invite the children to draw a picture of something they like to do and ask them to describe what is happening in their pictures.
- Cut photos from magazines. Help the children sort the photos into two categories: "things I like to do" and "things I do not like to do." Talk with them, as they sort the photos. Ask "why" questions to stimulate conversation.

Asking the child questions about her picture builds her vocabulary and her understanding of new concepts.

Reflecting on the Lesson

Ask the children:

- *What was an activity that one of your friends said they liked to do?*
- *Why do they like to do it?*

Special Needs Adaptations

Special Need	Adaptation
Visual Impairments	■ Because this child depends on touch to identify items, ask her to talk about her favorite toy. Then, invite a friend to close her eyes and hold the toy while the child with visual impairments describes it for her. This allows the peer to learn how the child with visual impairments uses touch to identify objects.
Hearing Impairments	■ If the child uses sign language, learn the sign that describes her favorite thing and teach it to the whole class. Teach the class the sign for "thank you" (see page 253 in the Appendix). After the child signs her favorite thing, tell the class what she has just signed for them. Then, ask them to use sign language to say "thank you."
Cognitive Challenges	■ A child with cognitive challenges may be limited by her language skills. Show her a picture of three items or activities (one she prefers and the two that are not her particular favorites). Ask the child to point to the activity she enjoys most. Encourage her to say the name of the activity or, if she does not know the name, say it for her and ask her to repeat it after you.
Motor Delays	■ A child with motor delays may be limited in the activities she can do. Help her identify an activity she enjoys. Remember to ask her family for suggestions of things she enjoys doing. ■ If the child is severely motor impaired and unable to talk, find a picture of an activity she enjoys and place it on a tabletop easel on the child's wheelchair tray when it is her turn.
Speech/ Language Delays	■ If the child is unable to tell you what she enjoys, show the child three pictures and ask her to point to the one she enjoys.
Emotional/ Behavior Issues	■ Sometimes, children with emotional issues can become very oppositional. That means they may yell out "No!" when you ask them a question. If this happens, try to coax the child into the activity by saying, "Oh, I thought you enjoyed _____ (fill in the blank with an activity you know the child enjoys)." For example, "Oh, I thought you enjoyed playing with blocks." The child may then respond with, "blocks." Add her response to the list you make of things each child enjoys. If she continues to yell "No!" add something for her, ignore her protest, and go on to the next child.

Prop Box Language

Children will:

■ expand vocabulary related to a specific topic.

Vocabulary

cheese	oven	sauce
cups	pepperoni	small
delivery	pizza	table
dine-in	pizza cutter	tablecloths
large	pizza tray	tomatoes
medium	plates	toppings
menu	roll	vocabulary
napkins	rolling pin	words

Materials

boxes
crayons or markers
paper
pizza parlor photos
pizza parlor supplies
Shanna's Pizza Parlor by Jean
   Marzollo, *Mrs. Hippo's Pizza
   Parlor* by Vivian French, or
   Moira's Birthday by Robert N.
   Munsch

Preparation

Create Prop Boxes. See page 280 in the Appendix for suggested topics and items to include. Rotate the Prop Boxes through the Dramatic Play Center each week. This literacy lesson is designed to be used with the Pizza Parlor Prop Box. The same basic lesson can be utilized with each box.

Introducing and Developing the Lesson

❑ Introduce the Pizza Parlor Prop Box by showing the children items that are included. Have them name each item, and provide vocabulary as needed.

❑ Tell the children that they are going to learn words and concepts related to a pizza parlor. Discuss what things happen in the pizza parlor. Show photos, if available.

❑ Read books about pizza parlors and/or pizza such as *Shanna's Pizza Parlor* by Jean Marzollo, *Mrs. Hippo's Pizza Parlor* by Vivian French, or *Moira's Birthday* by David N. Munsch.

Practicing the Lesson

❑ Place the Pizza Parlor Prop Box in the Dramatic Play Center. Encourage the children to set up and run a pizza parlor. Demonstrate how to take orders, fill orders, and collect payments.

❑ Encourage the children to make signs to accompany their pizza parlor. Where is the entrance? Where is the exit? Where are the restrooms? Ask a volunteer to draw a male and female figure to identify the bathrooms.

Reflecting on the Lesson

Ask the children:

❑ *What new words have you learned today?*

❑ *Which part of running a pizza parlor do you like best—taking orders, making pizzas, accepting payment for the pizza, or cleaning up?*

Special Needs Adaptations

Special Need	Adaptation
Visual Impairments	■ Invite the child and a peer to explore the pizza prop box before you introduce it to the class. Giving the child a few minutes to orient herself to the new items and objects in the prop box will make her more comfortable when it is time to discuss it, and when you set up a pretend pizza parlor for the class.
Hearing Impairments	■ Show the child each item in the prop box and give her a few minutes to examine each one. If the child has residual hearing, say the name of each item and invite her to repeat it after you.
Cognitive Challenges	■ Select three or four items from the prop box and show them to the child. Say the name of each item as you hand it to her. Invite her to repeat the name after you.
Motor Delays	■ Make sure that some of the items in the prop boxes have handles that are easy to grasp and are large enough for a child with motor limitations to pick up and use.
Speech/ Language Delays	■ Show the child each item and ask her to name it for you. To extend her language, encourage her to tell you something about the item (color, size, shape, and so on). If the child has difficulty coming up with a descriptor, ask her a leading question, such as, "What color is the _____?" "How is the _____ used?" When working with children with language delays it is important to use the name of the object when you describe that object.
Emotional/ Behavior Issues	■ To encourage more interaction with the class, ask the child to tell you about her favorite kind of pizza or ask her to be the leader and hold each item up for the class to see, as you describe it. Remember, many children with emotional issues have very low self-esteem. Being selected to help, and doing so successfully, builds a child's self-confidence.

Story Photos

Children will:

- expand vocabulary and sentences.
- retell a story.

Vocabulary

book
describe
favorite
retell
sequence
story

Materials

audio recorder
copy of teacher's favorite story
crayons
media for recording
paper

Introducing and Developing the Lesson

- ❏ Ask the children about their favorite books.
- ❏ Read your favorite story to the children. Be sure to tell the children why this book is one of your favorites. If possible, read a story that features a child with a special need (see the suggestions on the next page).
- ❏ This lesson is an opportunity to continue working with the class on tolerance and understanding of others. This is especially important if some of the children in your class have not been around other children with special needs until now.
- ❏ Ask questions after the story to make sure that the children understand the story.
- ❏ Encourage the children to draw a picture about their favorite part of the story. Have the children share their pictures later on in the day during Story Time.

Practicing the Lesson

- ❏ Challenge the children to place their pictures in a sequence that retells the story. Place photos in a horizontal line. Place photos that are about the same part of the story in a vertical line.
- ❏ Record the story and place the book and recording in the Listening Center.

Reflecting on the Lesson

Ask the children:
- ❏ *Which part of the story was your favorite part?*
- ❏ *Which parts of the story might really happen?*
- ❏ *Which parts of the story are pretend?*

Special Needs Adaptations

Special Need	Adaptation
Visual Impairments	■ *Knots on a Counting Rope* by Bill Martin, Jr. and John Archambault—A boy who was born blind is the subject of a story that is told by a grandfather to his grandson. ■ *Luna and the Big Blur* by Shirley Day—Luna has several adventures and mishaps until she learns that wearing glasses is not so bad after all.
Hearing Impairments	■ *Deana the Deaf Dinosaur* by Carol Addabbo—Deana runs away from home because her parents want her to use sign language. Alone in the forest, she learns that communication is very important.
Cognitive Challenges	■ *Be Good to Eddie Lee* by Virginia Fleming—A child with Down syndrome, Eddie Lee, wants to be included in the activities of the other children in his neighborhood. Although they initially reject him, they later learn to value him as a friend. ■ *My Brother, Matthew* by Mary Thompson—The story is told from the point of view of David, a boy with a younger brother who was born with a cognitive challenge.
Motor Delays	■ *Tibby Tried It* by Sharon and Ernie Useman—Tibby learns that a physical impairment does not mean that he can't do the same things as his friends, he just must learn to do them differently. ■ *Rolling Along: The Story of Taylor and His Wheelchair* by Jamee Riggio Heelan—Getting his first wheelchair opens up a whole new world to Taylor, who has cerebral palsy. ■ *Rolling Along with Goldilocks and the Three Bears* by Cindy Meyers—This traditional story has a new twist: Baby Bear is in a wheelchair and she is gone for physical therapy when Goldilocks arrives. Children enjoy this retelling of a favorite classic.
Speech/ Language Delays	■ *Charlie Who Couldn't Say His Name* by Davene Fehy—Charlie is teased because of his speech problem until a program at school helps him stand up for himself.
Emotional/ Behavior Issues	■ *Tobin Learns to Make Friends* by Diane Murrell—Told through the mind of Tobin the train engine, aspects of social skills development are explained in concrete terms that children can understand. ■ *I'm Like You, You're Like Me: A Child's Book About Understanding and Celebrating Each Other* by Cindy Gainer—Through interaction with others who are different, children learn to value others, even those who may not be able to do the same things they are able to do.

Yarn Tales

Children will:

- use complete sentences.
- listen with purpose.

Vocabulary

add
story
tale
tell
turn
yarn

Materials

ball
crayons
paper
photos from magazines
yarn

Preparation

- Roll yarn into a ball.

Introducing and Developing the Lesson

- ❑ Say a sentence with part missing, such as, "The three little pigs built homes. The first little pig built his home with _____." Ask for a volunteer to finish the sentence. Tell the children that they will be creating a group story.
- ❑ Ask children to sit in a circle. Hold the ball of yarn as you start a story. Make sure your story topic is one that children know something about. For example, "One day, Evan was playing in the park. He saw another little boy sliding down the slide. Evan walked over to the little boy and said…." Give the ball of yarn to the child beside you and invite her to add something to the story. Each person who adds to the story holds continues to hold onto the yarn so that the ball of yarn unravels as it is passed to each "storyteller."
- ❑ Continue passing the yarn with each child adding to the story for as long as the story holds the interest of the children.
- ❑ Learning to add on to a story takes practice. Children will get better at this each time you repeat it.

Practicing the Lesson

- ❑ Cut photos from magazines or draw pictures to create a deck of object cards. Divide the cards into two decks and turn the photos face down. Have the children take turns drawing one photo from each stack and then making up a sentence or a story that connects the two photos.
- ❑ Have the children draw pictures. Shuffle the pictures and pass them out so each child has a picture. Ask the children to make up a sentence about the pictures.
- ❑ Have the children sit in a circle. Hold a ball in your lap. Make up a couple of sentences for a story starter and then roll the ball to one of the children. When this child has added a sentence or two, she rolls the ball to another child to continue the story. Continue for as long as the story holds the children's interest.

Reflecting on the Lesson

Ask the children:
- ❑ *Which part of the story did you like best?*
- ❑ *Do you think stories are better when a lot of people add parts to them?*

Special Needs Adaptations

Encourage participation by showing the child what to do next.

Special Need	Adaptation
Visual Impairments	<ul><li>Invite the child to hold the yarn and feel it before starting the group story. Explain that each child will pass the yarn to the next person after she has made a sentence or added something to the story.</li><li>When the child next to the child with visual impairments passes the yarn to her, remind her to place the yarn in the palm of the child's hand, so she can feel it before adding her own sentence.</li></ul>
Hearing Impairments	<ul><li>Because a child with hearing impairments may not be able to hear the other children well, place her next to you and face her when you start the story.</li><li>Allow her to be the first child to add something to the story.</li></ul>
Cognitive Challenges	<ul><li>Help the child participate by asking her a question. For example, if the child before her says, "David missed the bus." You might say, "_____ (use the child's name), David missed the bus, how do you think he got to school?" If the child answers, "car" you might say, "Let's put that in a sentence." Make the sentence so that the child can fill in the blank, "David asked his mom to drive him to school in the _____." Invite the child to fill in the blank and then pass the yarn to the next child.</li></ul>
Motor Delays	<ul><li>If the child with motor delays is unable to hold the yarn, drape it gently around her wrist, before passing it on to the next child. If the child is unable to speak, ask her to point to a friend who can make a sentence for her.</li></ul>
Speech/ Language Delays	<ul><li>Making a sentence without cues can be very difficult for a child with limited vocabulary. Ask her questions to help her create the sentence she will add to the group story.</li></ul>
Emotional/ Behavior Issues	<ul><li>So that the child does not become frustrated by having to wait too long for her turn, try making several class stories and keeping the group size smaller, with five or six children at a time.</li></ul>

Show, Tell, and Share

Children will:
- complete sentences.
- tell a personal narrative.
- engage in conversation.

Vocabulary

answer

explain

share

show

tell

Materials

favorite storybook

photos of children at home or
    with family members

special toy or item from home

zipper-close plastic bags

Introducing and Developing the Lesson

- ❏ Tell the children that they are going to share information with each other about things they like.
- ❏ Share an object or picture that is special to you. Tell the children what it is, where it came from, why you like it, and, if applicable, how it works. Invite the children to ask you questions about your special item or picture.
- ❏ Set aside one day a week for a few children to share a special toy or item from home. Have the children take turns telling their friends about the toy or item. Encourage the children to ask the speaker questions. Encourage the speaker to answer the questions from her friends.
- ❏ Invite a few children to bring a photo to class each day for a week. Place the photos in zipper-close plastic bags to protect them.
- ❏ Have children pass their photo around the circle while telling who is in the photo and what is happening in the photo. Encourage classmates to ask children questions about their photos.

Practicing the Lesson

- ❏ During Story Time, have the each child share her favorite story book. Ask questions and encourage the other children to ask questions. *What is the book about? What characters are in the book?*
- ❏ Invite the children to tell their friends about a special vacation or trip they have taken. Encourage children to ask questions about the vacation or trip.

Reflecting on the Lesson

Ask the children:
- ❏ *Why do we ask questions?*
- ❏ *If there is something you want to know, how do you find out?*

Special Needs Adaptations

Special Need	Adaptation
Visual Impairments	■ Select an object rather than a picture. Remember to select something that is large enough for the child to see or feel. ■ When the child brings a favorite item from home, invite a few of her peers to feel the object, so they can understand that children with visual impairments often depend on touch to explore new things.
Hearing Impairments	■ When the child brings an item from home, teach the class how to sign the name of that item. Practice the sign with the children.
Cognitive Challenges	■ Ask the child's family to identify people in the photo she brings. Any other information that they can provide about the photo (where it was taken, when it was taken, and so on) will help you know how to encourage the child to describe it for the class. ■ It may be necessary for you to ask the child direct questions, so she can tell you about the photo.
Motor Delays	■ If the child's favorite item is a story book, ask her to show you her favorite character or point to her favorite part of the story.
Speech/ Language Delays	■ Use the item or pictures to reinforce her use of words that describe. Remember to ask her questions that prompt her to use words that describe. ■ Sometimes, it helps if you pretend to make a mistake. For example, if a child brings a stuffed bear, you might say, "Oh look! Thomas brought a cup to class." Hopefully, the child will correct you. If the child does not correct you wait a few seconds and say, "Oops, I made a mistake. It is a bear."
Emotional/ Behavior Issues	■ When the child shares a family photo, ask her questions about how she felt when the picture was taken. ■ It is very important that children, especially those with emotional issues, learn to talk about their feelings. ■ Some children with behavior/emotional issues have these issues because of the circumstances in their lives. They may not live in situations where they have access to family photos or preferred items. As an alternative, select an item from the classroom that is a preferred item for the child and ask her to describe it for the class.

Sentence development

Comic Conversations

Introducing and Developing the Lesson

❑ Photocopy and enlarge a simple comic strip, such as Peanuts, Garfield, Marmaduke, or Family Circus. Read it to the children. Call attention to the conversation that takes place between two characters. Tell the children that they will be learning about conversation, which is talking and listening between two or more people or characters.

❑ Photocopy and enlarge a second comic strip and provide a copy for each child. Use correction fluid to cover the existing conversation.

❑ Encourage children to use the pictures to make up what might be said in the bubbles above each character. Write their words in the bubbles. Read the comic strip to the children. How do they like the comic strip they created?

❑ Read *Don't Let the Pigeon Drive the Bus!* by Mo Willems. Point out that the words in the book are in bubbles, just like the words in comic strips. After having read the book once through, read it a second time and allow the children to tell you, in their own words, what should be in the conversation bubbles. Ask children who the pigeon is talking to in the book.

Practicing the Lesson

❑ Provide several comic strips. Use correction fluid to cover the words in the conversation bubbles. Allow individual children to create their own comic strips. Encourage them to take their comic strips home to share with family members.

❑ Provide puppets. Suggest that the children have the puppets talk with one another.

Reflecting on the Lesson

Ask the children:

❑ *Do you read comics (funny papers) at home? Which comic is your favorite?*

❑ *How is the print in comic strips different from print in books? How is it the same?*

Children will:

■ understand conversational rules.

Vocabulary

comic strips
conversation
sentences
words

Materials

comic strips (several simple copies)
correction fluid
Don't Let the Pigeon Drive the Bus! by Mo Willems
pen
puppets

Special Needs Adaptations

Special Need	Adaptation
Visual Impairments	■ It may be necessary to tell the child what is happening in each panel of the comic strip, so that she can suggest what the characters might say.
Hearing Impairments	■ Work one-on-one with the child and explain that a comic strip is like a book. It tells a story in a very short space. ■ Point to each panel of the strip before using correction fluid to cover the words. Invite the child to make up a new story for the comic strip.
Cognitive Challenges	■ Select a very short comic strip with only two or three panels and limited print. Invite the child to make up her own sentences. Don't be surprised if you need to prompt her with questions such as, "What might Snoopy say here?" or "What else could happen?"
Motor Delays	■ Make sure the child is seated and positioned so that she can see the comic strip as you show it to the class. It may be necessary to place the comic strip in front of the child on a small tabletop easel at about a 45° angle. Children with motor skills may have difficulty looking up at you when you talk, especially if they are unable to bend their necks.
Speech/ Language Delays	■ A child with limited language skills will need prompts or suggestions to tell you what a character in the comic strip might say. It will also help if you give her information that helps her understand what may be happening in the comic strip. For example, you could say, "Snoopy is unhappy because he has not had his dinner." Pause a moment. Then continue by asking, "What do you think he is saying here?" and point to the first panel in the comic strip.
Emotional/ Behavior Issues	■ Select a comic strip that will be of interest to the child. Children with autism are often reluctant to participate in activities that are of no interest to them. Because they are so literal they are more likely to be upset that you are covering the words with correction fluid. It is important to tell the child why you are doing this activity.

Story Tellers

Introducing and Developing the Lesson

❏ Sing "Five Flying Frogs" (see page 256 in the Appendix).
❏ Tell the children that they will be helping create a story about flying frogs.
❏ Read *Tuesday* by David Wiesner.
❏ Review the pages a second time. This time, ask the children to create the words for each page. If they need prompting, ask them questions: "What are the frogs doing? Where are they?" Print their text for each page on large stick-on notes. Encourage the children to use complete sentences.

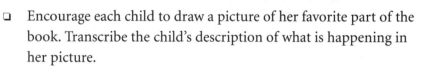

Children will:
- practice sentence structure.
- sequence a story.

Vocabulary
sentence
story
vocabulary
words

Materials
audio recorder
crayons
media for recording
paper
stick-on notes
Tuesday by David Wiesner

Practicing the Lesson

❏ Encourage each child to draw a picture of her favorite part of the book. Transcribe the child's description of what is happening in her picture.
❏ Record the children's text and place the recording and the book in the Listening Center.
❏ Invite the children to help create a story for *One Frog Too Many* by Mercer Mayer.

Reflecting on the Lesson

Ask the children:
❏ *Which part of the story is your favorite part?*
❏ *Do you like the book better with or without words?*

Special Needs Adaptations

Special Need	Adaptation
Visual Impairments	■ If the child can't see the book, invite a friend to tell her what is on each page. Encourage the child with visual impairments to suggest words for the page after her peer describes it for her.
Hearing Impairments	■ Introduce some hand motions to help the child understand what is happening in the song "Five Flying Frogs." For example, hold up five fingers when you say "five," flap your arms like wings when you say "flying." Hold up a picture of a frog when you say "frog." If possible, provide a picture of a frog and attach wings to it to demonstrate the song.
Cognitive Challenges	■ Instead of providing text for an entire book, ask the child to tell you what is happening on one page of the book. ■ If the child is unable to use a complete sentence, suggest that she tell you the names of each item shown in the picture. Learning to expand and build vocabulary is an important skill for children with cognitive challenges.
Motor Delays	■ Select books with illustrations that are large enough for the child to see. To help the child turn the pages of the book more easily, attach jumbo paper clips to each page. This provides a page turner that the child can use independently, without help from others.
Speech/ Language Delays	■ Instead of making up sentences about what might happen, ask the child to select one or two items in the book and tell you about the item. For example, if the child points to a picture of a frog, ask her to make up a sentence about a frog. If she is unable to make a complete sentence, ask her to tell you something about the frog, "What color is the frog?" "What size is the frog?" and so on.
Emotional/ Behavior Issues	■ It is critical for a child with emotional issues to understand that the song is about pretend frogs. Children with behavior issues, especially children with autism, are very literal. If you do not explain that the song is pretend, you may find that, long after you have finished singing the song with the children and moved on to other activities, the child is still telling you, "Frogs don't fly!"

Books That Support Oral Language

Vocabulary

Andy and his Yellow Frisbee by Mary Thompson *

The Boy Who Didn't Want to Be Sad by Rob Goldblatt *

Bread, Bread, Bread by Ann Morris

Chickens Aren't the Only Ones by Ruth Heller

Edward the Emu by Sheena Knowles

Exactly the Opposite by Tana Hoban

Fish Wish by Bob Barner

Freight Train by Donald Crews

From Head to Toe by Eric Carle

From Seed to Plant by Gail Gibbons

Lilly's Purple Plastic Purse by Kevin Henkes

My Granny's Purse by Paul Hansen

Planting a Rainbow by Lois Ehlert

Russ and the Firehouse by Janet Elizabeth Rickert *

Shelly the Hyperactive Turtle (Second Edition) by Deborah Moss*

Signs for Me: Basic Sign Vocabulary for Children, Parents & Teachers by Ben Bahan and Joe Dannis *

This Is the House That Jack Built by Simms Taback

This Is the House That Jack Built by Pam Adams

Tortilla Factory by Gary Paulsen

Trucks by Byron Barton

The Very Hungry Caterpillar by Eric Carle

Wheels! by Annie Cobb

Sentence Development

Alicia's Happy Day by Meg Starr

All Kinds of Friends (Even Green) by Ellen B. Senisi *

Amazing Grace by Mary Hoffman

Arnie and the New Kid by Nancy Carlson *

The Best Worst Brother by Stephanie Stuve-Bodeen *

Bob by Tracey Campbell Pearson

Brown Bear, Brown Bear, What Do You See? by Bill Martin, Jr.

Don't Let the Pigeon Drive the Bus! by Mo Willems

Down by the Bay by Raffi

Edward the Emu by Sheena Knowles

Gingerbread Baby by Jan Brett

Good Dog, Carl by Alexandra Day

Harold and the Purple Crayon by Crockett Johnson

Here Are My Hands by Bill Martin, Jr. and John Archambault

Imogene's Antlers by David Small

Koala Lou by Mem Fox

Moira's Birthday by Robert Munsch

Mrs. Hippo's Pizza Parlor by Vivian French

Over in the Meadow by Ezra Jack Keats

Pancakes for Breakfast by Tomie dePaola

Shanna's Pizza Parlor by Jean Marzollo

Tuesday by David Wiesner

We Go in a Circle by Peggy Perry Anderson *

We'll Paint the Octopus Red by Stephanie Stuve-Bodeen *

Where the Wild Things Are by Maurice Sendak

* Denotes books about children with special needs

Reading stories about children with special needs encourages acceptance of others.

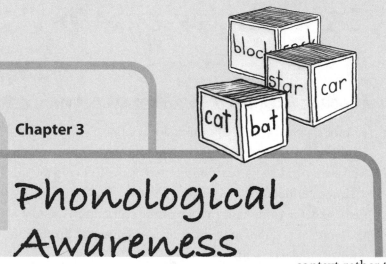

Chapter 3

Phonological Awareness

Overview

The sounds of language are the building blocks of literacy! Phonological awareness is sensitivity to sound. It is an umbrella covering everything from babbling and cooing to blending of sounds and decoding. For preschool children, the umbrella includes sound discrimination activities such as recognizing same and different sounds, playing with onomatopoeic words, matching rhyming word pairs, and identifying the repetitive sound in an alliterative phrase or sentence.

The foundation for sound discrimination is wired in the brain during the first year of life, as a neuron is assigned to every sound in a baby's native language (44 phonemes in English). The more the child is spoken to, sung to, and read to, the more discriminate the neurons become. The brain is so fertile to sound during the first year of life that it is capable of wiring sounds for as many different languages as it experiences.

Opportunities for the development of phonological awareness occur on a regular basis in the classroom. We can capitalize on alliteration, onomatopoeic words, and rhyming word patterns in songs that we sing, books that we read, and activities that we plan. We must be vigilant in watching for opportunities and turning those sound experiences into lessons.

We must become more intentional and purposeful in our instruction. Often, children with special needs do not develop awareness of the sounds they hear. Sometimes, they are unable to develop a phonological system that helps them decode words. For example, a child who is deaf will not learn how to sound things out and combine sounds to read words. Instead, it is important that the child learns how to use words in context rather than in isolation. Children with language delays need extra practice to develop their phonological awareness. It is, however, very important that children with special needs develop this skill, because there is a direct relationship between phonological awareness and future success with reading. This is also true for children with cognitive challenges as well. Research has shown that breaking down a task and allowing the child extra time to practice each step can help him as he learns the skills necessary to build his phonological awareness. Definitions for phonological awareness components are as follows:

Alliteration—The repetition of a consonant sound in a series of words, such as, "Peter Piper picked a peck of pickled peppers." Children can hear the repetition of the /p/ sound, but do not necessarily need to identify that the sound is made by the letter P.

Onomatopoeia—Words that sound like what they describe, for example, "pitter-patter," "moo," "quack," "beep," and so on.

Rhyming words—Words with the same ending sound.

Segmentation—The ability to isolate sounds from a stream of speech; to hear individual words within a sentence and syllables within a word.

Sound discrimination—The ability to hear differences in sounds; to determine likeness and differences in sounds.

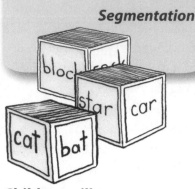

Segmentation

Segmenting Words

Children will:

- isolate individual words in a sentence.

Vocabulary

break apart
part
segment
sentence
whole
words

Materials

chart paper
favorite children's book
hole punch
interlocking cubes
marker
poster board (3" x 12" in colors)
scissors
sentence strips
shoelace or piece of yarn

Introducing and Developing the Lesson

- ❏ Ask for six volunteers. Tell them to form a line. Point out to the class that there are six children who are standing together to make a line.
- ❏ Make six word cards by printing each of the following words on 3" x 12" poster board: "I like to read good books." Print one word on each card. Give one card to each of the children in the line. Read the words. Explain that words make up sentences just like the children make up a line.
- ❏ On chart paper, print, "I like to read good books." Point out that it is a sentence. Tell the children that they will be listening for words that make up sentences.
- ❏ Read one of the children's favorite books, moving your hand beneath the words as you read.
- ❏ Pick a couple of sentences from the book and print them on sentence strips. Cut the sentence strip between the words as the children watch. Place the words in a pocket chart or on the floor to reconstruct the sentence. Invite the children to say the words as you place them into the chart. Read the sentence and have the children slap their hands on their thighs as they say each word.

Practicing the Lesson

- ❏ Give the children several interlocking cubes. Say several simple sentences slowly and ask the children to connect a cube for each word they hear in the sentences.
- ❏ Cut 3" diameter circles from colored poster board and punch a hole in each circle with a hole punch. Print words to a simple sentence on each circle. Print the sentence on chart paper and challenge the children to string the circles onto a shoelace or piece of yarn to copy the sentence.

Reflecting on the Lesson

Ask the children:

- ❏ *What are sentences made of?*
- ❏ *How many words are in the sentence, "I love you?"*

106 ■ **Inclusive Literacy Lessons for Early Childhood** ■

Special Needs Adaptations

Special Need	Adaptation
Visual Impairments	■ Adapt the activity by placing a white card in the child's hand and explain that you will be printing one word on it. It will help to use either white or yellow poster board and write with a black marker. Don't forget that if the child has residual vision, it is important to use large print.
Hearing Impairments	■ Explaining how a sentence is broken up into parts by using visual activities, such as the line activity or the pocket chart, will reinforce the child's understanding, especially if he has difficulty hearing.
Cognitive Challenges	■ Modify the activity by using shorter sentences. Instead of six children, make a sentence with three children.
Motor Delays	■ Remember to make sure the child is positioned so he can see you when you explain the activity. If he is unable to slap his thigh as you say each word, suggest that he beat a drum or clap his hands. For children with severe motor problems, use a bell, such as a "service" bell. The child can tap the bell when you say each word.
Speech/ Language Delays	■ Use words that the child can identify easily and pronounce. The visual representation of each word joined together to make a sentence will reinforce language understanding.
Emotional/ Behavior Issues	■ Group activities, such as the children standing in a line to make a sentence, may be challenging for a child with behavior issues. If he starts to get upset, use a technique called a "communication replacement." Give him a sign or gesture for him to do that lets you know he wants to leave the group. For young children, the gesture can be as simple as holding a hand up palm outward to make a "stop" gesture. This alerts those around him that

The child with special needs cues the teacher when he needs to leave the group.

he needs a few minutes away from the group. It is critical, however, that he uses this before he has a tantrum and that he be required to rejoin the group at some point, to decrease the likelihood of the child learning to use the "stop" gesture to get out of something he wants to avoid.

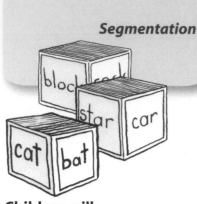

Segmentation

Chim-Chimmy-Chimpanzee

Children will:
- isolate individual words in a sentence.

Vocabulary

break apart
listen
part
segment
sentences
whole
words

Materials

butcher paper
chart paper
photos of animals and objects
    that might be in something (a
    dog or a book)
photos of places these objects
    might be in (a house or a
    wagon)
rhythm sticks or the cardboard
    tubes from a clothes hanger
    for each child
sentence strips of different colors

Introducing and Developing the Lesson

- ❏ Print "Chimpanzees eat bananas" on chart paper. Have the children clap for each word in the sentence.
- ❏ Tell the children that they will be listening for words in sentences.
- ❏ Give each child a rhythm stick or the cardboard tube from a clothes hanger. Invite the children to chant and tap to "Chim, Chimmy Chimpanzee" (see page 263 in the Appendix). While they say this rhythmic chant, they tap out words, not syllables.
- ❏ Challenge the children to make up additional sentences to tap.
- ❏ If children are ready, repeat the game, tapping syllables instead of words.

Practicing the Lesson

- ❏ Teach the children "Peas Porridge Hot" (see page 265 in the Appendix). Make up a simple clapping pattern to the rhyme.
- ❏ Print this sentence "The _____ is in the _____" on butcher paper, leaving blanks where indicated. Provide photos of animals and objects that might be in something, such as a dog, a book, a person, and so on. Provide photos of places these objects might be in, such as a house, a wagon, a car, and so on. Invite the children to place the photos in the blanks in the sentence. Count the words in the sentence each time you make a change. Does the number of words change?
- ❏ Make Silly Sentence Strips. Print the words to the silly sentences in the lesson on sentence strips. Put each sentence on a different color of sentence strip so the children will know which words go with each sentence. Cut the sentence strips between the words. Invite the children to reconstruct the sentences. If necessary, provide the original sentences on chart paper as a model for reconstruction.

Reflecting on the Lesson

Ask the children:
- ❏ *How many words do you hear in this sentence, "My name is Quinn"?*
- ❏ *Clap the words in this sentence, "Today is my birthday." How many words are there in the sentence? Clap the syllables in the word birthday. How many syllables do you hear?*

Special Needs Adaptations

Special Need	Adaptation
Visual Impairments	■ Make sure the child understands what you are asking him to do before beginning the clapping/tapping activity. Before you invite the class to clap the words, "Chimpanzees eat bananas," say the sentence one time without clapping. Say, "Now we will clap each word like this," and demonstrate by clapping each word.
Hearing Impairments	■ Make sure the child understands that you are making silly or pretend sentences. Provide extra picture cues to help the child participate in making the silly sentences. For example, a colorful picture of a chimpanzee swinging from a tree.
Cognitive Challenges	■ If the "Chim, Chimmy Chimpanzee" chant is too long, break it up and introduce one verse at a time. Remember, children with cognitive challenges need extra practice before they learn a new chant or rhyme.
Motor Delays	■ If the child cannot clap or tap, adapt the activity so he can participate. Attach a handle (such as a kitchen cabinet pull) to a large wooden block. The child holds the handle and taps the block on a table or wheelchair tray while his classmates clap. If his block tapping is too loud, place a piece of felt on the bottom to lower the impact of the block when it taps.
Speech/ Language Delays	■ Work one-on-one with the child so he understands that he is to tap each word he hears. ■ Tapping syllables will be confusing for a child with language delays. Be consistent and just ask him to tap words.
Emotional/ Behavior Issues	■ A therapy ball or a beanbag chair will make sitting in a large group easier for a child with emotional issues.

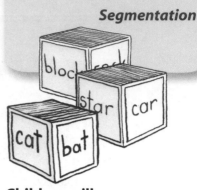

Segmentation

Segmenting Syllables

Children will:

- isolate syllables within words.

Vocabulary

clap
count
part
segments
snap
syllables
tap
whole

Materials

maracas
poster board (4" x 10" strips)
recording device
recording media

Introducing and Developing the Lesson

- ❏ Sing "Bingo" (see page 254 in the Appendix) more slowly than you may have previously sung it. Clap each letter of Bingo's name as you sing them, pronouncing the letters distinctly and clearly as you say them. Do not add the verses that clap out missing letters.
- ❏ Tell the children that you are going to be helping them break words into parts like the letters in Bingo's name. Explain that they will clap out parts of words, just as they clapped out the letters in Bingo's name.
- ❏ Teach the children "Hickey, Picky, Bumblebee" (see page 264 in the Appendix). Clap out the title of the song before starting.
- ❏ Ask the children how clapping, snapping, and tapping names in "Hickey, Picky Bumblebee" is like clapping the letters in Bingo. Explain that syllables are several letters together. Clap a child's name in syllables and then clap it again, one letter at a time, so that children can hear the difference.

Practicing the Lesson

- ❏ Make Word Puzzles with each child's name. Print children's names on 4" x 10" strips of poster board. Cut the name into syllables with a puzzle cut. Place the puzzles in the Language Center. Encourage children to work in pairs to determine if their names have the same number of syllables or a different number of syllables.
- ❏ Place maracas in the Music Center. Suggest that the children shake the syllables of their first and last name.

Reflecting on the Lesson

Ask the children:

- ❏ *When we were clapping, snapping, and tapping syllables in names, which names used a lot of claps, snaps, and taps? Which names used only one clap, snap, and tap?*
- ❏ *What is a long word that would take lots of claps to clap its syllables? What about some of the names of dinosaurs? Ask the children to clap the syllables in the names of their favorite dinosaurs. Have them clap the syllables in "supercalifragilisticexpialidocious."*

Special Needs Adaptations

Special Need	Adaptation
Visual Impairments	■ Let the child feel your hands as you clap out "Bingo" the first time. This will help him understand what is happening.
Hearing Impairments	■ Sit behind the child and place your hands gently on his wrists. Slowly move his hands to clap out the names. ■ Tap on the child's arm lightly to demonstrate how each name is broken down.
Cognitive Challenges	■ Show the child how to clap when each letter in the song is spoken or sung. For example, sing "B" (clap) then let the child says "B" and claps. ■ Allow extra time to practice clapping or tapping his name so he understands how to clap or tap each syllable. ■ If he taps or claps without regard for the sounds, provide extra practice by helping him clap out simple words, such as cup-cake, in-side, out-side, and so on.
Motor Delays	■ Use whatever motor skills the child has to help him participate. If he cannot move his hands, teach him to bob his head with each syllable or tap his foot with each syllable. ■ Provide a service bell for the child to ring or tap for each syllable.
Speech/ Language Delays	■ Help the child clap out his name, saying each syllable as you clap. Have him repeat what you just said. ■ Provide additional opportunities for him to practice clapping or tapping out words.
Emotional/ Behavior Issues	■ Sit the child near you and monitor how he is responding to the noise level. If he becomes overwhelmed, allow him to go to a quieter area of the room for a few minutes then rejoin the group.

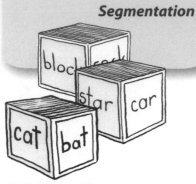

Segmentation

Animal Syllables

Children will:

- isolate syllables within words.

Vocabulary

breaks

listen

part

segments

sentences

syllables

whole

words

Materials

chart paper

scissors

sentence strips of different colors

Introducing and Developing the Lesson

❑ Print "The elephant ate a cookie" on chart paper. Read the sentence. Ask the children to listen carefully to each word you read. Ask the children to clap the syllables (parts) of each word in the sentence.

❑ Print the names of the animals in "Animal Cookie Jar Chant" (see page 262 in the Appendix) on chart paper, showing the breaks for syllables. Clap or tap the syllables in each animal's name.

❑ Explain that some words are made up of more parts than others. Clap the syllables of the other animal names and discuss the number with the children. *Which animal name has the most parts?*

❑ Tell the children that they are going to be listening carefully for breaks in the animal names that are used in the chant.

❑ Invite the children to play a variation of the game "Who Took the Cookie from the Cookie Jar?" called "Animal Cookie Jar Chant."

Practicing the Lesson

❑ Play "Who Took the Cookie from the Cookie Jar?" (see page 262 in the Appendix) using the children's names. Stop to clap syllables in each name.

❑ Print the animal names on sentence strips of different colors and then cut the names apart between syllables using a puzzle cut. Challenge the children to reconstruct the animal names.

Reflecting on the Lesson

Ask the children:

❑ *How many syllables (breaks) do you hear in "gorilla?"*

❑ *Clap the word "Monday." Clap the syllables in "Monday." How many parts are there in the word "Monday"?*

Special Needs Adaptations

Special Need	Adaptation
Visual Impairments	■ Make sure the animal names are written in large print on either white or yellow sentence strips. If necessary, bring in a real cookie jar and invite the child to explore it before playing the game.
Hearing Impairments	■ Show the child how words are made up of syllables by cutting apart each syllable of a word while the child is watching. ■ Say each syllable separately and then put them together with tape.
Cognitive Challenges	■ While the child may not yet be able to understand the concept of syllables, this is a good opportunity to teach the concept of part/whole. ■ Look for some items in the classroom that you can use to demonstrate the concept, for example, a piece of construction paper that you cut in half.
Motor Delays	■ If the child cannot clap or tap the syllables, let him ring a service bell instead.
Speech/ Language Delays	■ Help the child learn to count syllables by making a list of five or six words that he knows. Write each word on a sentence strip and then draw a line between each syllable break. Ask the child to say the word with you. Cut the words apart and repeat the process with each syllable. Finally, arrange the word with each separated part touching so it forms a complete word again. Repeat this activity several times.
Emotional/ Behavior Issues	■ If the child gets anxious during the large group activity, allow him to take a "work break." Remember, whenever a child takes a work break, it is important that he return to the activity he was doing before the break. Teach the child that breaks are allowed, but they cannot be used to avoid an activity altogether.

Clapping animal syllables may be easier with a friend.

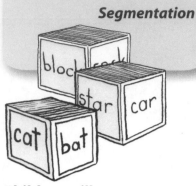

Kitchen Part Sort

Children will:
- isolate syllables within words.

Vocabulary

graph
name
part
syllables
whole

Materials

bag
bucket
Chrysanthemum by Kevin Henkes
kitchen utensils (several types)
paper bag full of crayons
paper plates
plastic animals
tub

Preparation

Place a kitchen utensil (spatula, wooden spoon, and so on) inside a paper bag. Place kitchen items inside a bucket and crayons in a paper bag.

Introducing and Developing the Lesson

- ❑ Take a kitchen utensil out of the bag and ask the children to identify the item. Ask how many syllables are in the item's name.
- ❑ Tell the children that they will be practicing counting syllables.
- ❑ Have the children sit in a circle. Pass a bucket of kitchen items around the circle. Have each child reach inside the bucket and remove an item. Challenge them to say the name of the item and then count the syllables in the name.
- ❑ Sort the kitchen items by the number of syllables in the item's name.

Practicing the Lesson

- ❑ Place plastic animals inside a tub. Have the children remove them one at a time and determine how many syllables are in the animal's name. Encourage the children to sort the animals by number of syllables in their name. Provide paper plates to use as sorting trays. Print the numbers 1–4 in the center of the plates.
- ❑ Read *Chrysanthemum* by Kevin Henkes. Clap the syllables in Chrysanthemum's name. *How many syllables do you hear?* Make a graph for name syllables. Have the children count the number of syllables in their names and then place a mark on the graph in the column that matches the number of syllables in their names.

Reflecting on the Lesson

Ask the children:
- ❑ *How many syllables are in your name? Do you have more or fewer syllables in your name than* Chrysanthemum?
- ❑ *What is the name of a kitchen item with only one syllable in its name?*

Special Needs Adaptations

Special Need	Adaptation
Visual Impairments	■ Instead of crayons in the paper bag, use color markers. Because they are larger than crayons, markers will be easier for the child to identify.
Hearing Impairments	■ Encourage the child to say the name of each item before counting the number of syllables in that item's name. Model for the child exactly what you expect him to do, so he understands. Select items with fewer numbers of syllables for the child to identify.
Cognitive Challenges	■ If this activity is too difficult, modify it by sorting everyday items rather than crayons. Instead of sorting the items by syllable, invite the child to sort the items by other attributes, such as color. For example, you might supply a red car, small blue ball, blue cup, red marker, blue paper square, and red paper square. Provide the child with two paper plates or boxes. Glue a red square in one plate or box and a blue square in the other. The child can sort the items by color. As the child becomes more familiar with colors, add more boxes or plates and more items. Add additional items in red or blue (or add objects with other attributes) to encourage generalization.
Motor Delays	■ Instead of using paper plates for sorting in the Literacy Center activity, use a shoebox or plastic container. It will be easier for the child to place the items into a box when he sorts them. If the child has difficulty picking up the item, provide kitchen tongs (like those used with spaghetti) to help him.
Speech/ Language Delays	■ Before sorting the plastic animals by the number of syllables in their names, make sure the child can recognize each animal. If the child does not know the animal's name, ask him to repeat it after you. Encourage the child to make a sentence with each animal's name.
Emotional/ Behavior Issues	■ Some children with sensory issues will not touch hard plastic. Instead of using plastic animals, the child may respond better to everyday objects. Select some items from around the room and encourage the child to sort them by the number of syllables in each name. Using a box rather than a paper plate may be easier for the child.

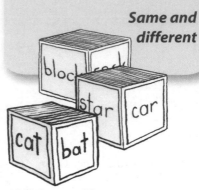

Same and Different

Children will:

- recognize differences between same and different.

Vocabulary

different
same

Materials

basket of items for the children to group (two that are alike and one that is different)

construction paper (several sheets)

glue

items that are the same and different (for example, three blocks, two that are square and one that is a rectangle)

magazines

Introducing and Developing the Lesson

- Ask for three volunteers and tell them to stand. Whisper an action in their ears. Give two children the same action and the other a different action. For example, you might ask two children to clap their hands and the third child to turn around. Ask the class which children are doing the same thing and which child is doing something different.
- Tell the children that they will practice recognizing things that are the same and things that are not the same. When things are not the same they are *different.*
- Show children two items that are exactly alike and one that is different. For example, you might show children three blocks, two that are square and one that is a rectangle.
- Discuss things that are the same and things that are different. Show as many examples as possible. Show two same letters and one different letter, two same-color crayons and one different-color crayon, two same cups and one different cup. Children will need to understand the concepts of *same* and *different* before they will be able to identify same and different sounds in words.

Practicing the Lesson

- Suggest that the children look through magazines for pictures of things that are alike. Have them cut the pictures out and glue them in pairs on a sheet of construction paper. When they have several pairs of items glued to their paper, have them look for items that are different, to add to each pair of items, so that they have sets of three items with two that are alike and one that is different.
- Provide a basket of items for the children to group. Have them make sets of three items—two that are alike and one that is different.

Reflecting on the Lesson

Ask the children:

- *Are you the same as or different from your friends? In what ways are you the same (for example, each friend has two eyes)? In what ways are you different from your friends (for example, the eyes may be a different color)?*
- *Are all puppy dogs the same? How are they different?*

Special Needs Adaptations

Special Need	Adaptation
Visual Impairments	▪ When showing the child same and different items, it is important to make the different items as different as possible. For example, for the same items, allow the child to examine three blocks; for the different items, show him a block, a ball, and a small toy car. Allow him time to touch and feel each item. Again, it will help if the items are in a tray or on a cookie sheet, so he can feel the boundaries for each set.
Hearing Impairments	▪ To reinforce the concept of the lesson, bring in a few pictures that illustrate the same and different, such as animals. (Three dogs in one picture; a cat, dog, and hen in the next picture; or a picture of three red blocks and three blocks of different colors.) To really understand the concept, the child will need multiple examples.
Cognitive Challenges	▪ To understand *same* and *different*, the child will need examples that are very similar and those that are very different. Three blocks of three different colors may be too difficult.
Motor Delays	▪ If the child has severe motor delays, it may be necessary for him to lean toward an item that he selects and you or a peer buddy can move it for him. ▪ Don't forget that children with motor delays do not necessarily have cognitive challenges. With simple adaptations, they can participate and learn the same way as their typically developing peers.
Speech/ Language Delays	▪ When discussing things that are the same or different, use the activity as an opportunity to reinforce learning new vocabulary. One-on-one with the child, say the name of each item you will use to demonstrate the concepts of *same* and *different* and ask him to repeat it after you. Select a few items that he already can identify so he feels successful. If the child is just learning language, he may initially just have to point to the ones that are the same and different.
Emotional/ Behavior Issues	▪ Children with emotional/behavior issues, especially a child with autism spectrum disorder, may be very attached to a certain type of object, for example, blocks, toy cars, or a specific book. Sometimes, those objects are less functional, such as an attachment to spoons or lids. If the child has an object he is attached to, use this item or one that is similar to teach the concepts of *same* and *different*.

Same and Different Sounds

Children will:
- recognize differences between same-sounding words.

Vocabulary

alike
different
same
sound

Materials

ball
basket of objects that includes
   pairs of objects with similar
   sounding names (for example,
   block and sock)
film canisters or pill bottles and
   items to fill them (gravel,
   paper clips)
two rhythm band instruments

Introducing and Developing the Lesson

❑ Use two rhythm band instruments to create a series of three sounds. For example, use the bells and the sticks to make two ringing sounds and one tapping sound. Ask the children which two sounds are alike and which sound is different.

❑ Tell the children that you are going to be talking about words that sound alike and words that sound different. Say three words, for example, "ball," "ball," and "cat." Ask the children which two words sound alike. Try other sets of three words, two the same and one different; for example, "blue," "blue," "car"; "day," "day," "child"; or "block," "block," "ball."

❑ After a few examples using two of the same words and one word that is different, try two words that sound alike and one that sounds different, such as: "ball," "call," "dog"; "blue," "two," "car"; "day," "bay," "child"; or "block," "sock," "phone."

❑ Repeat each of the rhyming word pairs: ball/call, blue/two, day/bay, and block/sock. Tell the children that when two words have similar ending sounds, like these words, they are called *rhyming words*.

Practicing the Lesson

❑ Play "Let the Ball Fall." Have the children stand in a circle. Provide a ball. Explain that you will be saying several words that sound similar. As long as the children hear a word that sounds similar to the previous word, they pass the ball to the child beside them. When they hear a word that sounds different from the previous word, they are to let the ball fall to the ground. When the ball falls, the child who dropped it picks it up and a new list begins. Here are some word lists you can use for this game:
pet, vet, met, bet, set, let, mouse
sat, rat, mat, bat, at, fat, pat, cat, dog
bit, sit, mitt, fit, pit, hit, wit, kit, ball

Reflecting on the Lesson

Ask the children:

❑ *Does a game called Let the Ball Fall sound like more fun than Drop the Ball? Why?*

❑ *Describe one of the sets of items you put together that had two items with names that sound similar and one item that sounds different.*

Special Needs Adaptations

Special Need	Adaptation
Visual Impairments	■ A child with visual impairments should have no difficulty participating in all of these activities as long he understands exactly what he is expected to do. ■ A child who is blind has different ways of orienting himself to his "space." Invite a friend to escort the child to the circle. Give him time to touch the child on either side of him. He will probably do this by feeling their shoulders.
Hearing Impairments	■ For a child with a moderate hearing loss it may be necessary, at first, to use words that are very dissimilar in sound as these will be easier for him to understand.
Cognitive Challenges	■ The concept of words that sound alike, especially those that rhyme, may be too difficult for a child with cognitive challenges. Modify the activity for him by helping him first understand the concept you are teaching. Say two words, such as "ball, ball" and then say one word that is very different, such as "out" or "rock." It may be necessary to do this multiple times before the child understands the idea behind *same* and *different*. Reinforce the difference by reviewing the previous lesson and showing him objects that are the same and those that are different.
Motor Delays	■ Adapt this activity by using larger containers to make the sound canisters. Try an oatmeal container or potato chip can, as they will be easier to pick up and handle.
Speech/ Language Delays	■ Using the rhythm band instruments will be especially useful for a child with limited language skills. To reinforce the learning, reverse roles so that you say a word and invite him to make a sound, then say a different word and invite him to make a different sound. Repeat the activity several times. As he starts to understand that when you say the same word, he plays the same instrument again, and when you say a different word, he should play a different instrument, it will make it easier for him to understand the difference in how words sound.
Emotional/ Behavior Issues	■ Children with emotional issues may be sensitive to the environment. Before beginning any new activity, check the environment for things that might be very distracting for the child, such as harsh lighting, sounds that are too loud, and so on. If the children sit on carpet squares to participate in group activities, try to identify if a child with behavior issues reacts better if he is sitting on something else, such as a soft cushion or beanbag chair. ■ Sometimes a simple environmental adjustment can make the difference in not only how much a child participates but, more importantly, how much a child learns.

Weather Sounds

Children will:

- recognize and use onomatopoeic words.

Vocabulary

crash
describe
drip drop
onomatopoeia
pitter-patter
sounds
swoosh
weather

Materials

crayons or paint
Listen to the Rain by Bill Martin
paper
ribbons
sticks

Introducing and Developing the Lesson

- ❏ Invite the children to recite "Five Little Sparrows" (see page 263 in the Appendix). Tell the children that they will be learning about words that describe the sounds of weather. Ask the children which words in the fingerplay were words that describe the sound of the wind and the rain (swoosh, pitter-patter). Explain that these words are called onomatopoeia.

- ❏ Ask for a volunteer to describe the sound of rain. He may say "pitter-patter" or "drip-drop" or even "splish-splash." These words are also examples of onomatopoeia—words that sound like what they are describing.

- ❏ Invite the children to participate in *A Weather Story* (see page 266 in the Appendix). Have the children sit on the floor. Give half of them sticks and the other half ribbons. Tell them that they are to listen for specific words in the story. They should tap their sticks when they hear the words walk, run, and thunder, and shake their ribbons when they hear the words, wind, rain, and lightning.

- ❏ Discuss the sounds that the sticks and ribbons made. Have the children use onomatopoeic words to describe the sounds.

Practicing the Lesson

- ❏ Take the children outdoors. Engage them in a discussion about the weather conditions. Is the wind blowing? What does it sound like? Is the sun shinning? How does it feel? Is the word that describes how the sun feels onomatopoeic?

- ❏ Invite the children to draw or paint weather pictures. Encourage them to describe the weather scene they have created. With their permission, print their descriptions on the back of their drawing.

- ❏ Read *Listen to the Rain* by Bill Martin, Jr. Discuss the onomatopoeic sounds in the story.

Reflecting on the Lesson

Ask the children:

- ❏ *Which onomatopoeic word for falling rain is your favorite?*
- ❏ *What onomatopoeic word would you use to describe thunder?*

Special Needs Adaptations

Special Need	Adaptation
Visual Impairments	■ Instead of ribbons, which will be difficult for the child to hear, use either handmade drums (an oatmeal container or a plastic dish with a lid) or bells.
Hearing Impairments	■ Show the child some weather pictures, so he has a frame of reference to use when you explain the activity to the class.
Cognitive Challenges	■ While learning about onomatopocia may be too difficult for some children, learning to participate in an activity and learning about the sounds that words make can be fun. ■ Even if the child does not fully understand what you are talking about, he can learn to listen for certain sounds in his environment.
Motor Delays	■ If the child is unable to tap, adapt the activity by using something he can shake, such as maracas.
Speech/ Language Delays	■ Select three of the words you have used in class, such as "pitter-patter," "splash," and "swoosh." Talk to the child about what each word means. Use each word in a sentence for him, and invite him to tell you about the word. Play a game with the child where you listen for sounds in the environment and describe them to each other.
Emotional/ Behavior Issues	■ If the weather story is too long to engage the child, tell the story in three segments. It is important to remember that you want the child to be able to recognize how words *sound* like the noise they make.

Onomatopoeia

Animal Sounds

Children will:

- recognize and use onomatopoeic words.

Vocabulary

animals
describe
moo
oink
onomatopoeia
quack
sounds
words

Materials

chart paper
marker
paper
paper bag
plastic animals

Introducing and Developing the Lesson

- Sing "Old MacDonald Had a Farm" (see page 258 in the Appendix). Discuss the sounds the animals make in the song. Explain that words that sound like what they are describing are called onomatopoeia.
- Tell the children they will be learning about words that describe the sounds animals make.
- Place a variety of plastic animals inside a paper bag. Ask for volunteers who, one at a time, draw an animal from the bag and describe the sound the animal makes.
- Make a list on chart paper of the onomatopoeic words that the children use to describe animal sounds.
- Give the children several plastic animals. Invite them to create a sequence of animals and point to each animal while making the sound for the animal instead of saying the animal's name. *What happens if you arrange the animals into patterns? Do the sounds they make also create a pattern?*

Practicing the Lesson

- Play "Quack, Quack, Honk," just as you would "Duck, Duck, Goose." Children sit in a circle. One child—IT—walks around the outside of the circle, tapping each player on the head and saying "Quack." Eventually IT taps a player and says "Honk" instead. The tapped player gets up and chases IT around the circle. If he taps IT before they get around the circle, he gets to go back to his place. If he doesn't, he becomes the new IT and the game continues.
- Sing songs that have animal onomatopoeic words in them. For example, "Six White Ducks," "Zzzz, Zzzz! Snort, Snort!" and Five Little Ducks" (see the Appendix for listed songs) and so on.

Reflecting on the Lesson

Ask the children:

- *Do dogs make a different sound when they are happy than when they are angry? What about cats?*
- *Can you think of an animal that doesn't make a sound?*

Special Needs Adaptations

Special Need	Adaptation
Visual Impairments	<ul><li>Use plastic animals that are easily recognizable by touch and do not have a lot of fine detail.</li><li>Remember to use plastic animals that are large enough for the child to investigate by touching.</li></ul>
Hearing Impairments	<ul><li>Hold up a picture of each animal as you sing about it. This helps give the child a clue as to what will be sung next.</li></ul>
Cognitive Challenges	<ul><li>Some children may not be familiar with the names of the animals in the song. Start by showing the child pictures of animals in the song (pig, goose, horse, cow, and so on), and asking him to identify each. You can also play a game with the child where you say the animal's names and he makes the sound that the animals make. If he does not know the sound, invite him to make it with you.</li></ul>
Motor Delays	<ul><li>Provide the child with his own plastic animals to use. Make sure they are large enough for him to pick up and hold.</li></ul>
Speech/ Language Delays	<ul><li>Encourage the child to build his vocabulary by talking about characteristics of the animals in the song. For example, ducks swim, pigs have snouts, and so on.</li></ul>
Emotional/ Behavior Issues	<ul><li>Make sure the child is familiar with the song and knows what he is expected to do in the activity. You can avoid a tantrum or outburst from the child by explaining and modeling how the song is sung, before introducing it to the class.</li></ul>

Onomatopoeia

Food Sounds

Children will:
- recognize and use onomatopoeic words.

Vocabulary

chomp
crunch
describe
onomatopoeia
slurp
sounds

Materials

chart paper
Slop Goes the Soup: A Noisy Warthog Word Book by Pamela Duncan Edwards
foods or photos of foods
fruits and snack foods that make a variety of crunchy sounds and no sound
popcorn

Preparation

Gather food or photos of foods.

Introducing and Developing the Lesson

- Sing "Chew! Slurp! Crunch!" (See page 255 in the Appendix) to the tune of "She'll Be Comin' 'Round the Mountain." Point out the onomatopoeia in the song.
- Tell the children that they will learn words that describe the sounds made when eating.
- Gather foods or photos of foods. Show the food or photos to the children. Ask them to describe the sound they would make eating or drinking the food item.
- Print the sound words they use on chart paper. When you are finished with the list, read the words to the children. Have them name foods that make that sound when chewed or swallowed.

Practicing the Lesson

- Serve a variety of fruits for snack. Have the children identify the sounds that they make as they eat the various fruits.
- Provide snacks that make a crunchy sound when chewed, such as crackers and cookies. At the same time, serve snacks that do not make a noise when eaten, such as yogurt or gelatin. Encourage the children to predict, in advance, if the snack will make noise when it is eaten.
- Read *Slop Goes the Soup: A Noisy Warthog Word Book* by Pamela Duncan Edwards. Discuss the sounds the warthog makes as he attempts to prepare soup.
- Pop popcorn. Ask the children to describe the sounds of the popping corn. Tell them it is a popcorn "serenade."

Reflecting on the Lesson

Ask the children:
- *What did you eat for breakfast this morning? Which of the foods made sounds when you chewed them?*
- *Do animals make sounds when they eat? Describe the sounds you have heard them make.*

Special Needs Adaptations

Special Need	Adaptation
Visual Impairments	■ Be sure to select toy food, real food, or pictures that match the child's visual abilities. For example, a child with gross form perception (one who can see objects, but not their detail) might respond best to brightly colored objects placed on a high-contrast color background, such as a carrot stick on a yellow piece of paper.
Hearing Impairments	■ The child may be unable to hear the sounds that foods make. It may be necessary for you to explain that, sometimes, when we eat food, it makes a sound. If the child has residual hearing, he may be able to hear louder food sounds, such as a celery or carrot crunch.
Cognitive Challenges	■ It may not be possible for the child to identify the sound a food makes. In fact, he may not even know the word name for all the foods you discuss. Adapt the activity by inviting him to help you sort food pictures into things you eat and things you drink.
Motor Delays	■ Remember to use foods that the child can eat. Depending on his motor involvement, he may not be able to eat some foods, such as popcorn.
Speech/ Language Delays	■ Select three foods and talk with the child about the sound each one makes when eaten. Make sure the child knows the names of the foods you have selected. Ask him questions that encourage him to talk about each. For example, "Which food would we put into a salad?" (Show a picture or a real carrot and a picture or a real container of gelatin.) Follow up with more questions, such as, "What other foods might go in a salad?"
Emotional/ Behavior Issues	■ Many children with behavior issues, especially those with autism spectrum disorder, relate better to real objects than to pictures. If possible, use real food to demonstrate the onomatopoeic words.

Children who do not know the names of common foods will benefit from picture cues.

Onomatopoeia

Travel Sounds

Children will:

- recognize and use onomatopoeic sounds.

Vocabulary

beep
clink
describe
onomatopoeia
sounds
swish

Materials

photographs representing the
    sound
recording of traffic and car
    sounds
transportation vehicles for Block
    Center

Preparation

Gather items to make sounds
mentioned in "The Wheels on the
Bus" (for example, a horn, coins
and a metal can, and a squeegee).

Introducing and Developing the Lesson

- Sing "The Wheels on the Bus" (see page 261 in
  the Appendix).
- Discuss the sounds described in the song.
  Tell the children that they will be exploring
  sounds that accompany transportation.
- Demonstrate the sound of items mentioned
  in "The Wheels on the Bus,"
  for example,
  honk a horn,
  clink money
  into a metal
  can, and run
  a squeegee
  over a window
  to represent a

  wiper. Ask the children if the sounds you demonstrate actually
  sound like the words in the song. Remind them that the words
  describing the sounds are called onomatopoeia.
- Record traffic and car sounds. Provide photographs and challenge
  the children to match the sound to the picture that represents
  the sound.

Practicing the Lesson

- Sing other songs with travel sounds in them, such as "Little Hunk
  of Tin" and "Little Red Caboose" (both on page 258 in the
  Appendix).
- Provide transportation vehicles for the Block Center. Encourage
  children to use the sounds the vehicles make when they play.

Reflecting on the Lesson

Ask the children:

- *What sound does your car make when the motor is turned on?*
- *In the song, "The Wheels on the Bus," the sound for the horn is beep.
  What other sound might be used for a horn?*

Special Needs Adaptations

Special Need	Adaptation
Visual Impairments	■ Whenever possible, provide three-dimensional objects for the child to hold. For example, holding a toy bus with wheels that turn when you are singing "The Wheels on the Bus" will help him relate to the song.
Hearing Impairments	■ Keep in mind that some sounds will be more easily identified by the child than others. Softer sounds such as "swish" may be more difficult for the child to hear.
Cognitive Challenges	■ Remember, the child's only experience with riding a bus may be a school bus or van. So, it will be necessary to explain phrases that may be new to him, such as "the money on the bus goes 'clink'!"
Motor Delays	■ Glue each photograph or picture on an index card and attach a wooden clothespin to each card. As the child identifies a sound and reaches for the card that matches the sound, the clothespin provides something to hold, so he can easily pick up the card.
Speech/ Language Delays	■ As the child matches the mode of transportation with the sound it makes, encourage the child to describe one thing about the vehicle.
Emotional/ Behavior Issues	■ If the child cannot stay involved while you and the class sing "The Wheels on the Bus," try shortening it and only singing two verses. If the child becomes frustrated with an activity, such as the sound-matching activity, allow him to leave for a few minutes and take a work break. Remind him that he must return after the break and finish the activity.

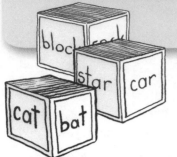

Onomatopoeia

Children will:
- recognize and use onomatopoeic sounds.

Vocabulary
buzz
crash
describe
hiss
onomatopoeia
ring
rum-pum-pum
rum-tum
sounds
toot
twang
words

Materials
boxes
chart paper
circles of wax paper
cardboard tubes
coat hanger tubes
crayons or markers
empty cardboard tubes (use paper
    towel tubes or wrapping
    paper tubes cut into
    4"–6"sections)
marker
pencils
rhythm band instruments
rubber bands
straws

Musical Sounds

Introducing and Developing the Lesson

- ❏ Play a rhythm band instrument. Ask the children to describe the sound it makes. Print the sound word on chart paper.
- ❏ Continue playing instruments, one at a time. Encourage the children to describe the sound. Print their descriptions on chart paper.
- ❏ Explain that the sounds used to describe the sounds made by musical instruments are called onomatopoeia.
- ❏ Help the children make kazoos. Provide each child with a cardboard tube, a circle of wax paper, and a rubber band. Let them decorate the tube using crayons and markers. Help them secure the waxed paper with a rubber band around one end of the tube. Show them how to hum into the open end of the tube to create a kazoo sound.

- ❏ Ask them to describe the sounds they make.

Practicing the Lesson

- ❏ Help the children make drums to play. Use box bottoms for drums and coat hanger tubes for drum sticks. Have the children describe the sounds they make with their drums.
- ❏ Change drumsticks to rhythm sticks. Does the sound change? Try using straws for drumsticks. Does the sound change?
- ❏ Take children on a field trip to a local high school so they can hear the band play. Ask them to describe the sounds they hear.

Reflecting on the Lesson

Ask the children:
- ❏ *Which instrument sound do you like best?*
- ❏ *Which instrument makes a crashing sound?*

Special Needs Adaptations

Special Need	Adaptation
Visual Impairments	■ Make sure the child is seated where he can see each instrument as you play it. If the child has significant visual impairments, hand him each instrument and let him explore it before playing it.
Hearing Impairments	■ The child with some residual hearing will probably be better able to hear the instruments that are louder, such as the drums or cymbals. As an alternative to a kazoo, try playing something louder. ■ Utilize the traditional method of taking two kitchen spoons and "playing the spoons" by knocking them together on your thigh.
Cognitive Challenges	■ Changes in the daily routine can be very overwhelming to a child with cognitive challenges. Before going on the band field trip, play some band music for the child and then tell him the field trip will be going to hear more band music.
Motor Delays	■ If the child does not have the motor skills to play a kazoo, you could make a "jingle bells bracelet" by attaching bells to a simple cloth headband and placing them on his wrist or his ankle. He can shake his wrist or his feet, if he has limited use of his upper body. Then, he can play the bells with the kazoo band.
Speech/ Language Delays	■ Children with language delays may not know the names of the instruments you are using. Describe each one in detail for the child before you play it. As a review, ask the child to hand you an instrument. For example, say, "Please hand me the cymbals."
Emotional/ Behavior Issues	■ Some children are very sensitive to sound. If the child grabs his ears when you play the instruments, allow him to wear headphones so the noise will not overwhelm him. Headphones may also be used when the class visits the school band.

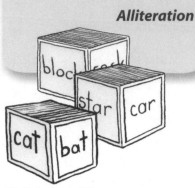

Alliteration

Peter Piper

Children will:

■ recognize the repetition in beginning consonant sounds of a series of words.

Vocabulary

alliteration
letters
repetition
sounds
tongue twister
words

Materials

blocks
chart paper
grocery bags
multicolored pompoms
newspaper
pail
tape
tongs

Preparation

Print the tongue twister "Peter Piper" on chart paper. Fill grocery bags ¾ full of crumpled newspaper and then fold the top of the bag over and tape closed.

Introducing and Developing the Lesson

❑ Display the "Peter Piper" tongue twister. Move your hand under each word as you read it to the children.
Peter Piper picked a peck of pickled peppers.
If Peter Piper picked a peck of pickled peppers,
Where's the peck of peppers that Peter Piper picked?

❑ Ask a volunteer to identify the sound he hears repeated in the tongue twister. It is not important to state the sound is made by the letter "P." Tell the children that the repetition of an initial consonant sound in a series of words is called *alliteration* (Daffy Duck, pink pansies, five frogs, and Maggie Mae).

❑ Ask for a volunteer and then direct that child to underline all the "Ps" in Peter Piper in the first line, another child to underline all the "Ps" in the second line, and a third child to underline all the "Ps" in the third line.

❑ Recite the tongue twister again. Move your hand under each letter "P" as you say the rhyme.

❑ Place the Bag Blocks (see Preparation) on the floor. Suggest that the children stack the blocks into a tower and say, "Tumble, tumble, tumbling towers," as they knock the towers over.

Practicing the Lesson

❑ Play "Pink and Purple Pompom Pickup." Drop multicolored pompoms onto the floor. Give each child a pail and a pompom picker-upper (a pair of tongs). Challenge the children to pick up the pink and purple pompoms and drop them into the pail. Print "Pink and Purple Pompom Pickup" on chart paper. Point out the repetition of the letter "P" and ask the children to tell you what sound the letter makes.

❑ Sing alliterative rhymes, such as "Miss Mary Mack" (see page 264 in the Appendix) and songs, such as "Billy Boy" (see page 254 in the Appendix).

Reflecting on the Lesson

Ask the children:

❑ *Which sentence sounds best to you,* "Billy builds big buildings" *or* "Tiffany builds large towers"?

❑ *What is it called when a beginning consonant sound is repeated in two or more words?*

Special Needs Adaptations

Special Need	Adaptation
Visual Impairments	■ Give the child a "bag block" to explore closely and handle, before introducing the tumbling towers game. If the child has significant visual challenges, place the bag blocks on the floor and provide a large box for the child to build his tower in. The sides of the box will serve as a guide to the child so he will know where to build the tower.
Hearing Impairments	■ If the child is having difficulty distinguishing the /p/ sound, invite him to hold his palm a few inches away from your mouth, so he can feel the air coming out when you say the /p/ sound.
Cognitive Challenges	■ Identify words that the child may not know and tell him about them before beginning this activity. Examples may include "pickled," "peppers," "tumble," and "piper."
Motor Delays	■ If the child can't participate in the tumbling towers activity, make smaller bag blocks and place them on his wheelchair tray. ■ If the child has limited motor control, look for other ways he can help knock over the tower, such as with his feet or with a kitchen utensil like a spatula.
Speech/ Language Delays	■ If the child is unable to say the whole tongue twister, break it into smaller phrases and ask him to repeat each phrase after you. ■ Help the child identify other words that he knows that start with the letter "P."
Emotional/ Behavior Issues	■ Remind the child to take turns and give everyone a chance to add to the tumbling tower. Before beginning the activity, tell the child that the purpose of the activity is to stack the blocks up until they fall.

Chocolate Chip Cookies

Children will:

- recognize the repetition of a beginning consonant sound.

Vocabulary

alliteration
repetition
same
sounds

Materials

chart paper
chocolate chip cookies
seashells
simple tongue twisters

Introducing and Developing the Lesson

- ❑ Print "chocolate chips" on chart paper. Have the children say "chocolate chips" several times. Underline the letters "ch" in each word. Pronounce the words slowly and ask children to listen to the repetition of sounds. Can they hear the /ch/ sound repeated?
- ❑ Tell the children that they will practice listening for the repetitive sound /ch/. Remind them that the repetition of beginning sounds of several words in a row is called *alliteration*.
- ❑ Sing "Chocolate Chip Cookies" (see page 255 in the Appendix) to the tune of "Mary Had a Little Lamb."
- ❑ Ask children which words in the song had the /ch/ sound.
- ❑ Print "It's chocolate chip cookies a choosy child chews" on chart paper. Underline each /ch/ sound. Have the children repeat the sentence a couple of times. Can they hear the /ch/ sound?
- ❑ Teach the children some simple tongue twisters.
  - She sells seashells by the seashore.
  - How much wood would a woodchuck chuck if a woodchuck could chuck wood?
- ❑ Have the children try saying these simple phrases three times quickly.
  Big black bear
  Six sick sheep
  Quinn quits quietly

Practicing the Lesson

- ❑ Serve chocolate chip cookies for snack. Ask the children to think of other snacks that have alliterative sounds. For example, peppermint patties, buttered bread, crumb cake, candy corn, and so on.
- ❑ Bring some seashells to class and put them in the Science/Nature Center. Invite children to say "She sells seashells" three times.

Reflecting on the Lesson

Ask the children:

- ❑ *If you created an alliterative name for yourself what would it be?*
- ❑ *Which of the following Disney characters have alliterative names: Donald Duck, Pluto, Mickey Mouse, Goofy, or Daisy Duck?*

Special Needs Adaptations

Special Need	Adaptation
Visual Impairments	■ Bring chocolate chips to class in a small plastic bag. Invite the child with visual impairments to hold one and smell it. Then, tell him you will be talking about chocolate chip cookies today. ■ Bring seashells to class. Invite the child to hold a seashell while you say the tongue twister.
Hearing Impairments	■ Teach the class the sign for "cookie" (see page 252 in the Appendix). It is an easy sign to use and the children will enjoy signing the word as you discuss chocolate chip cookies with the class. If the child with hearing impairments has some residual hearing, invite him to place his palm a few inches from your mouth and feel the /ch/ sound as you make it.
Cognitive Challenges	■ Because children with cognitive challenges often have speech and language delays as well, it is a good idea to help the child follow the same procedure described above. By feeling the breath as it comes out of your mouth when you make the /ch/ sound, the child can better understand how to reproduce it himself.
Motor Delays	■ A child with motor delays may be unable to say the entire tongue twister. Instead, invite him to say, "I choose chocolate chip cookies."
Speech/ Language Delays	■ Work with the child one on one to say the /ch/ sound before beginning this activity. Say, "ch-ch-choo-choo" several times and invite him to join you. It may be necessary for you to show him how to make the /ch/ sound by placing his tongue behind his bottom teeth.
Emotional/ Behavior Issues	■ Show the child a picture of chocolate chip cookies and tell him that you will be talking about the /ch/ sound. Follow the same procedure with a seashell.

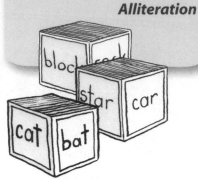

Alliteration

Flea Fly Flow

Children will:
- recognize the repetition of a beginning consonant sound.

Vocabulary

alliteration
beginning
repetitive
sounds
tongue twisters

Materials

black chenille wire
bowl
chart paper
clear carbonated drink (Ginger Ale or Sprite)
marker
raisins

Preparation

Print "One Flea Fly Flew" (see page 258 in the Appendix) on chart paper.

Introducing and Developing the Lesson

❏ Teach the children "The Fly and the Flea." After reading it aloud a couple of times, point out the repetition of the /fl/ sound.
A fly and a flea in a flue (clap, clap)
Were caught, so what could they do? (clap, clap)
"Let us fly," said the flea.
"Let us flee," said the fly.
So they flew through a flaw in the flue. (clap, clap)

❏ Tell the children that they will be sound detectives. You will be trying to find repetition of beginning sounds in songs and chants.

❏ Sing "One Flea Fly Flew" (see page 258 in the Appendix).

❏ Display the chart paper with the song written on it. Encourage children to help locate the /fl/ sounds.

❏ Ask for a volunteer and then direct that child to underline the /fl/ sounds.

Practicing the Lesson

❏ Teach the children "Flea Fly Flow" (see page 263 in the Appendix). Can they hear the repetition of the /fl/ sound?

❏ Serve Fly Floats for snack. Place raisins in a clear carbonated drink such as Ginger Ale or Sprite. The carbonated bubbles will make the "flies" (raisins) float.

❏ Teach the children how to play "Flea Flickers." Cut a black chenille wire into small segments to represent fleas. Place the "fleas" on the table top. Show the children how to use their index finger or their ring finger to flick the fleas from the table top to the floor below, then pick them up and do it again. When they get more skilled at flicking, provide a bowl and challenge the children to flick the fleas into the bowl on the floor.

Reflecting on the Lesson

Ask the children:

❏ *What repetitive sound do you hear in the words "flea, fly, flow?"*

❏ *Which word makes "fly" an alliterative phrase, black fly or flower fly?*

Special Needs Adaptations

Special Need	Adaptation
Visual Impairments	■ Make an additional copy of "One Flea Fly Flew" in large print. Laminate it, if possible, and invite the child to look at it while you are using the chart paper version for the rest of the class.
Hearing Impairments	■ Work with the child one on one and show him how to make the /fl/ sound. After the child watches you make the sound a few times, invite him to make it with you.
Cognitive Challenges	■ Words, such as "flaw" and "flue" and even "shoo" may be new for the child. Tell him the meaning of each word and, if possible, show him a picture of a flue.
Motor Delays	■ If the child is unable to clap when you say "The Fly and the Flea" chant, invite him to ring a bell or tap on a table.
Speech/ Language Delays	■ Talk to the child about words that sound the same but have different meanings. For example, "flew," "flue," and "flu." Help the child make a list of other words that sound the same, such as "to" and "two" or "know" and "no."
Emotional/ Behavior Issues	■ Remember, some children have very short attention spans. It may be necessary to break the lesson into several parts. Review each part before going on to the next.

Alliteration

Alliterative Alerts

Children will:
- recognize the repetition of beginning consonant sounds.

Vocabulary
alike
alliteration
beginning
sounds

Materials
beads
blocks
bows
buttons
chart paper
marker
paper
pink paint

Preparation
Print "Terry the Terrifying Tiger" on chart paper.

> Terry the terrifying tiger.
> Terrifying teeth.
> Terrifying toes.
> Terrifying tail.
> Terry the totally terrifying
>   tiger.

Introducing and Developing the Lesson

- Read "Terry the Terrifying Tiger" to the children, moving your hand beneath the words as you read them.
- Underline each beginning letter "T."
- Remind the children that repetitive beginning sounds are called *alliteration*.
- Tell the children that they will be learning more about alliteration. Tell them to keep their ears open and be on "Alliteration Alert."
- List the children's names on chart paper. Challenge the group to make up an alliterative name for each child.
- Encourage the children to use their alliterative names throughout the day. Be sure to acknowledge children when they use their classmate's alliterative names.

Practicing the Lesson

- Invite the children to paint "pink pictures" or to build "ten tall towers." Point out the alliteration in each phrase.
- Provide beads, buttons, and bows for the children to use to make a Buttons, Beads, and Bows Collage. Point out the alliteration in the phrase "buttons, beads, and bows."

Reflecting on the Lesson

Ask the children:
- *Which alliterative activity did you enjoy the most?*
- *Which alliterative phrase sounds best, "terrifying teeth" or "terrifying toes"? Why?*

Special Needs Adaptations

Special Need	Adaptation
Visual Impairments	■ Remember to print the words to the poem large enough for the child to see. It may be necessary to provide a copy of the poem on a small easel in front of him, so he can follow along.
Hearing Impairments	■ To reinforce the /t/ sound in the poem, invite the child to hold his palm a few inches from your mouth and feel the breath that comes out when you say the /t/ sound.
Cognitive Challenges	■ The child will enjoy making an alliterative name for himself. You will need to help him by suggesting words he may use. For example, if his name is Marcus, you could say, "Marcus, you like music. What about *Musical Marcus*?" or "Laquisha, you laugh a lot. What about *Laughing Laquisha*?"
Motor Delays	■ Remember to position the child in such a way that he can see you and what you are doing when you underline the /t/ sound.
Speech/ Language Delays	■ If the child has a speech/language delay, he may not be able to make a /t/ sound. Demonstrate how the sound is made and invite the child to watch closely, as you place your tongue just behind your front teeth when you make the sound.
Emotional/ Behavior Issues	■ Be sure to mention a preferred toy or activity when helping the child create an alliterative name for himself. ■ Children with autism spectrum disorder usually have an easier time understanding concepts that are concrete, so the "Alliteration Alert" may not make sense to them. Remember to smile, so a child with autism knows you are playing a "pretend" game when you use a "silly" name for him.

Rhyming words

Nonsense Rhymes

Children will:
- identify rhyming words.

Vocabulary

nonsense rhymes
rhyming words

Materials

The Hungry Thing by Jan Slepain
and Ann Seidler or *There's a
Wocket in My Pocket* by Dr.
Seuss
paper bag
photos of different types of food
large stew or soup pot

Introducing and Developing the Lesson

- ❑ Tell the children that they will be playing with nonsense rhymes and stories.
- ❑ Read *The Hungry Thing* by Jan Slepain and Ann Seidler. Allow the children to guess what the hungry thing wants to eat before you read the correct item in the story. Discuss the nonsense rhymes the hungry thing used to communicate his request for food.
- ❑ Challenge the children to make up a rhyming name for the hungry thing, such as Needy Feedy or Starvin' Marvin.
- ❑ Provide a large stew or soup pot. Invite the children to make up a Rhyme Stew to put into the pot. Challenge them to make up a string of nonsense rhymes that will go into the pot. Give them a starting word, such as banana. They might then add hana, mana, rana, tana, lana, and so on.

Practicing the Lesson

- ❑ Give the children a paper bag and photos of different types of food. Encourage the children to place a food photo in their paper bag and then provide nonsense rhyming clues to their friends that will reveal the rhyming contents of their bag.

- ❑ Read *There's a Wocket in My Pocket* by Dr. Seuss. Talk with the children about the nonsense rhymes in the book.

Reflecting on the Lesson

Ask the children:
- ❑ *What nonsense word rhymes with your name?*
- ❑ *What is your favorite food? What nonsense word would rhyme with that food?*

Special Needs Adaptations

Special Need	Adaptation
Visual Impairments	■ To participate in the rhyming stew activity, the child will need additional word clues to help him. For example, you might ask the child to listen while you make up a rhyme.
Hearing Impairments	■ Hearing differences between words, especially words that sound similar, may be very difficult for the child. Before beginning the rhyming stew activity, ask the child to name some words that rhyme. If this is difficult for him, say some words for him.
Cognitive Challenges	■ While making nonsense rhymes may not be feasible for a child with cognitive challenges, he can still participate in the Rhyme Stew activity. Instead of nonsense rhymes, invite him to provide a word that rhymes with a familiar word, such as when you say "bat" and he says "cat" or "hat." ■ If necessary, stand beside the child and whisper hints in his ear to help him participate.
Motor Delays	■ Place the stew pot near the child. If he is unable to reach into it to add his rhyming word, offer to let a friend help him.
Speech/ Language Delays	■ Before beginning this activity, review rhyming pairs with the child. Play a game where you say one word, such as "ball" and the child says a word that rhymes with it, like "tall," "fall," "call," and so on.
Emotional/ Behavior Issues	■ The child may be more likely to participate in the rhyming stew activity if he is in a very small group (three or fewer). Remember to model for him exactly what you want him to do.

Humpty Dumpty

Children will:

- identify the rhymes in familiar words.

Vocabulary

rhyme
rhyming
word pairs

Materials

chart paper
crumpled newspaper
Henny Penny by Paul Galdone
lunch-size brown paper bags
marker
masking tape
plastic eggs
plastic farm animals

Introducing and Developing the Lesson

- ❑ Recite the "Humpty Dumpty" rhyme (see page 264 in the Appendix) with the children. Point out that "Humpty Dumpty" is an egg, and that he has a rhyming name.
- ❑ Ask the children to say Humpty's full name, "Humpty Dumpty," several times. Ask the children, "Who likes the sound of the name?"
- ❑ Write "Humpty Dumpty" on a piece of chart paper. Look at the letters. *Which letters are the same? Which letters are different?*
- ❑ Lead children to discover that only the first letter of each part of Humpty's name is different.
- ❑ Challenge the children to create a rhyming name by using their first names and made-up second names. For example, Madison Wadison or Ben Len.

Practicing the Lesson

- ❑ Read the traditional Henny Penny story (one example is *Henny Penny* by Paul Galdone). Discuss the rhyming names of the characters. Place plastic farm animals in the Block Center and encourage the children to re-enact the story.
- ❑ Suggest that the children play "Humpty Dumpty Dumpty." Give each child two plastic eggs. The children stand with their arms out to their side with a plastic egg resting in each hand. Tell the children that when you say "go," they are to stand on one foot while balancing their Humpty Dumpty eggs on their hands. Count to 10. *How many eggs get dumped?*

Reflecting on the Lesson

Ask the children:

- ❑ *Would the "Humpty Dumpty" rhyme be as much fun if the egg's name was Eggbert instead of Humpty Dumpty? Why or why not? Say the rhyme using different names that the children suggest. What makes "Humpty Dumpty" such a good name?*
- ❑ *Why do you think the author of "Humpty Dumpty" chose the name Humpty Dumpty?*

Special Needs Adaptations

Special Need	Adaptation
Visual Impairments	■ Object cues are objects that represent things. For example, using a plastic egg to represent Humpty Dumpty would allow a child with vision impairments to understand the lesson better. ■ A large plastic egg helps the child *see* and understand the lesson by exploring the egg with his hands. If the child is hesitant, place one of your hands over his and explore the egg together. Invite the child to hold the egg as you recite the rhyme. ■ It is important for a child with visual challenges to know what will happen next and the boundary of where to stand. With careful planning, the child with visual impairments can participate in the "Humpty Dumpty Dumpty" game. Explain each step and invite him to act it out. Say, "First, stand up and hold out your hands." It may be necessary for you to position his hands for him.
Hearing Impairments	■ A child with hearing impairments may not fully understand the words in the rhyme. To make optimal use of the child's residual hearing, make sure he is facing you with the light behind him. Say one line of the rhyme and then invite him to say it with you.
Cognitive Challenges	■ Playing "Humpty Dumpty Dumpty" may provide a good opportunity for a child with cognitive challenges to begin to learn about reciprocity or the give-and-take that is necessary when two friends work together. First, invite the child to play the game with you so you and the child can take turns. Start with one egg before adding a second one.
Motor Delays	■ A child with severe motor delays will be unable to play "Humpty Dumpty Dumpty." Look for opportunities to help the child partially participate. Partial participation means that the child does as much or as little of an activity as he can.
Speech/ Language Delays	■ A child with delays in either speech or language will benefit from learning the rhyme associated with this lesson by using picture cues. Make a picture cue to go with each line in the rhyme. Place them, in order, in front of the child. Later, when he is more familiar with the rhyme, he may be able to sequence them for you.
Emotional/ Behavior Issues	■ Use sequence cards to let the child know what is going to happen. Knowing what will happen and what he is expected to do helps the child with behavior issues feel more in control. Emotional outbursts are often the result of a child not knowing what to expect will happen next.

Nursery Rhyme Time

Children will:
- identify familiar rhyming word pairs.

Vocabulary

nursery rhyme
rhyme
rhyming

Materials

basket of items that can be arranged into rhyming pairs (for example, a sock and a rock)
recording device
recording media

Introducing and Developing the Lesson

- Recite "Hey, Diddle, Diddle" (see page 264 in the Appendix).
- Recite the rhyme a second time, stopping as you come to a rhyming word and letting the children fill in the blank. Tell the children that you are going to be working on helping them identify rhyming words.
- Teach the children "Hickory, Dickory, Dock" (see page 264 in the Appendix).
- Recite the rhyme in a normal voice, except whisper the rhyming words. Recite the rhyme in a whisper, except say the rhyming words in a normal voice. Recite the rhyme in a normal voice, stopping on rhyming words. Point to a child to fill in the rhyming words.
- Provide a basket of items that can be arranged into rhyming pairs. You could include a sock and a rock, a book and a hook, a car and a star, and so on.

Practicing the Lesson

- Record several nursery rhymes. Place the recording in the Listening Center.
- Teach the children how to play "One Potato" (see page 265 in the Appendix). Have them sit facing a partner. As they say the rhyme, they tap one fist on top of the other, except when they come to a rhyming word ("four," "more," "ten," "again"). On the rhyming words they clap hands with their partner. Repeat the rhyme three or four times.

Reflecting on the Lesson

Ask the children:
- *Which nursery rhyme is your favorite? Why? What are the rhyming words in the rhyme?*
- *What rhymes with "dock" other than "clock"?*

Special Needs Adaptations

Special Need	Adaptation
Visual Impairments	■ Bring in a toy mouse and invite the child to hold it and feel it. He will enjoy the activity more if he knows what he is talking about. ■ If the child is not tactilely sensitive, let him help you as you say the rhyme. Ask him to hold out his arm when you say "the mouse ran up the clock"; you can run your fingers along his arm to simulate the mouse running up the clock. Stop at his shoulder. When you say, "The mouse ran down," repeat the motion, but this time, run your fingers down to his hand. The other children will enjoy this reenactment as well.
Hearing Impairments	■ Make a series of picture sequence cards to demonstrate the rhyme: for example, a picture of a mouse, a mouse running up a clock, and a mouse running down a clock. As you say each part of the rhyme, hold up the corresponding picture.
Cognitive Challenges	■ Make sure the child knows the vocabulary before you introduce the rhyme. In addition, if the child is going to sort items, select fewer items and items that are familiar for him to sort. ■ While the rest of the class may be ready for items that sound alike, the child with cognitive challenges may only be able to practice sorting items that are very dissimilar, such as those introduced in the lesson about same/different.
Motor Delays	■ If the child is unable to pick up the objects used in the rhyming pair activity, ask him to invite a friend to help him.
Speech/ Language Delays	■ Use the picture sequence cards previously mentioned to reinforce the child's vocabulary. Show him the picture of the mouse and invite him to tell you about the mouse. Do the same with the clock picture. ■ Even if the child has problems pronouncing the words in the rhyme, such as saying "hickory, dickory, dock," encourage him to participate anyway. ■ For a child with speech pronunciation problems, learning to say the words "mouse," "ran," "up," and "clock" are more functional (useful) than learning "hickory, dickory, dock."
Emotional/ Behavior Issues	■ Make sure the child is engaged and attending to the activity before asking him to provide a rhyme for you. ■ Model for him exactly what you expect him to do.

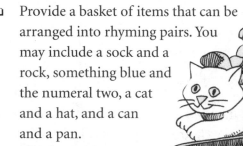

Rhyme Time

Children will:
- identify familiar rhyming word pairs.

Vocabulary
rhyme
rhyming
sounds
words

Materials
basket of items that can be
    arranged into rhyming pairs
    (for example, a sock and a
    rock)
chart paper
construction paper pears
marker
photos from magazines
recording device
recording media

Introducing and Developing the Lesson

- ❏ Sing "Down by the Bay" (see page 256 in the Appendix). List the rhyming word pairs, for example, "pig/jig" and "cat/hat" on chart paper.
- ❏ Challenge the children to write a new verse for the song.
- ❏ Play "Say and Touch" (see page 262 in the Appendix). Follow the directions in the text.
- ❏ Encourage the children to think of additional lines to add to the chant.
- ❏ Provide a basket of items that can be arranged into rhyming pairs. You may include a sock and a rock, something blue and the numeral two, a cat and a hat, and a can and a pan.

- ❏ Tell the children to match the rhyming pairs with a friend.

Practicing the Lesson

- ❏ Record "Say and Touch" and place the recording in the Listening Center. Invite the children to practice the rhyme.
- ❏ Invite the children to play Pick a Pear. Use photos from magazines to make a set of rhyming word cards or use commercial rhyming words. Mount the cards on construction paper shaped like pears. Encourage the children to make rhyming pears (pairs) with the cards.

Reflecting on the Lesson

Ask the children:
- ❏ *Which word rhymes with "Jill"—"Jack" or "hill"?*
- ❏ *What rhymes with "tongue"?*

Special Needs Adaptations

Special Need	Adaptation
Visual Impairments	- Place items in the rhyme-pair basket that the child can identify by touch. For example, "pan" and "can" are easier to identify by touch than "two" and "blue." When the child is participating in a group activity that requires movement, remember to show the child the boundaries for his personal space so he does not run into his classmates.
Hearing Impairments	- Look for items to put in the rhyme pair basket that the child knows and that he can easily identify either by lip-reading or using sign language. Place the child in a position that enables him to see you while you play the "Say and Touch" game. Even if he cannot hear all the words you are saying, by watching you he can participate in the movements.
Cognitive Challenges	- Instead of using all the verses in the "Say and Touch" rhyme, begin with three. Repeat them until the child can complete each one. It will be easier for a child with cognitive challenges to learn a few verses (three or four) and enjoy singing them and participating in the activity than to overwhelm him with multiple verses.
Motor Delays	- Change the "Say and Touch" activity so that it includes things the child, is able to do, such as, "Say, 'Snap and clap!' Clap! Clap!" or "Say, 'Three' and look at me."
Speech/ Language Delays	- Because a child with language delays may have limited vocabulary, select four verses of the "Say and Touch" game for him to work on. Teach each step in reverse. For example, you may say, "Touch your head." If the child does not touch his head, take his hand and gently place it on his head. After you practice saying, "Touch your head" a few times add the first verse. Continue with the other verses, until he can complete three or four without your prompting or helping him.
Emotional/ Behavior Issues	- It will be easier for the child if he does not become too frustrated. Use fewer items in the rhyming pair basket and be sure to select items that he knows. A child may respond better to the rhyming pears (pairs) activity if the cards are mounted on pears that are his favorite color.

Rhyming Story

Children will:

■ use rhyming words in sentences.

Vocabulary

rhyme
sound
story
words

Materials

basket full of rhyming objects (for example, a cat and a mat)
box
The Cat in the Hat by Dr. Seuss, *Over in the Meadow* by Ezra Jack Keats, and/or *There Was an Old Lady Who Swallowed a Fly* by Simms Taback
rhyming word cards

Preparation

Gather rhyming word objects. For example, you may collect a sock, a lock, a block, and a smock.

Introducing and Developing the Lesson

❏ Tell the children that you will be reading stories that use rhyming words and that they will be using rhyming words to create stories.

❏ Read stories that are rich in rhyme, such as *The Cat in the Hat* by Dr. Seuss, *Over in the Meadow* by Ezra Jack Keats (or other authors), or *There Was an Old Lady Who Swallowed a Fly* by Simms Taback (or other authors).

❏ Provide a basket full of rhyming objects, for example, a cat, mat, hat, and bat or a sock, rock, lock, and block. (Use the ones from the previous lesson or add new ones.)

❏ Help the children create a story using the rhyming objects as props.

Practicing the Lesson

❏ Place the basket of rhyming word objects in the Language Center. Invite the children to create rhyming object stories.

❏ Provide rhyming word cards. Challenge the children to make up a sentence or two using both words in the rhyming pair.

Reflecting on the Lesson

Ask the children:

❏ *If we made up a rhyming story with "ball" in it, which word would be more likely to be part of the story, "fall" or "big"?*

❏ *Here are some rhyming words: "vet," "bet," "met," and "wet." What other words rhyme that with these words?*

Special Needs Adaptations

Special Need	Adaptation
Visual Impairments	■ Select objects for the rhyming stories that are easily identified and can be examined by touch as well as sight. ■ Remember to select objects with different textures and without a lot of intricate detail.
Hearing Impairments	■ Before asking the child to make up a sentence using rhyming pair words, work with him individually to be sure he understands the concept of rhyme. Begin by showing him an object from the rhyming-pair basket and asking him to select another object that rhymes with it.
Cognitive Challenges	■ Use no more than four pairs of rhyming objects. Place them on the table in front of the child and pick up one object in your right hand and the object that rhymes with it in your left hand. Say the name of each object, then put them on the table in front of him, side by side. Point out that they are a rhyming pair. Select another object and ask him to help you find the object in the basket that rhymes with the one you selected. It may be necessary for you to model this for him. If he is having trouble with four pairs, start with just two or three pairs. Remember, he will need to practice this more than the other children.
Motor Delays	■ If the objects in the basket are too difficult for the child to pick up, adapt them by hot-gluing a plastic shower curtain ring to each object. (Do this when the children are not around.) This provides a handle for the child to use when picking up the object.
Speech/ Language Delays	■ Making up a story using the rhyming objects will be too difficult for many children with limited vocabulary. Instead, adapt the activity by making up a sentence about one of the objects and inviting the child to select the object you are talking about from the basket. Later, as he becomes more familiar with the words, see if he can match objects that rhyme.
Emotional/ Behavior Issues	■ Select objects for the basket that the child enjoys playing with. If he refuses to make up a story, ask if he would like to select a peer to help him. Encourage them to work together to make up a story.

Rhyming Songs

Children will:
- recognize rhyming words.

Vocabulary
rhyme
sounds
words

Materials
chart paper
marker

Introducing and Developing the Lesson

- ❑ Sing "The Itsy Bitsy Spider" (see page 258 in the Appendix).
- ❑ Print the rhyme on chart paper.
- ❑ Tell the children that "itsy" and "bitsy" are rhyming words.
- ❑ Ask for a volunteer and tell that child to point out the letter in "bitsy" that is different from "itsy."
- ❑ Tell the children that they will learn songs with rhyming words.
- ❑ Sing "Down by the Bay" (see page 256 in the Appendix). Invite the children to help add a verse to the song.
- ❑ Sing "Say and Rhyme" (see page 259 in the Appendix) to the tune of "Mary Had a Little Lamb."

Practicing the Lesson

- ❑ Invite the children to make up their own verses to "Say and Rhyme" (see page 259 in the Appendix).
- ❑ Pick a favorite nursery rhyme and challenge the children to change the rhyming word pairs. For example:

  Humpty Dumpty sat on a chair.
  Humpty Dumpty had no hair.
      or
  Humpty Dumpty sat on a bed.
  Humpty Dumpty scratched his head.

- ❑ Sing "Catalina Magnalina" (see page 254 in the Appendix). Challenge the children to make up a name for Catalina's brother, Angelino Magnalino.

Reflecting on the Lesson

Ask the children:
- ❑ *What is the rhyming word for the second line of these rhymes?*
  Jack and Jill   *Little Bo Peep*
  Went up the _____.   *Lost her _____.*
- ❑ *Are there songs that don't have rhyming words in them? ("Are You Sleeping?")*

Special Needs Adaptations

Special Need	Adaptation
Visual Impairments	■ Invite the child to help you as you sing "The Itsy Bitsy Spider." Wiggle your fingers on the back of his hand, walk your fingers up his arms, and slide your fingers down his arm to show "washed the spider out." Thank the child for helping you!
Hearing Impairments	■ Show the child the sign for "spider." (See Appendix page 252.) Invite the rest of the children to use the sign for "spider" as you sing the song.
Cognitive Challenges	■ Be sure the child knows any new vocabulary associated with this lesson, such as "itsy" and "spout." Explain that a spout is the same thing as a gutter on a house or building.
Motor Delays	■ Remember to position the child so he can see what you are saying and doing.
Speech/ Language Delays	■ A child with limited vocabulary may be unable to sing all the words of the songs. Invite the child to sing it with you. Pause after each verse. Review any unfamiliar vocabulary.
Emotional/ Behavior Issues	■ Some children are very sensitive to touch and do not enjoy singing songs with movements. Suggest that the child sing along without doing the hand movements or gestures that accompany the song.

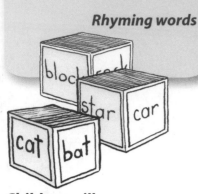

Clapping, Snapping, and Tapping Games

Children will:
- recognize and use rhyming words.

Vocabulary
rhyme
rhyming words

Materials
drum or box
rhythm sticks, dowels, or paper towel tubes

Introducing and Developing the Lesson

- ❑ Ask the children to clap their hands when they hear the rhyming words ("sea" and "see") as you sing "A Sailor Went to Sea" (see page 259 in the Appendix).
- ❑ Tell each child to find a partner. Repeat the song and tell the partners to clap hands with their partners on the rhyming words.
- ❑ Tell the children that they will be playing rhyming word games.
- ❑ Take the children outside. Have them stand in a circle. Say the rhyme "I Had a Little Puppy" (see page 264 in the Appendix). Have the children clap their hands on the second word in a rhyming word pair.
- ❑ Recite the rhyme a second time. This time, have the children jump (or snap their fingers) on the second word in rhyming word pairs.
- ❑ Give the children two rhythm sticks, dowels, or paper towel tubes. Sing "Rhyme Time" (see page 259 in the Appendix) to the tune of "The Addams Family." Have the children tap their sticks for each rhyming word introduced in the song.

Practicing the Lesson

- ❑ Have the children clap with a partner rhythmically to one of the following rhymes: "Bo-bo Ski Watten Totten" on page 263 or "Have You Ever?" on page 264. Challenge the children to identify the rhyming word pairs.
- ❑ Give each child a drum or a box to turn over and use as a drum. Have them tap their drum when they hear the rhyming words in "Miss Mary Mack" (see page 264 in the Appendix) or another song that has distinct rhymes.

Reflecting on the Lesson

Ask the children:
- ❑ *Which word doesn't belong in this group of words?* (clap, snap, *and* jump).
- ❑ *Which words in "Miss Mary Mack" are rhyming words?*

Special Needs Adaptations

Special Need	Adaptation
Visual Impairments	■ Make sure the child understands that sometimes words have two different meanings, such as "see" and "sea."
Hearing Impairments	■ Using hand motions or pictures will help the child understand what is happening in the rhymes. For example, when you say, "sailor," you should hold up a picture of a sailor. When you say, "to see what he could see," cup your hand on your forehead like you are looking around.
Cognitive Challenges	■ Reinforce the lesson for the child by giving him three words and asking him to identify the one that does not belong. Use simple words that he knows. Knowing how to determine when something does not belong in a series is an important skill to acquire.
Motor Delays	■ If the child does not have the motor skills to clap or snap his fingers, invite him to tap the words with a cardboard drum stick. Look for other ways he could participate, such as tapping his feet or tapping his hand on a table.
Speech/ Language Delays	■ The rhymes used in this lesson may be too much for a child who has limited language. Select one or two and work on those with the child. Also, find opportunities to say three words for the child and ask him to tell you which one does not belong.
Emotional/ Behavior Issues	■ The child may resist clapping with a partner. Reduce the requirements of the activity by asking him to clap one verse with a partner. Learning to work cooperatively is a very important life skill to acquire.

Packing Rhymes

Children will:
- create rhyming word pairs.

Vocabulary
pack
rhyming words
suitcase

Materials
ball
basket of items that rhyme with
    star (for example, car, jar)
nonrhyming objects for the basket
rhyming word cards
rhyming word starter
suitcase

Preparation
Gather a suitcase, a star, and items
that rhyme with "star." Gather
other sets of rhyming word items.

Introducing and Developing the Lesson

❑ Read the poem, "I Took a Trip" (see page 264 in the Appendix) to the children. Let them fill in the packed items in the second verse. Tell the children that they will practice creating sets of rhyming words.

❑ Provide a suitcase and a basket of items that rhyme with "star" (for example, "car," "jar," "bar," and "tar"—use black playdough for the tar). Include some nonrhyming objects in the basket.

❑ Tell the children that you are placing a star in the suitcase. Ask them to add items that rhyme with "star" to the suitcase. You can use rhyming word pictures if items are too difficult to gather.

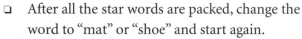

❑ After all the star words are packed, change the word to "mat" or "shoe" and start again.

❑ Provide rhyming word cards. Ask the children to place the cards into sets.

Practicing the Lesson

❑ Place the suitcase in a center and let the children practice packing rhyming words.

❑ Give pairs of children a rhyming word starter and have them toss a ball back and forth as they say words that rhyme with the starter word.

Reflecting on the Lesson

Ask the children:

❑ *What things would you pack in a suitcase if all the items needed to rhyme with "moon"?*

❑ *What rhymes with "sun" but can't be packed? (fun!)*

Special Needs Adaptations

Special Need	Adaptation
Visual Impairments	■ Use a star made from a shiny substance or one that is easily recognizable by its shape or texture.
Hearing Impairments	■ To reinforce the child's understanding of the concept of rhyming, go through the basket of rhyming objects once and select two items that rhyme. Then, ask the child to select two that rhyme. ■ If he does not select two that rhyme, say the name of each item for him and talk about how you recognize words that rhyme.
Cognitive Challenges	■ Use the rhyming word cards or objects to help the child understand about rhyming words. Select a few items (six, or three pairs) and start with those. Choose one and ask the child to select the one that rhymes with it. Make sure the child can identify all six items before you begin.
Motor Delays	■ As an alternative to using rhyming cards, it may be easier for the child to put together real objects that rhyme.
Speech/ Language Delays	■ Play a game with the child where you start a sentence and he ends it with a rhyming word. For example, "The cat sat on a _____." The child could say any word that rhymes, such as "rat," "mat," "hat," or "bat." If the child does not select a word that rhymes with "cat," help him by making a list of words that rhyme with "cat." Then, repeat the sentence and ask him to use one of the rhyming words in the sentence.
Emotional/ Behavior Issues	■ Before you begin, tell the child that this will be a pretend activity. Make sure the child understands that you would not really pack a star in a suitcase. Remember, children with certain types of behavior/emotional issues are very concrete and may interrupt the activity or be unable to concentrate on the game because of a concern that you would not really pack a star.

Books That Support Phonological Awareness

Onomatopoeia

Barnyard Banter by Denise Fleming

Chicka Chicka Boom Boom by Bill Martin, Jr. and John Archambault

Freight Train by Donald Crews

In the Tall, Tall Grass by Denise Fleming

Listen to the Rain by Bill Martin, Jr.

Mice Squeak, We Speak: A Poem by Arnold Shapiro

Over in the Meadow by Ezra Jack Keats

Roar and More by Karla Kuskin

The Listening Walk by Paul Showers

The Seals on the Bus by Lenny Hort

Where the Wild Things Are by Maurice Sendak

Who Took the Farmer's Hat? by Joan Nodset

Alliteration

The Baby Uggs Are Hatching by Jack Prelutsky

Featherless/Desplumado by Juan Felipe Herrera

Four Famished Foxes and Fosdyke by Pamela Duncan Edwards

Miss Mary Mack: A Hand-Clapping Rhyme by Mary Ann Hoberman

Piggy in the Puddle by Charlotte Pomerantz

Six Sleepy Sheep by Jeffie Ross Gordon

The Three Billy Goats Gruff (traditional)

Rhyming Words

Andy: That's My Name by Tomie dePaola

Anna Banana: 101 Jump Rope Rhymes by Joanna Cole

Bringing the Rain to Kapiti Plain by Verna Aardema

The Cat in the Hat by Dr. Seuss

Catalina Magdalena Hoopensteiner Wallendiner Hoga Logan Bogan Was Her Name by Tedd Arnold

Chicken Soup with Rice by Maurice Sendak

The Day the Goose Got Loose by Reeve Lindbergh

Down by the Bay by Raffi

"Fire! Fire!" Said Mrs. McGuire by Bill Martin, Jr.

Green Eggs and Ham by Dr. Seuss

Henny Penny by Paul Galdone

Hi! Fly Guy by Tedd Arnold

How Much Is that Doggie in the Window? by Iza Trapani

Is Your Mama a Llama? by Deborah Guarino

Itsy Bitsy Spider by Iza Trapani

Jamberry by Bruce Degan

Jen the Hen by Colin and Jacqui Hawkins

The Lady with the Alligator Purse by Nadine Bernard Westcott

Mig the Pig by Colin and Jacqui Hawkins

Old Mother Hubbard and Her Wonderful Dog by James Marshall

One Duck Stuck by Phyllis Root

One Fish, Two Fish, Red Fish, Blue Fish by Dr. Seuss

Pat the Cat by Colin and Jacqui Hawkins

Sheep in a Shop by Nancy Shaw

Silly Sally by Audrey Wood

Sing a Song of Popcorn by Beatrice Schenk de Regniers et al.

Special People, Special Ways by Arlene Maguire*

There's a Wocket in My Pocket by Dr. Seuss

Twinkle, Twinkle Little Star by Iza Trapani

Rhythm

Brown Bear, Brown Bear, What Do You See? by Bill Martin, Jr.

Chicka Chicka Boom Boom by John Archambault and Bill Martin, Jr.

The Grouchy Lady Bug by Eric Carle

A House Is a House for Me by Mary Ann Hoberman

Pat, the Cat by Frances Dinkins Strong *

Polar Bear, Polar Bear, What Do You Hear? by Bill Martin, Jr. and John Archambault

Quick as a Cricket by Audrey Wood

Multilingual Books

Chinese Mother Goose Rhymes [Ju tzu ko t`u] by Robert Wyndham—A collection of nursery rhymes translated from Chinese, which also includes the rhymes in Chinese characters.

Grandmother's Nursery Rhymes/Las Nanas de Abuelita: Lullabies, Tongue Twisters, and Riddles from South America/Canciones de cuna, trabalenguas y adivinanzas de Suramerica by Nelly Palacio Jaramillo—A collection of traditional Spanish rhymes from Mexico and South America.

Los Amigos en el trabajo y en el juego by Rosabello Bunnett *

* Denotes books about children with special needs

Chapter 4

Letter Knowledge and Recognition

Overview

Letter knowledge and recognition is the understanding of the alphabetic principle. It means that children are able to recognize all 26 letters of the alphabet in both uppercase and lowercase forms. It also means that they understand that letters are the foundation of words.

It is important to teach the alphabet to children in such a way that they understand that it is flexible and moveable. This concept is often hampered by the fact that we usually teach children the alphabet song early in their lives and then encourage them to sing it over and over again. The initial wiring for letter knowledge gets connected and reinforced in a low-functioning part of the brain, far away from the place where it will be needed in rational thought. When children continually say and sing the alphabet starting with "A" and ending with "Z," they tend to think of the alphabet as linear—that it always must start with "A" and end with "Z." This creates a challenge when they begin to move from letters into words.

Children need to sing the alphabet song forward and backward. They need to sort letters by type of line used to make the letter. They need to see letters as independent components that have many ways to be

organized. This is especially true for children with special needs who often do not generalize information well. In other words, although a child might be able to participate in singing the alphabet song she may not understand that letters are combined to make individual words.

For children who cannot see letters, it is important that they learn what letters look like by other means, such as touching letter cutouts. It is also imperative that children with special needs learn new concepts in context. So,

Identifying the first letter in his name encourages a child to notice the differences between letters.

learning letters in isolation may have little meaning for a child with cognitive challenges, whereas learning the letters in her name and the sound that each letter makes is a very important functional (lifelong) skill that will be of benefit.

Same and Different

Children will:

- see the likenesses and differences in letters.

Vocabulary

alike
different
letters
see

Materials

chart paper
magnetic letters that are the same and that are different
marker
two blocks that are different
two blocks that are the same
two paintbrushes that are different
two paintbrushes that are the same

Introducing and Developing the Lesson

- ❏ Show the children two blocks that are the same and then two blocks that are different. Hold up two paintbrushes that are the same in one hand and two paintbrushes that are different in the other hand. Ask the children which pair of brushes has two brushes that are the same and which pair has two brushes that are different. Tell the children that they will be looking for letters that are alike and letters that are different.
- ❏ Place three magnetic letters on the board—two that are the same and two that are different.
- ❏ Continue creating sets of letters with two or more letters that are the same and the remainder of the letters that are different.
- ❏ Ask the children how they know if the letters are the same or different. Lead them to understand that they should look carefully at the shape of each letter.
- ❏ Encourage children to create sets of letters that have two letters that are the same with the rest of the set members being different.

Practicing the Lesson

- ❏ Encourage children to use the magnetic letters to write their names. Are any of the letters the same?
- ❏ Print "Ram Sam Sam" on chart paper. Ask the children to identify the letters that are the same in each word and the letter that is different in one of the words.

Reflecting on the Lesson

Ask the children:

- ❏ *How do you know if letters are the same or different?*
- ❏ *Which classmates have names that start with the same letters?*

Special Needs Adaptations

Special Need	Adaptation
Visual Impairments	■ Adapt the activity by using item pairs that the child can easily identify by touch. For example, instead of paintbrushes, use stuffed bears. Make sure the two have different characteristics that the child can easily identify, such as one stuffed bear with clothes on and one without. When a child is learning to identify differences in letters, provide letters that she can feel. Talk about the differences as she examines each one.
Hearing Impairments	■ Before identifying items that are the same and items that are different, make sure the child understands the concept. Show her several pairs of items that are the same and several that are different. Take a piece of poster board or large paper and draw a line down the middle. Place the items that are the same on one side and say or sign "same/alike," and then place the items that are different on the other side of the paper and say or sign "different."
Cognitive Challenges	■ Children with cognitive challenges don't understand subtle differences. Because the goal is to help the child discriminate between items that are the same and items that are different, it will be necessary to reinforce the concept by having the child first understand the meaning of the words. Start by showing the child two paintbrushes. In the second pair, instead of two different paintbrushes, show her one paintbrush and one toothbrush. Show her other pairs (one identical and one very dissimilar), to be sure she understands the concept of same and different before showing her two items that are the same with a subtle difference, such as size or color.
Motor Delays	■ For the child in a wheelchair, it will be important that she be able to access the letters presented in the literacy lesson. It may be necessary to place a cookie sheet on her wheelchair tray. Elevate the cookie sheet to an angle that is comfortable for the child. Use magnetic letters that are large enough for her to see and move.
Speech/ Language Delays	■ Children with language delays may have difficulty discriminating between letters, especially if they are just learning the letter names. Use only a few letters (three or four) and work with those first. It may be necessary for you to tell the child how they are different, "This one has a round part or this one is straight," and so on. For this child, the goal may be to identify letters and the sounds they make, rather than to be able to identify subtle differences between letters.
Emotional/ Behavior Issues	■ Getting the attention of children with behavior issues is a major obstacle. Look for ways to help the child focus as you introduce this activity. For example, select pairs of items that will be of interest to the child. If she likes dinosaurs, use dinosaurs, or if she prefers trains, use trains.

Moveable Alphabet

Children will:
- understand the alphabet as a moveable and flexible group of letters.

Vocabulary
alphabet
backwards
direction
family
forward
group
letters
movable

Materials
alphabet wall cards
chart paper
felt letters
magnetic letters
marker

Introducing and Developing the Lesson

- ❑ Sing "The Alphabet Song" (see page 254 in the Appendix).
- ❑ Tell the children that you are going to show them that the letters in the alphabet are moveable and that they do not have to stay in A-to-Z order.
- ❑ Ask for a volunteer and tell that child to demonstrate moving forward and moving backward.
- ❑ Print "The Alphabet Song Forward and Backward" (see page 254 in the Appendix) on chart paper and then sing it with the children.
- ❑ Talk with the children about singing the song backward. *How does it sound?* Point out that the letters of the alphabet are a family of letters, but they do not have to be sung or written in only one direction (from A to Z). They do not have to be used in the order that they are displayed on your alphabet wall.
- ❑ Place alphabet cards on the floor. Ask a child to pick up the letters of her name and help her to arrange the letters to spell her name.

Practicing the Lesson

- ❑ Place the alphabet wall cards on the floor in the Language Center and suggest that the children use the letters to spell their names.
- ❑ Give the children magnetic letters. Challenge them to arrange the letters in reverse alphabetical order.
- ❑ Provide felt letters. Have the children arrange the letters in reverse alphabetical order. Provide the letters in reverse alphabetical order on chart paper, so the children have a point of reference.

Reflecting on the Lesson

Ask the children:
- ❑ *Which way do you like the alphabet the best—forward or backward?*
- ❑ *Which letter is last when the alphabet is sung backward?*

Special Needs Adaptations

Special Need	Adaptation
Visual Impairments	■ If the child has some vision, it may be necessary for you to make the alphabet cards larger. Also, consider using cards that are printed on white paper with black writing because this will be easier for the child to see.
Hearing Impairments	■ Record the song as it is sung forward and as it is sung backward. Provide the child with an opportunity to listen to both versions using headphones. Children with residual hearing will find it easier to follow the premise behind the lesson.
Cognitive Challenges	■ If the child does not know all her letters, it would not be beneficial for you to attempt to teach her the alphabet backwards. Instead, spend extra time helping her select and arrange the letters in her name. Print her name on a white card and invite her to match the letters using magnetic letters. Ask her to name each letter as she selects it. If she does not know the name of the letter, say it for her, and then ask her to repeat it.
Motor Delays	■ Place magnetic letters on a cookie sheet and let the child select the ones in her name. If she can move the letters, make an adaptive stick to help her. Use a dowel rod that is approximately 6" long. Wrap tape around a small area on the rod several times, to build up a surface that can help the child grasp the stick. The stick can be used to help the child move the letters into place.
Speech/ Language Delays	■ It is important that children with language delays learn to identify the letters in their names. Invite the child to say each letter name as she uses it to spell out her name.
Emotional/ Behavior Issues	■ If the child becomes frustrated trying to sing the song backward, break it down into small segments. For example, sing "A-B-C-D-E-F-G," then "G-F-E-D-C-B-A."

Provide cues to help the child learn the letters in his name.

Letter knowledge and recognition

Letter Sort

Children will:

- understand the alphabet as a moveable and flexible group of letters.

Vocabulary

alphabet
curved
letters
movable
sort
straight

Materials

blocks
magnetic letters
paper
pencils

Introducing and Developing the Lesson

- ❑ Ask for a volunteer and then ask that child to show how she can make her body form a straight line. Ask a second volunteer to show how to make her body form a curved line.
- ❑ Tell the children that they will learn to determine which letters in the alphabet are straight and which letters are curved.
- ❑ Place magnetic letters on the floor. Ask the children to help find the letters that are made with only straight lines.
- ❑ After they identify all the letters made with straight lines, ask the children to help find letters that are made only with curved lines.
- ❑ Finally, ask the children to find letters that are made using both straight and curved lines.

Practicing the Lesson

- ❑ Place magnetic letters in the Literacy Center. Suggest that the children sort them into three categories: letters made using only straight lines, letters made using only curved lines, and letters made using both straight and curved lines.
- ❑ Have the children write their names on sheets of paper. Ask them to circle the straight letters in their names and underline the curved letters in their names.
- ❑ Challenge the children to use blocks to form letters made with straight lines. Ask, "Can you make letters that have curved lines with blocks? Why not?"

Reflecting on the Lesson

Ask the children:

- ❑ *Do you have more straight-line letters or curved letters in your name?*
- ❑ *Which curved letter do you like best? Which straight-line letter do you like best?*

Special Needs Adaptations

Special Need	Adaptation
Visual Impairments	■ Before beginning this activity, place an object that is straight in the child's hand. For example, a ruler or the letter l. Invite the child to explore the item, pointing out the straight part of the letter. ■ Next, place a curved object such as a circle or the letter O in the child's hand. Make sure the object is raised or large enough so the child can trace the curved part with her fingers. When the child is asked to sort letters that are straight and letters that are curved, make sure the letters themselves are clearly recognizable by touch only. If possible, use large magnetic letters or letters that have been cut out of a material that is three-dimensional.
Hearing Impairments	■ Use the same objects (one curved and one straight) that were used above. Take the child's hand and help her gently trace each part with her finger. To help the child be successful, provide fewer letters for her to sort. Sorting more than six or seven letters may be overwhelming.
Cognitive Challenges	■ Use the same procedure described above (see Hearing Impairments). As the child sorts the letters, invite her to say each letter name. If she cannot identify all her letters, use only those she can identify for the letter-sorting activity.
Motor Delays	■ If the child is in a wheelchair, place the magnetic letters on a cookie sheet in front of her. If she has difficulty moving the letters, provide a magnet to help her move the letters.
Speech/ Language Delays	■ If the child is able, invite her to write her own name; if not, write it for her. Take her finger and help her trace a letter. Talk about how the letter is made. Ask her to show you which letters are straight and which are curved. ■ If she does not understand what to do, take her hand and help her trace a letter while you point out the straight and the curved parts of that letter.
Emotional/ Behavior Issues	■ Remember that children with emotional issues may have trouble attending and staying engaged in an activity. To help maintain the child's interest, give her a piece of paper with a picture at the top of something she likes. For example, a dinosaur or a train. After she writes her name on the paper, it may be necessary for you to model for her and circle a letter that is curved and underline a letter with straight lines.

Sorting letters takes time and practice.

Letter knowledge and recognition

Pair, Think, and Share

Children will:
- recognize letters of the alphabet.

Vocabulary
alphabet
letters
pair
shapes
share
think

Materials
alphabet wall cards

Introducing and Developing the Lesson

- ❏ Select eight alphabet letters from your wall cards. The letters T, L, H, F, O, V, X, and Y will be easiest to replicate. Ask the children to identify the letters.
- ❏ Tell them that they are going to have some fun using their bodies to form alphabet letters. Tell the children that they are going to play Pair, Think, and Share.
- ❏ Ask the children to select partners. Give each pair of children a letter card. Instruct them to work together to find a way to use their bodies to make the letter.
- ❏ After a few minutes, ask the children to sit in a circle. Have partners demonstrate their letter, one pair at a time. Challenge the other children to guess which letter the pair is forming.
- ❏ Place all eight alphabet cards on the floor in the Gross Motor Area. Encourage the children to work with a partner to make all eight letters with their bodies.

Practicing the Lesson

- ❏ Challenge the children to make the letters T, X, W, and C with their fingers.
- ❏ Show children how to spell Y-O-U using their bodies. Make a Y by standing tall and spreading arms overhead in a V. Make an O by connecting arms in a circle overhead. Make a U by lifting arms overhead—curved and unconnected.

Reflecting on the Lesson

Ask the children:
- ❏ *Can you make one of the letters in your name with your body or your hands?*
- ❏ *Which letter did you and your partner make?*

Special Needs Adaptations

Special Need	Adaptation
Visual Impairments	▪ Remember, alphabet wall cards are usually very colorful with bright pictures. For a child with visual impairments, use cards that show a single letter in bold print on a plain background.
Hearing Impairments	▪ Working collaboratively with a peer will be easier if the child understands exactly what she and the peer are expected to do. Invite a child to be your partner and tell the child with hearing impairments to watch while you and your partner make a letter using your body. Once the child sees what you are doing, it will be easier for her to copy it with a partner.
Cognitive Challenges	▪ Assign the child to a peer buddy who will be patient and understanding with the child. It is important they both understand that the object of this activity is to try to make a letter with their bodies and it is not a competition. Assign the pair of children a letter that is easy to make.
Motor Delays	▪ It is unlikely that a child with significant motor delays will be able to make letters using her body. However, she can still participate by being your personal assistant and helping you monitor the progress of the other letter-making teams.
Speech/ Language Delays	▪ Talk about the letters T, X, W, and C. Help the child make each letter with her hand. Then, see if she can think of a word that starts with each letter. Invite her to use that word in a sentence.
Emotional/ Behavior Issues	▪ Tell the child that you will help her work with a friend. Select the friend (peer partner) ahead of time and invite the peer buddy to be your helper on just this activity. Explain that you want her to help, as you teach _____ (use the name of the child with emotional challenges) to work in a group. Once the peer buddy has been assigned, explain that you want the two children to work together and use their bodies to form a letter. Monitor their progress and remind them that the purpose of this activity is to learn and have fun.

Assign a peer buddy who will be patient and understanding with the child.

Letter knowledge and recognition

E-I-E-I-O Change-O

Children will:
- recognize letters of the alphabet.

Vocabulary
letters
alphabet
sing

Materials
Old MacDonald Had a Farm by Pam Adams
chart paper
magnetic letters
marker
strips of paper with "__-__-__-__-O" written on it

Preparation
Print the first verse of "Old MacDonald Had a Farm" on one sheet of chart paper. On a second sheet of chart paper, print the first verse (authors, is this correct?) again, except this time use "A-U-A-U-O" instead of "E-I-E-I-O."

Introducing and Developing the Lesson

- Sing "Old MacDonald Had a Farm" (see page 258 in the Appendix). Ask the children what "E-I-E-I-O" means.
- Tell the children that they will learn about the part of the song that says, "E-I-E-I-O."
- Show the children the chart paper with the first verse of "Old MacDonald Had a Farm" written on it. Sing the song again, pointing to the words (and letters) as you sing them.
- Ask for a volunteer and tell that child to show you on the chart the part of the song that is letters only. Ask the children to identify the letters.
- Turn to the second sheet of chart paper and sing the song again with the letter substitution, "A-U-A-U-O." Ask for a volunteer to identify the new letters.
- Allow the children to pick a new pair of letter to use in the song and sing it with their letter choices.
- Give the children magnetic letters. Ask them to create an E-I-E-I-O pattern with the letters.

Practicing the Lesson

- Give the children a strip of paper with "__-__-__-__-O" written on it. Challenge them to fill in the Es and Is.
- Read *Old MacDonald Had a Farm* by Pam Adams. Ask a volunteer to find the letters E-I-E-I-O in the text.

Reflecting on the Lesson

Ask the children:
- *Can you think of another song that has letters in it?*
- *Do you like "Old MacDonald's Farm" better with "E-I-E-I-O" or with "A-U-A-U-O"?*

Special Needs Adaptations

Special Need	Adaptation
Visual Impairments	■ Cut out the letters E, I, and O from cardstock or other heavy material. Place the letters on a large cookie sheet in front of the child. Feeling the sides of the cookie sheet helps her recognize the boundaries. Suggest that she handle or outline each letter before you sing the song.
Hearing Impairments	■ If the child is beginning to use sign language, show her the letter signs for E, I, and O (see page 281 in the Appendix for a list of letter signs). If others in the class are interested in learning the signs that accompany the song, teach them as well. Use the letter signs for E, I, and O when you sing the song. Invite the rest of the class to use the signs while they sing the "E-I-E-I-O" part of the song.
Cognitive Challenges	■ Use magnetic letters to write E-I-E-I-O on a cookie sheet. Invite the child to trace each letter as you say it. Review what the child learned in previous lessons by asking her to point to the letters with straight lines and the letters that arc curved. As you are singing the song with the children, encourage the child to sing along, even if the only part she knows is "E-I-E-I-O."
Motor Delays	■ It is important that the child with motor delays be viewed by the rest of the children as a valuable class member. This lesson requires minimal use of motor skills and allows you to show off the strengths of a child with motor delays. Invite the child to lead the class as they identify other combinations of letters to use in the song.
Speech/ Language Delays	■ Unlike many letters in the English alphabet, E, I, and O are very easy to say. Hold up the letter and invite the child to say the sound it makes with you. Use a mirror and tell the child to watch her mouth in the mirror when she is making the sounds E, I, and O. Vowel sounds are often much easier for the child with a speech problem to make than consonants.
Emotional/ Behavior Issues	■ Don't be surprised if a child with autism or obsessive compulsive issues interrupts the song, when you try to tell the child to use letters other than E-I-E-I-O. The child may yell out "That's wrong. It's not 'A-U-A-U-O.'" ■ Remember that some children have great difficulty when a familiar pattern is changed. To avoid an outburst, it is very important that you tell the child before you start singing the song that you are going to change it.

Letter knowledge and recognition

Children will:

- recognize letters of the alphabet.

Vocabulary

letters
name
Scrabble
scramble

Materials

construction paper (tan)
glue
black marker
paper
paper bag
Scrabble™ letters

Preparation

Cut tan construction paper into 9" squares to represent Scrabble letters. Use a black marker to print the letters of the alphabet on the squares. Trim the corners, if desired. Make additional vowels and a few popular consonants, such as R, S, B, C, and M.

Scrabble™ Scramble

Introducing and Developing the Lesson

- ❑ Ask, "Have you ever seen adults or older siblings play a game called Scrabble?" Show the children a game of Scrabble. Tell them that they will be using Scrabble letters to spell some important words.
- ❑ Place Scrabble letters into a paper bag. Ask for a volunteer and tell that child to draw a letter from the bag and identify the letter. Help her identify the letter, if necessary.
- ❑ Place the construction paper Scrabble letters on the floor. Use them to spell some words that are familiar to the children. Some examples include words such as "mom," "dad," "dog," "cat," "ball," or perhaps the name of your school.
- ❑ Ask one of the children to use the large letters to spell her name.
- ❑ Pick up the real Scrabble letters that spell a child's name. Hold all of the letters in your hand and then drop them onto the floor. Ask the child whose name you chose to arrange the scrambled letters into her name.

Practicing the Lesson

- ❑ Place Scrabble™ letters in the Writing Center and invite the children to spell their names.
- ❑ Place the large teacher-made letters in a center and invite the children to use the letters to spell their names on the floor.
- ❑ Provide blank 2" tan construction paper squares. Encourage the children to print the letters in their names on the squares and then glue them, in the proper order, onto sheets of paper.

Reflecting on the Lesson

Ask the children:
- ❑ *Which letters did you use to spell your name?*
- ❑ *Did you use the letters to spell another word or someone else's name? What name or word did you spell?*

Special Needs Adaptations

Special Need	Adaptation
Visual Impairments	■ Using raised letters (foam or cardboard) to attach to the teacher-made scrabble pieces makes it easier for the child to identify the letters. Be sure to use dark-colored letters printed with bold black marker. ■ Remember that children with visual impairments may be hesitant to put their hands into something unfamiliar (such as the paper bag containing letters). Tell the child that you will do it with her, and place your hand on top of hers while she draws a letter out.
Hearing Impairments	■ Before beginning the activity, demonstrate one-on-one with the child what you will be doing. A child with a hearing impairment will be able to participate in an activity more easily if she is familiar with what is expected.
Cognitive Challenges	■ This lesson provides practice at letter identification, and it is also an opportunity to help the child recognize survival words such as "stop," "go," "on," and "off." Use the Scrabble letters to spell out survival words and ask the child to help you say them.
Motor Delays	■ Attach a 1" square of cardboard (use an old box) to the back of each teacher-made letter (use hot glue or glue). This prevents the letters from laying flat on the floor so the child with motor delays can move the slightly raised letters more easily.
Speech/ Language Delays	■ To provide more practice in recognizing the sound that each letter makes, suggest that the child say each letter of her name before she uses the Scrabble letters to spell it. Select one of the teacher-made letters and ask the child to help you name as many words as possible that start with that letter. If she does not know any words, give her a hint, such as, "It barks." When the child says "dog," reinforce her answer by saying, "Yes, the word 'dog' starts with the sound that the letter "d" makes."
Emotional/ Behavior Issues	■ If the child does not want to put her hand in the bag and draw out a letter, ask her if a classmate can draw for her. If she still says no, skip her and go to the next child. ■ Remember that there are times when you can honor the child's request not to participate and other times when you must insist that she participate.

Letter Songs

Children will:

- recognize letters of the alphabet.

Vocabulary

letters
songs
words

Materials

chart paper
magnetic letters
index cards
marker
tracing paper

Preparation

Print the words "smile," "grin," and "laugh" on chart paper. Print the words "smile," "grin," "laugh," and "ha" on index cards.

Introducing and Developing the Lesson

- ❏ Sing "Bingo" (see page 254 in the Appendix). Sing the song slowly so the children can hear the letters that make up Bingo's name.
- ❏ Tell the children that they will learn another song with letters that spell words.
- ❏ Teach the children, "S-M-I-L-E" (see page 260 in the Appendix).
- ❏ Display the chart paper with the words "smile," "grin," and "laugh" written on it. Move your hand under the letters of each word as you sing the song a second time. Call attention to the word "ha." Ask for a volunteer to say which letters are used to spell "ha."

- ❏ Print "smile," "grin," and "laugh" on chart paper. Provide magnetic letters and invite the children to copy the words.

Practicing the Lesson

- ❏ Sing other songs that have words spelled within them, such as "The Weather Song" on page 260 and "Y-O-U Spells You" on page 261.
- ❏ Give the children the index cards with the words "smile," "grin," "laugh," and "ha" written on them. Provide tracing paper for the children to trace over the words.

Reflecting on the Lesson

Ask the children:

- ❏ *How do you spell "smile"?*
- ❏ *Which verse of the song do you like best? Why?*

Special Needs Adaptations

Special Need	Adaptation
Visual Impairments	■ Show the child, with your body, what a smile, grin, and laugh are like. Invite the child to smile (it may be necessary for you to gently position her mouth for her) and to feel what a smile looks like. ■ Encourage the child to touch her chest when she laughs, so she can feel her own laughter. Children with visual impairments often cannot understand abstract concepts, so take a few minutes and explain the difference between a smile, grin, and laughter.
Hearing Impairments	■ Show the child your face as you smile, grin, and then laugh. Invite the child to imitate you, as you smile, grin, and laugh.
Cognitive Challenges	■ Draw a smile on a piece of paper. Tell the child that people smile when they are happy. Ask the child to smile. Invite the child to tell you about things that make her smile.
Motor Delays	■ Instead of index cards with the words "smile," "grin," "laugh," and "ha" written on them, use ¼ sheets of poster board. The larger surface will be easier for the child to use. Provide tracing paper and invite the children to trace over the words. If the child cannot hold the paper in place, tape it to the poster board so it will not slide off.
Speech/ Language Delays	■ Write the words "smile," "grin," and "laugh," on a piece of paper. Talk with the child about things that make her smile, laugh, and grin. Talk about the differences between the three words. If possible, invite her to pick a word and use it in a sentence.
Emotional/ Behavior Issues	■ A major obstacle to social development for children with emotional issues is their inability to use emotions appropriately. For example, laughing when another child falls down or grinning when someone else in the class is corrected by the teacher. It is even more difficult for a child with autism, as they often show no emotional response at all to situations going on around them. For this reason, it would be useful when talking about smiling, laughing, and grinning to ask the child to talk about a situation where she might grin and a situation where a grin would not be appropriate. Talk about expressing feelings and how it is important to try to understand how someone else feels when they fall down or when they are sad about something.

Letter knowledge and recognition

What's the Weather?

Children will:

- recognize that letters make up words.

Vocabulary

letters
part
whole
words

Materials

chart paper
index cards
magnetic letters
marker
newspaper
pictures of different kinds of weather
sentence strips

Preparation

Print "s-u-n-n-y," "c-l-o-u-d-y," "w-i-n-d-y," and "f-o-g-g-y" on chart paper. Print the weather descriptions, "sunny," "cloudy," "windy," and "foggy" on index cards. Print "Today is _____." on a sentence strip. Print the weather description words on sentence strips that can be used to fill in the blank.

Introducing and Developing the Lesson

- ❑ Ask the children to describe the weather outside. Print their descriptive words on chart paper.
- ❑ Show the children pictures of different kinds of weather.
- ❑ Ask for a few volunteers to tell the class something about each weather picture.
- ❑ Tell the children that they will be learning how to spell some weather words.
- ❑ Sing "The Weather Song" (see page 260 in the Appendix).
- ❑ Point out that each weather word is made up of letters. Have the children clap the letters as you sing again the verse of the song that describes today's weather.

Practicing the Lesson

- ❑ Place the index cards with weather descriptions in the Writing Center. Encourage children to use magnetic letters to copy the words.
- ❑ Place the sentence strip words, "Today is _____." in the Science Center. Have the children use the sentence strip words to fill in the blank.
- ❑ Show the children where the weather forecast is printed in the newspaper.

Reflecting on the Lesson

Ask the children:

- ❑ *What is your favorite kind of weather? How do you spell it?*
- ❑ *What is today's weather? How do you spell it?*

Special Needs Adaptations

Special Need	Adaptation
Visual Impairments	■ Describe the pictures for the child as you show them to the rest of the class. If possible, provide a prop, such as ice, for the child to touch when you describe cold weather, and so on.
Hearing Impairments	■ If the child cannot tell you something about each picture, ask her to point to something that she notices in each picture.
Cognitive Challenges	■ Ask the child direct questions, such as, "Do you think it is cold?" Hold up a picture of a winter day. Continue to ask questions such as, "What kind of clothes do you wear in cold weather?"
Motor Delays	■ If the child does not have the motor skills to clap the letters as you sing the weather song again, let her tap or ring a service bell while her classmates clap.
Speech/ Language Delays	■ Use this lesson as an opportunity to build on the child's vocabulary. Invite her to describe each picture you hold up that depicts various types of weather. ■ For children with very limited vocabulary, ask them yes/no questions about each picture.
Emotional/ Behavior Issues	■ Make sure the child understands that you will be asking different people to describe the pictures you hold up. ■ If the child has poor impulse control, suggest that she help you by holding up each picture.

Weather pictures seem more real to children when they feature people doing weather-related activities.

My Name

Introducing and Developing the Lesson

❑ Print your name on chart paper. Point out the individual letters that make up your name.

❑ Point out that names begin with an uppercase letter that is followed by all lowercase letters.

❑ Tell the children that they will practice recognizing their names and the letters that make up their names.

❑ Show the children the Name Cards. Ask the children to stand when they see their names and to say the letters that make up their names. Explain that each child's name is a word that is made up of letters. The name is the whole and the letters are the parts, like puzzle pieces in a puzzle.

❑ Go through the names again and see how many of the names the children recognize.

❑ Give the children their Name Puzzles. Ask each child, "How many puzzle pieces do you have?"

Practicing the Lesson

❑ Suggest that the children copy the names in the Classroom Name Box (a recipe box that contains each child's name printed on an index card).

❑ Encourage the children to spell their names using magnetic letters and then count the number of letters in their names.

Reflecting on the Lesson

Ask the children:

❑ *What is the first letter of your name?*

❑ *How many letters are in your name?*

Children will:

■ recognize the letters in their names.

Vocabulary

letters   part

name   whole

Materials

box to hold index cards

chart paper

envelopes

index cards

laminate

magnetic letters

marker

scissors

sentence strips

Preparation

Print each child's name on a sentence strip and laminate them to make Name Cards. Print the children's names on index cards and place them into a Classroom Name Box. Print children's names a second time onto sentence strips, this time leaving a space between each letter. Make puzzle cuts between each letter to create Name Puzzles. Place each set of letters into an envelope and print the child's name on the outside.

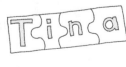

Special Needs Adaptations

Special Need	Adaptation
Visual Impairments	■ Children who are visually impaired need concrete experiences to make the connection between an object and its name or use. The child may not understand that her name is unique. For her name card, use dark-colored foam letters and mark her card in the box with a visual cue, such as a paper clip. The child can feel in the box, find the card with the paper clip, withdraw the card, feel each letter in her name, and match it using the magnetic letters.
Hearing Impairments	■ If the child is using sign language, she may be using a letter sign to indicate her name. (Young children with hearing impairments who are learning to sign may not use "letter signs" to represent their names. They are usually the first letters of their names.) Copy the sign beside her name on the name card. Even if a child is using sign language, it is important that she learns about written language.
Cognitive Challenges	■ Learning to recognize, read, and write your name is a critical life skill for all children. If the child is unable to write or copy her name, help her learn to select and match the letters in her name. Again, you may want to narrow the choices for her. For example, if the child's name is Karen, you might select the magnetic letters K, A, R, E, and N and three or four additional letters. Start by asking the child to select the letter K and match it to the letter on the sentence strip. If this is too difficult, offer her a choice between two letters. For example, put the letters K and O in the palm of your hand and hold them out for the child to see. Ask the child to find the K. Place the letter K over the K on the written card. Use a cookie sheet or other metal to help hold the magnetic letters in place.
Motor Delays	■ Position the child so she can successfully use her motor skills. If the child is not in a wheelchair, make sure the child's feet touch the floor, because this will help stabilize her overall posture. If her feet do not touch the floor, use a box or small foot stool for the child to rest her feet. Make sure her arm is placed on the table in a way that her elbow is bent to an angle of approximately 90°.
Speech/ Language	■ Provide extra practice in using pronouns by encouraging the child to say, "My name is _____ (inserts her name)" while she is working with her name card.
Emotional/ Behavior Issues	■ Make sure the child understands that when she hears her name she is supposed to stand. If the child refuses to stand, walk over to her and say, "_____, I called your name. You may now stand." If she refuses, ignore her and go on to the next child. When the next child stands, say to the group, "Thank you, _____ (child's name), for standing." Smile, and continue the activity. After you call a few more names, return to the child who refused to stand and call her name again.

If Your Name Starts with P

Children will:
- recognize letters of the alphabet.

Vocabulary
begin
first
letters

Materials
index cards
markers
crayons
drawing paper
magnetic letters
markers
paper bag

Preparation
Make Letter Cards by writing one letter of the alphabet on each index card. Write each child's name on a separate index card.

Introducing and Developing the Lesson

❑ Give each child a card with her name written on it. Ask the children to identify the first letter in their names. Tell the children that they will practice listening for the first letters of their names.

❑ Play The Name Game. Have children sit in a circle. Make up an action for each letter of the alphabet and call out the letter and the action. For example, "If your name starts with P, pat your tummy. If your name starts with T, tap your toe. If your name starts with B bounce up and down." Call out one letter at a time; the children who have that letter as the first letter of their names perform the action.

❑ Continue with letters and actions until all letters have been called. Hold up a letter card for each letter as you call it. You can call more than one letter at a time if you would like. Tell the children that every letter of the alphabet is the first letter in some child's name.

❑ Place magnetic letters in a paper bag. Ask for a volunteer to reach into the bag and pull out a letter. Challenge the volunteer to name the letter and then give it to a child in the room whose name starts with that letter. Continue the game by letting the child whose first name began with the drawn letter select the next letter.

Practicing the Lesson

❑ Suggest that the children make Letter Cards. Encourage them to print the first letters of their names as large as they would like in the middle of a sheet of paper. They can then use crayons and markers to make designs for their Letter Cards.

❑ Challenge the children to write their names with magnetic letters.

Reflecting on the Lesson

Ask the children:

❑ *Are there other children in the room whose name starts with the same letter as your name? Who?*

❑ *Does anyone in your family have a name that starts with the same letter as your name?*

Special Needs Adaptations

Special Need	Adaptation
Visual Impairments	<ul><li>Provide the child with a card with her name written boldly in dark colors.</li><li>To help the child see as well as feel the difference between letters and how they are made, use raised letters, such as letters made from craft foam or cardboard.</li></ul>
Hearing Impairments	<ul><li>Remember to use gestures when showing the child the motions that accompany each letter for The Name Game. For example, when you say, "If your name starts with P, pat your tummy." Pat your own tummy.</li></ul>
Cognitive Challenges	<ul><li>Remember, the child may not be able to identify the first letter in her name and may require extra clues from you to help her. If the child still cannot identify the letter, say it for her. Then, invite her to repeat it after you.</li></ul>
Motor Delays	<ul><li>If the child is unable to draw her letter card, perhaps she could make a letter collage with pictures of objects whose names that start with the first letter of her name.</li></ul>
Speech/ Language Delays	<ul><li>Reinforce learning letter names by asking the child to help you name other words that start with the same first letter as her name.</li></ul>
Emotional/ Behavior Issues	<ul><li>If the child resists the activity, encourage her to try part of the activity. Perhaps, instead of a motion to accompany the first letter of her name, she could tell you another word that starts with that letter.</li></ul>

Letter knowledge and recognition

Name Comparisons

Children will:
- recognize letters of the alphabet.

Vocabulary

alphabet
count
graph
letters
long
lowercase
short
uppercase

Materials

chart paper
letter building blocks or letter
    cards taped to building blocks
marker
premade graph
Scrabble™ letters

Preparation

Make a graph that along one side provides one space for each child in the classroom and also has the numerals 1–12 written across the top. (See sample graph on page 267 in the Appendix.)

Introducing and Developing the Lesson

❑ Tell the children that they are going to make a graph that shows which children have the longest names.

❑ Ask several children if they think their names are long are short. Print their names on chart paper as they give you their answers.

❑ After every child's name has been printed on chart paper, have them count the letters in each name.

❑ Place their names on the graph you have made and make a check in the column that corresponds to the number of letters in their names. Which child has the longest name? Which child has the shortest name? How many letters must a name have in order to consider it a long name? (Let the children decide.)

❑ Give the children Scrabble letters. Have them spell their names and compare the lengths of their names (number of Scrabble tiles) to friends' names.

Practicing the Lesson

❑ Print letters on building blocks or tape letter cards to building blocks. Encourage the children to spell their names with blocks. Have them use one-to-one correspondence to compare the number of letters in their names to their friends' names. Whose names are longer?

❑ Make a graph of letters of the alphabet with which the children's names begin. Place the alphabet letters on the floor. Have the children come and stand behind the letters that are the first letters of their names. Transfer the information to a graph. Which letter is the most common first letter of children's names?

Reflecting on the Lesson

Ask the children:

❑ *Do you have a long name or a short name? What makes you think so?*

❑ *Can you tell if a name is long or short just by listening to the name?*

Special Needs Adaptations

Special Need	Adaptation
Visual Impairments	■ To help the child understand the purpose behind the activity, write out several names on a piece of paper attached to a tabletop easel (see page 249 in the Appendix for instructions on how to make a tabletop easel). Ask the child to point to the longest name and the shortest name.
Hearing Impairments	■ Before inviting the child to spell and compare the length of her name, model the activity for her by doing it with another child. Use gestures to point out which name is longest.
Cognitive Challenges	■ Demonstrate for the child what you mean by *long* and *short*. Encourage the child to show you things in the classroom that are longer than or shorter than other objects. Talk about the differences. ■ When you are introducing the letter graph, explain to the child that when you say a name is long, it means the name has more letters in it, while a short name will have fewer letters in it.
Motor Delays	■ Instead of Scrabble letters, which may be too difficult for the child to manipulate, use large magnetic letters and a cookie sheet. Tell the child to invite a friend, so the two of them can spell their names with the magnetic letters on the cookie sheet and compare them to see which one is longer.
Speech/ Language Delays	■ Demonstrate for the child how to compare the number of letters in her name with those in her friend's name. Encourage the child to count aloud the number of letters in her name. If necessary, review the concepts of *long* and *short* with the child before she begins the activity.
Emotional/ Behavior Issues	■ Working collaboratively with a peer can be very challenging. Before asking the child to use the scrabble letters to spell her name with a peer, review the rules of cooperative work. For example, say, "Take a turn, wait for your friend to have a turn, be kind, speak softly," and so on.

Sensory Letter Makers

Children will:

- recognize letters of the alphabet.
- use their senses to recognize letters.

Vocabulary

alphabet	mold
curved	shape
draw	straight
feel	touch
first	write
letters	

Materials

glue
hair gel
index cards
Letter Cards—4" x 8" sheets of tag board
marker
quart-size resealable plastic bags
Sandpaper Letter Cards— sandpaper and magnetic letters
scissors
Tactile Letter Cards—glue and sandpaper letters
Tactile Playdough—playdough and sand
Wikki Stix® or chenille wires

Introducing and Developing the Lesson

- ❑ Prepare Letter Cards (see page 280 in the Appendix).
- ❑ Tell the children that they will be using all of their senses to make letters.
- ❑ Show the children one of the Letter Cards. Ask the children to pretend to write letters in the air. Turn your back to the children and demonstrate writing the letter in the air. Encourage the children to copy your movements.
- ❑ Have the children practice air-writing the first letters of their names.
- ❑ Tell the children to stand in a circle with their backs to the people behind them. Have the children practice writing a letter (you select one) on the backs of the people in front of them.
- ❑ Invite the children to shape the first letters of their names with Tactile Playdough.
- ❑ Give the children the Sandpaper Letter Cards. Encourage them to find the letters in their name with their eyes closed.
- ❑ Provide Wikki Stix® or chenille wires. Encourage the children to shape the first letters of their names.

Practicing the Lesson

- ❑ Print letters on 4" x 6" index cards. Suggest that the children use a bottle of glue to make glue drops over the shapes of the letters. When the glue dries, you will have a set of tactile alphabet cards.
- ❑ Sing "The Alphabet Song" (see page 254 in the Appendix).

Reflecting on the Lesson

Ask the children:

- ❑ *Was it easier to shape the first letter of your name with playdough or with Wikki Stix?*
- ❑ *Does the first letter of your name have straight lines, curved lines, or both types of lines?*

Special Needs Adaptations

Special Need	Adaptation
Visual Impairments	<ul><li>When standing in a circle, encourage the child to put her hand on the shoulder of the child in front of her before she writes a letter on her back.</li><li>Remind peers that children with visual impairments often need to use "soft touches" to help them explore the world around them.</li></ul>
Hearing Impairments	<ul><li>Make sure you direct the child's attention to you when you are writing letters, so she can watch what you are doing. For the back-writing part of the lesson, it may be necessary to demonstrate what you will be doing by first writing on the child's back.</li></ul>
Cognitive Challenges	<ul><li>If the child does not know how to make a letter, encourage her to try.</li><li>Select letters to write on a peer's back that the child knows how to write.</li></ul>
Motor Delays	<ul><li>If the child can't participate in the back-writing part of the lesson, let her be the leader and pick the letters the children will write.</li></ul>
Speech/ Language Delays	<ul><li>Provide extra practice for the child to help her identify other words that may start with the first letter of her name.</li><li>Remember to include her family and encourage them to practice with her at home.</li></ul>
Emotional/ Behavior Issues	<ul><li>Children with autism often do not do well in activities that involve touching other people or working with art mediums (clay, paint, and so on). If the child has a preferred art medium, encourage her to use that one to write the first letter of her name.</li></ul>

Wikki Stix® make learning letters more fun.

Letter Hunt

Children will:
- recognize letters of the alphabet.

Vocabulary
find
hunt
letters
names

Materials
advertisements from magazines and newspapers, laminated
paper bags
plastic letters
sand table
strainer

Preparation
Cut out advertisements from magazines and newspapers. Select ads that have easy-to-read words and letters. Laminate each ad.

Introducing and Developing the Lesson

- Hide plastic letters throughout the classroom.
- Tell the children that they will be looking for letters in the classroom.
- Give each child a paper bag. Explain that they are going to have a letter hunt in the same way they might have an egg hunt. Tell them that when they find letters they are to put them into their letter bags.
- After the children find all the letters, have them empty their bags and name the letters they have found.

Practicing the Lesson

- Photocopy and enlarge advertisements from magazines and newspapers. Laminate the copies. Give the children the laminated copies and challenge them to find a specific letter. For example, find all the letters M or B. Provide a marking pen so that they can circle the specified letters.
- Hide plastic letters in the sand table and invite the children to use a strainer to find them. Have them name the letters they find.

Reflecting on the Lesson

Ask the children:
- *Which letters did you find during the letter hunt? Were any of the letters you found the same letters as those in your name?*
- *Which letters did you find with the strainer?*

Special Needs Adaptations

Special Need	Adaptation
Visual Impairments	■ To help the child participate in the letter hunt, give her verbal cues and allow her time to walk the boundaries where the letters are hidden. For example, you might tell her the letters are only hidden in and around objects that are on the carpet or just in the Dramatic Play Center. If she is having difficulty finding any letters, ask her if she would like to invite a friend to work with her.
Hearing Impairments	■ Invite the child to work with a friend on the letter hunt. Remember to model for her exactly what she is to do. For example, you may want to walk to a place where a letter is hidden, retrieve it, and put it in your bag while the child watches.
Cognitive Challenges	■ Give the child extra help by giving her a specific letter to look for and a verbal cue where the letter may be hidden. ■ After the child finds the first letter, say, "Good job" or "Great, you found the letter M."
Motor Delays	■ Instead of a paper bag, give the child a basket to hold her letters. The handle may be easier for her to hold. ■ Remember to place letters where the child can reach them.
Speech/ Language Delays	■ When the child returns to the group with the letters she found in the letter hunt, ask her to tell you a word that starts with that letter.
Emotional/ Behavior Issues	■ Because this activity requires that children move around in the classroom, review the rules of group activities, such as *wait for your turn* or *walk, don't run*. If the child shoves or pushes others out of the way so she can look for a letter, gently redirect her to somewhere else in the classroom. It will also help if you tell the children that there are plenty of letters hidden so that everyone will be able to find at least two letters.

Letter Walk

Children will:
- recognize letters of the alphabet in environmental print.

Vocabulary

alphabet	record
count	signs
letters	tally
match	words

Materials

chart paper
clip board
notebook
pencils
recording sheets—premade grid on notebook paper

Preparation

Print the alphabet on notebook paper in a grid to make a recording sheet. Make several copies of the recording sheet. Place one of the recording sheets on a clip board to use with the lesson. (See a sample on page 268 in the Appendix.)

Introducing and Developing the Lesson

- ❑ Sing "If You're Happy and You Know It," changing "clap your hands" to "point to the letter ___" (see page 257 in the Appendix). Instead of clapping, have the children say, "Hello" as they point.
- ❑ Tell the children that they are going on a letter walk to hunt for letters. Walk around the school both inside and outside in search of signs. Tell the children that they are going to look for letters and when they find them you are going to make a tally mark by that letter on your recording sheet.
- ❑ Ask the children to predict which letter they think they will see most often. Write their predictions at the top of your recording sheet.
- ❑ Look for letters on exits, bathroom signs, outside signs, and so on. Read the signs first and then ask for volunteers to identify the letters within the words. Keep a record of the letters that you find.
- ❑ When you return to the classroom, count the letters. *Which letter did you see most often?*
- ❑ On another day or later on the same day, walk around a different part of the school or outside area. Was the result the same?

Practicing the Lesson

- ❑ Give each child an individual recording sheet. Have the children search individually for letters in the classroom. Show them how to place tally marks beside letters as they find the letters.
- ❑ Print a simple sentence on chart paper. Give the children individual recording sheets and tell them to mark the letters they see in the sentence.
- ❑ Invite the children to use a recording sheet to tally and count the letters on a page of their favorite storybook.

Reflecting on the Lesson

Ask the children:
- ❑ *Which letters did you see most often today?*
- ❑ *What do the letters by the doors outside say?*

Special Needs Adaptations

Special Need	Adaptation
Visual Impairments	■ Make sure the child is familiar with the places you are going on your letter walk. Place the child near you at the front of the line, so that you can direct her attention to the object or sign that the class is observing.
Hearing Impairments	■ Walk around the room with the child and point out a few signs. Point to the first letter on the sign and explain to the child that later on you will be taking the whole class on a letter walk.
Cognitive Challenges	■ As you take the letter walk, keep in mind that the child may not know all her letter names. Be sure to select a few signs or written words starting with a letter that she knows. ■ Children with cognitive challenges have difficulty generalizing information from one setting to another; she may recognize a letter when her first name is written, but not recognize the same letter when she sees it on a sign or in another written word.
Motor Delays	■ If the child is in a wheelchair, it may be difficult for her to look up at signs or written words. Whenever possible, show her signs at her eye level. Select a few signs and written words that are in her line of vision.
Speech/ Language Delays	■ Because the child may have limited knowledge of letters and counting, you may need to help her participate in the letter walk. It may be necessary for you to say something such as, "I see the letter S" and then point to that word. Then ask her to show you that letter.
Emotional/ Behavior Issues	■ Transitions, such as when the class is preparing to go on the letter walk, are especially challenging for children with emotional issues. Remember to tell the child what will happen and, if necessary, limit the walk to places in the school that are familiar to the child. If the child becomes very anxious or upset, discontinue the walk and return to the classroom.

Letter Spotlight Game

Children will:
- identify letters of the alphabet.

Vocabulary
letter
spotlight

Materials
alphabet cards
flashlight
hanging sheet or curtain
large cutout alphabet letters
magnetic letters
overhead projector

Preparation
If you do not own large cutout alphabet letters, make a set from poster board.

Introducing and Developing the Lesson

- ❏ Tell the children that they are going to practice identifying and naming letters of the alphabet.
- ❏ Play the Letter Spotlight Game. Have the children sit in a circle. Place a set of alphabet cards on the floor in random order in the middle of the circle. Give a flashlight to one child. Turn out the classroom light. Ask the child to shine the light on a specific letter. Have the child pass the flashlight to the child next to her.
- ❏ Say another letter and have the child shine her light on the letter.
- ❏ Continue until the children tire of the game.

Practicing the Lesson

- ❏ Give the children the flashlight and letter cards. Encourage them to play the Letter Spotlight Game on their own.
- ❏ Play Alphabet Shadows. Provide large cutout alphabet letters. Place a light source between the wall and a hanging sheet or curtain. Display a letter between the light source and the curtain. Have the children identify the letter by the shadow it casts. Make the game more challenging by using both uppercase and lowercase letters.
- ❏ Provide magnetic letters and an overhead projector. Place a letter on the overhead and ask children to identify the letter shadow they see on the wall.

Reflecting on the Lesson

Ask the children:
- ❏ *Are letters easier to identify with a light shining on them or when they are in shadow form?*
- ❏ *What are some letters that look alike?*

Special Needs Adaptations

Special Need	Adaptation
Visual Impairments	■ Provide the child with her own set of letters. As you shine the light on each letter, invite the child to touch the letter you are saying. ■ Select letters that look alike (B/D/P, M/N, or C/O). Even letters that do not look exactly alike can be very confusing for a child with poor visual discrimination skills. Give the child time to examine each letter. If possible, provide a cutout and invite the child to trace it with her fingers while you talk about it. Say the letter and ask the child to say it after you.
Hearing Impairments	■ As you shine the light on each letter, be sure the letter is where the child can see it.
Cognitive Challenges	■ Children with cognitive challenges may have difficulty with letters that look alike. Take a few extra minutes and review the differences between the letters B, P, and D. Invite the child to think of a word that starts with each letter.
Motor Delays	■ If the child is unable to direct the spotlight, perhaps she could partially participate by asking a friend to help her.
Speech/ Language Delays	■ A child with language delays may not recognize or be able to identify all the letters used in this activity. Adapt the activity by shining the light on the letters she does know.
Emotional/ Behavior Issues	■ For the child to feel more at ease and less overwhelmed, you may want to introduce the activity first in a small group. Then when you bring in the whole class the child will feel more in control, because she knows what will happen next.

Name Bingo

Children will:
- recognize letters of the alphabet.

Vocabulary
erase
letters
names
words

Materials
basket
chart paper
construction paper
drawing paper
magnetic letters
name cards
paper
pencils
Scrabble™ letters
small index cards

Preparation
Cut 3" diameter circles from construction paper. Make Name Cards for each child by printing their names on sheets of paper. If children are able, allow each of them to print their names on sheets of paper. Make Letter Cards by printing an alphabet letter on each small index card. Place the Letter Cards in a basket.

Introducing and Developing the Lesson

- Sit with the children in a circle.
- Print your name on chart paper and put it in the middle of the circle. Ask for a volunteer to name one of the letters in your name. When the letter is named, cover it with one of the construction paper circles. Tell the children that you have just played a version of Name Bingo.
- Tell the children that they are going to play letter games. Give the children their name cards or have them print their names on sheets of paper. Give each child some construction paper circles.
- Tell the children that you will be drawing Letter Cards from a basket and that when they hear letters that are in their names they are to cover those letters with one of their construction paper circles. If a child has two or more of a letter in her name, she can cover all the letters.
- Call letters until all children have all their letters covered.

Practicing the Lesson

- Print the children's names in pencil on pieces of paper. If they are able, have the children print their own names. Play the game again. This time, have the children erase the letters in their names as they hear each one called.
- Give the children Scrabble letters to spell their names. Play again. This time, have the children turn over each letter when they hear it.
- Provide magnetic letters. Pull Letter Cards from the basket and announce them to the children. Have the children collect the letters for their names as they hear them called.

Reflecting on the Lesson

Ask the children:
- *Does it take longer to cover a long name than it does a short name?* (Help children work through this question. Help them determine that the length is not what causes the name to be covered quickly or slowly. It is the order in which the letters are called and the number of multiple letters in a name.)
- *Which version of the game do you like best? Why?*

Special Needs Adaptations

Special Need	Adaptation
Visual Impairments	■ Instead of construction paper circles, use checkers, because they will be easier for the child to see and manipulate.
Hearing Impairments	■ When you call out a letter, also write it on a piece of chart paper. This way, the child with hearing impairments will be able to see which letter you are calling.
Cognitive Challenges	■ When the first letter in the child's name is called, walk over and cover that letter for her. Invite her to help you. This will reinforce her understanding that she is to cover a letter when she hears it called out.
Motor Delays	■ Print the child's name on heavy paper or cardstock and use larger checkers or round jar lids to cover each letter. These will be easier for the child to pick up and manipulate than paper circles.
Speech/ Language Delays	■ Play the bingo game one-on-one with the child before introducing it to the group. This helps the child understand what she is expected to do and will make participation in the large group activity more fun for her.
Emotional/ Behavior Issues	■ Review the rules for playing games with the child before you start. Remind her to listen to your instructions and that it is not important whether she wins or loses the game. What matters is that she enjoys playing.

Shake a Letter

Children will:

- recognize and name letters of the alphabet.

Vocabulary

down
draw
letter
names
shake
up

Materials

laminate
Scrabble™ letter tiles or a
    homemade version of
    Scrabble letters
sheet of construction paper, tray,
    or rug square
small index cards
Styrofoam cup

Preparation

Print the letters of the alphabet on small index cards. Laminate the cards to make a deck of Letter Cards. Make two or three sets of cards.

Introducing and Developing the Lesson

- ❑ Read the poem, "Words and Letters" (see page 265 in the Appendix) to the children. Ask them to name places in the classroom where they see words and letters. Tell the children that they will be playing a game with alphabet letters.
- ❑ Place eight Scrabble letter cubes or a homemade version of Scrabble letters in a Styrofoam cup. Shake the cup and dump the letters onto a sheet of construction paper, tray, or rug square.
- ❑ Ask for a volunteer to name the letters that land facing up. Ask a second volunteer to turn the other letter cubes up and name the letters on them.
- ❑ Play the game several times. Change the letters in the cup each time you play.
- ❑ Give the children the cup and cubes and encourage them to play Shake a Letter with a friend. Have each child keep the letter cubes she is able to name. At the end of the game, the children can count their letter cubes to see just how skilled they are at recognizing letters.

Practicing the Lesson

- ❑ Ask the children to select a partner. Give each pair of children a deck of Letter Cards (see Preparation). Help them shuffle the cards and place the deck face down. Instruct them to take turns drawing a card and identifying the letter. If the child correctly identifies a letter, she keeps the card. If not, she places it in a stack face down beside the deck of playing cards. At the end of the game the children count their cards to see just how skilled they have become at recognizing letters.

Reflecting on the Lesson

Ask the children:

- ❑ *How many letters did you recognize today? Can you name some of them?*
- ❑ *Where in our classroom do you see letters that make up words?*

Special Needs Adaptations

Special Need	Adaptation
Visual Impairments	■ If the child has some residual vision, make sure the letter cards are large enough and bold enough for her to see. Remember to place them at an angle because the cards will be easier for her to see.
Hearing Impairments	■ Encourage the child to face her partner when they are playing the letter card games. Make sure the child can see her partner's mouth when the partner talks.
Cognitive Challenges	■ Use fewer letter cards and include only one or two that the child does not know. It is important that children with cognitive challenges experience success in a lesson. If the child is shown too many letters, it will be confusing for her.
Motor Delays	■ If the child can't turn over the letters or place the ones that she knows into a pile, suggest that she ask her partner in the game to help her.
Speech/ Language Delays	■ After the child has identified some letters with a partner, look at the stack of cards she kept (the ones that she knew). Ask her to use each one in a word. ■ If she can't think of a word that starts with that letter, ask her to find a friend to help her.
Emotional/ Behavior Issues	■ Before beginning any group activity, remind the children of the rules for group play: wait your turn, don't get upset if you don't win, share your materials, and so on. If the child gets upset and asks to quit playing, allow her to do so. ■ If the child throws her cards or screams, sit with her and insist that she complete the activity. It is very important for a child with emotional issues to learn that she can use words to express displeasure, but that she cannot use violence.

String a Word

Children will:

- recognize the part-to-whole relationship of letters to words.

Vocabulary

letters   together

string   words

Materials

beads

blocks

chart paper

construction paper of different colors

hole punch

sturdy string or laces

laminate

marker

small index cards

string

tape

Preparation

Cut 3" circles from construction paper. Print alphabet letters on each circle. Laminate and punch a hole in the top of the circle to allow for stringing to create Letter Circles. Print alphabet letters on small index cards. Laminate to create Letter Cards. Cut the string into appropriate lengths to make a necklace. Wrap tape around the ends of the string pieces, to facilitate lacing the necklaces.

Introducing and Developing the Lesson

- Tell the children they will make a necklace. String a few beads onto a string and tie the necklace around your neck. Ask the children what the necklace is made from. When they answer "beads," discuss the part-to-whole relationship of the beads to the necklace.
- Tell the children that they will focus on the whole-part relationship that letters have to words.
- Ask for a volunteer to suggest a word. Using the Letter Circles (see Preparation) string the letters to create the word suggested by the volunteer. Say the name of each letter as you string it.
- When you are finished, place the string of letters on the floor in front of you and say the word.
- Allow another volunteer to provide another word, and do the activity a second time.
- Discuss the part-to-whole relationship of letters to words.
- Give the children the Letter Circles and string. Encourage them to string the letters of their names together.

Practicing the Lesson

- Write color words on chart paper. Encourage the children to string the Letter Circles to spell the color words. Challenge them to use only the color of Letter Circles that match the color word they are stringing.
- Tape Letter Cards to blocks. Have the children stack the blocks in sequences that will spell their names. Point out that it takes several letter blocks to make up their names.

Reflecting on the Lesson

Ask the children:

- *Which letters did you string to make your name?*
- *Was it easier to string your name or stack your name?*

Special Needs Adaptations

Special Need	Adaptation
Visual Impairments	■ Because the child may not have well-developed visual motor skills, adapt the activity by creating letter circles on brightly colored piece of paper. ■ Select only the letters needed to spell the child's name. Invite the child to arrange the letters in the correct order before stringing them.
Hearing Impairments	■ In order for the child to understand that she is to use the circles with letters printed on them to spell her name and place the letters on the string, demonstrate the activity for her.
Cognitive Challenges	■ Preselect the circle cards needed to string the child's name. Give her only those letter circles she will need. If the child is unable to write or identify her name, begin by stringing the first letter for her. ■ Then, ask her to show you the next letter. Continue taking turns with the child until her name is on the string. Ask the child to point to each letter as you say it.
Motor Delays	■ If the child cannot string her name, invite her to ask a peer to help her.
Speech/ Language Delays	■ As the child adds each letter to her name string, encourage her to name the letters for you. Ask her to tell you other words that start with the letters.
Emotional/ Behavior Issues	■ Allow the child to choose the colors for her necklace. Choice is not only important, but also it helps children learn to make decisions and build confidence.

Letter knowledge and recognition

Letter Detectives

Children will:

- recognize letters of the alphabet by oral descriptions.

Vocabulary

clues
consonant
curved
letters
read
spell
straight
vowel
words

Materials

audio recorder
bag
magnetic letters
playdough
recording media

Preparation

Make a Mystery Letter recording that describes four different letters (for example, L-O-V-E).

Introducing and Developing the Lesson

- ❑ Talk with the children about detectives. *What do detectives do?* Make sure the children understand that detectives look for clues.
- ❑ Tell the children that they are going to be Letter Detectives.
- ❑ Place a magnetic letter inside a bag. Give the children clues as to which letter is inside. For example, for the letter T you might say the following:
    - This letter is made of straight lines.
    - This letter is the first letter of Tanya's name.
    - This letter makes a /t/ sound.
    - This letter is the last letter in "cat" and "mat."
- ❑ When someone guesses the letter correctly, change the letter and play again. Continue playing the game for as long as children show an interest.
- ❑ Encourage each child to select a partner and play Guess the Letter in My Hand. Have one child hold a letter behind her back and then describe the letter to her partner. When the partner guesses the letter, the children change roles.

Practicing the Lesson

- ❑ Invite the children to shape letters with playdough and use their own words to describe the letter they have shaped.
- ❑ Provide pairs of letters that look alike, such as B/D, M/N, and V/W. Ask the children to describe how the letters in each pair are different.

Reflecting on the Lesson

Ask the children:
- ❑ *Which letter of the alphabet is a circle?*
- ❑ *Which letter is a single straight line?*

Special Needs Adaptations

Special Need	Adaptation
Visual Impairments	■ Show the child the bag and make sure she understands that there is a letter inside. Explain that you will give clues about the letter.
Hearing Impairments	■ When playing the Guess the Letter in My Hand game, make sure the child with hearing impairments is seated directly in front of her partner where she can see her partner's face as the letter is described.
Cognitive Challenges	■ Give the child very concrete clues about the letter you have hidden in the bag. For example, you may say, "The letter is the first sound you hear in the word 'bat' and in the word 'ball.'" Keep in mind that there will be some letters she does not know.
Motor Delays	■ If the child is unable to hold the letter behind her back in the Guess the Letter in My Hand game, allow the child to place the letter in front of her and her peer partner can close her eyes while she describes the letter.
Speech/ Language Delays	■ Adapt the mystery letter recording activity for a child with limited language skills by recording a word and then pausing. Ask the child to select the letter card that matches the first sound in the name of the word you recorded.
Emotional/ Behavior Issues	■ Remind the child that this is a game and it does not matter who wins. Sometimes, children with emotional issues get very upset if they don't "win" a game. Smile often and praise the child for participating with her peers in this activity.

The Alphabet March

Introducing and Developing the Lesson

- Read *Chicka Chicka Boom Boom* by Bill Martin, Jr. and John Archambault. Discuss the "mama and papa" letters and how they are different from the baby letters.
- Tell the children that they will be practicing matching uppercase and lowercase letters.
- Place the lowercase alphabet cards on the floor in random order and scattered several feet apart.
- Give each child an uppercase magnetic alphabet letter.
- Sing "The Alphabet March" (see page 251 in the Appendix) to the tune of "The Ants Go Marching." Have the children march around until they locate the lowercase letter on the floor that matches the uppercase letter in their hand. When they find their match, they stand beside it until the lyrics direct them to switch their letters with a friend.

  Note: It is best to divide the class into two groups, so that neither group is so large it prevents the children from moving freely.

- Discuss the game when it is over. *Which lowercase letters look just like their uppercase matches? Which lowercase letters look different from their uppercase matches?* (b, d, a, g, r)
- Give the children the uppercase and lowercase magnetic letters to match.

Practicing the Lesson

- Copy and enlarge advertising text from magazines. Have the children pick a letter and then circle the uppercase letters in red and lowercase letters in green.
- Sit children in a circle. Give each child two or three uppercase letter cards. Tell them to hold up the matching uppercase letter to the lowercase letter that you hold up.

Reflecting on the Lesson

Ask the children:

- *Which lowercase letters look just like the uppercase letters, but smaller? (s, x, c, o)*
- *Does your name begin with an uppercase or a lowercase letter? Does the first letter of your name look like the lowercase letter that is its match?*

Children will:

- recognize and match letters of the alphabet.

Vocabulary

letters
lowercase
march
match
uppercase

Materials

advertisements from magazines
alphabet cards for both uppercase and lowercase letters
Chicka Chicka Boom Boom by Bill Martin, Jr. and John Archambault
crayons or markers (red and green)
magnetic letters (uppercase and lowercase)

Preparation

Gather or make a set of alphabet cards that show both the uppercase and lowercase letters.

Special Needs Adaptations

Special Need	Adaptation
Visual Impairments	■ Show the child how to play the Alphabet March. If the child is blind, invite a friend to walk with her. Review with the friend the correct way to lead a person who is visually impaired (see page 17 in the Introduction).
Hearing Impairments	■ Before beginning the game, walk with the child and invite her to match a few letters. Hand her an uppercase letter to match to the lowercase letter to help the child orient herself as to how the game will be played.
Cognitive Challenges	■ More than likely, the child will not know the names of all the letters. Be sure to give the child a letter to match that she is familiar with. Keep in mind that she may be familiar with the uppercase letter and not the lowercase letter or vice versa.
Motor Delays	■ Modify the game for the child who is not mobile by giving her her own set of uppercase and lowercase letters. Stack the lowercase letters face down in a deck. Place six to eight uppercase letters in front of the child. Invite her to pick one from the deck and match it to the uppercase letter in front of her. It will be necessary to use fewer letters, because the child's range of motion (area where she can reach) may not be large enough to place more than a few cards.
Speech/ Language Delays	■ Don't assume that just because a child can match letters she understands the name of the letter or the sound it makes. As the children match their letters, ask each one to tell you the sound made by that letter. Begin by giving the child a lowercase letter that she knows how to match to the uppercase letter. Later, add letters that she is learning.
Emotional/ Behavior Issues	■ Instead of dividing the class in half, which may result in too much noise and movement for the child, try dividing the class into four small groups to complete the activity. ■ Remember to model the activity (walking around and matching, when directed, and exchanging cards with a friend) several times before asking the child to participate.

Look for opportunities during the day for children to practice identifying letters.

Books That Support Letter Knowledge and Recognition

A Walk in the Rainforest by Kristin Joy Pratt

AA Is for Aardvark by Mark Shulman

ABC Helpers by Rochelle Bunnett *

ABC: A Child's First Alphabet Book by Alison Jay

Alligator Arrived with Apples: A Potluck Alphabet Feast by Crescent Dragonwagon

Alphabatics by Suse MacDonald

Alphabet City by Stephen T. Johnson

C Is for China by Sungwan So

Chicka Chicka Boom Boom! by Bill Martin, Jr. and John Archambault

The Dinosaur Alphabet Book by Jerry Pallotta

Dr. Seuss's ABC by Dr. Seuss

Eating the Alphabet: Fruits and Vegetables from A to Z by Lois Ehlert

The Farm Alphabet by Jane Miller

The Frog Alphabet Book by Jerry Pallotta

The Graphic Alphabet by David Pelletier

The Handmade Alphabet by Laura Rankin *

The Hidden Alphabet by Laura Vaccaro Seeger

Marti and the Mango by Daniel Moreton

My First Book of Sign by Pamela Baker *

My First Book of Sign Language by Joan Holub *

The Ocean Alphabet by Jerry Pallotta

Simple Signs by Cindy Wheeler *

*   Denotes books featuring children with special needs

Chapter 5

Print Awareness

Overview

Print awareness is the knowledge that printed words move from left to right and from top to bottom. It is also the awareness that print has many functions—labeling items, creating lists, conveying information in newspapers, telling stories in books, identifying exits and entrances, and so on.

Print awareness begins when children start to identify their favorite restaurant by its logo or sign or point out that a stop sign means stop. This is referred to as environmental print.

Some children will begin to combine letters to make words, usually starting with their own names. Others will actually pretend to write a message by making pretend letters (using letter approximations) (see page 286 in the Appendix—Writing Continuum).

Research has shown that to learn to recognize print in the environment, children with special needs require more visual cues, such as pictures, to help them. Children with special needs need additional opportunities to practice print awareness, and often group lessons may need to be repeated and expanded. It is important that children with special needs have multiple opportunities to practice what they learn in a variety of settings.

First, Next, Last

Children will:
- understand position words— "first," "next," and "last"

Vocabulary
first
last
next
position
second
words

Materials
beads in various colors
string
"The Three Billy Goats Gruff"
    (many versions are available)

Introducing and Developing the Lesson

- ❑ Teach the children the action rhyme, "Saying Goodbye" (see page 265 in the Appendix). What is the first part of saying goodbye in the rhyme? What is the last part of saying goodbye in the rhyme?
- ❑ Tell the children that they will be learning about the position words "first," "next," and "last."
- ❑ Read or tell the children the story of "The Three Billy Goats Gruff" (many versions are available). Discuss the order in which the goats went across the bridge. Which goat went across the bridge first? Which goat went across last?
- ❑ Invite the children to re-enact the story. After they have completed the re-enactment, ask the children who played the parts of the goats to line up in the order in which they crossed the bridge.

Practicing the Lesson

- ❑ Give the children three-step directions and challenge them to follow the directions. Discuss the first direction, second direction, and last direction.
- ❑ Prepare rebus directions that are three or more steps. For example, you could show a pattern for stringing beads: first the red bead, then the yellow bead, and last the green bead. Discuss the order of the beads on the string.

Reflecting on the Lesson

Ask the children:
- ❑ *What is the first thing you do in the morning when you get out of bed? What is the last thing you do at night before you get into bed?*
- ❑ *What is the first thing you do when you brush your teeth? What is the last thing you do as you finish brushing your teeth?*

Special Needs Adaptations

Special Need	Adaptation
Visual Impairments	■ Demonstrate the meaning of the words in this lesson by lining up the child with two friends. Talk about who is first in the line, who is next, and who is last.
Hearing Impairments	■ Show the child an example of first, next, and last by lining up three objects or items. Ask the child to show you which one is first, next, and last.
Cognitive Challenges	■ To help the child understand the concepts of "first," "next," and "last" look for opportunities throughout the day to demonstrate the meaning of the words for the child: for example, when you line up to go outside, when you get ready to have lunch (talk about what you do first, next, and last), and when you put away the toys or objects used in an activity.
Motor Delays	■ Look for a part the child can play in the reenactment of the story. For example, could the child be the narrator or the director of the reenactment?
Speech/ Language Delays	■ The child may understand "first" and "last" but not "next." Collect several objects and ask the child to show you the one that is first, next, and last. See if the child will describe the object to you or use it in a sentence.
Emotional/ Behavior Issues	■ To encourage the child to participate in the story reenactment, invite the child to pick the character he wants to be.

Spatial relationships

Top to Bottom

Children will:
- understand that print is read from top to bottom.

Vocabulary
body
bottom
middle
move
print
top

Materials
baby doll or stuffed animal
children's favorite book,
    preferably a big book
crayons
paper
red, yellow, and blue blocks

Introducing and Developing the Lesson

- Ask the children to stand. Have them touch their heads, then their waists, and then their feet. Ask the children which body part is at the top of their bodies. Which body part is in the middle of their bodies? Which body part is at the bottom of their bodies?
- Sing "Head, Shoulders, Knees, and Toes" (see page 257 in the Appendix). Ask the children, "If your waist is the middle of your body, which body parts mentioned in the song are in the top half of your body? Which body parts mentioned in the song are in the bottom half of your body?"
- Tell the children that they will be learning about "top" and "bottom."
- Select one of the children's favorite books, preferably a big book. Open the book to the first page of print. Ask for a volunteer to show you the first word on the page. Ask the class if the word is at the top of the page or bottom of the page. Ask a second volunteer to identify the last word on the page. Ask the class if the last word is at the top of the page or the bottom of the page.
- Read the page, moving your hand beneath the words as you read. Point out that the words start at the top of the page and end at the bottom of the page.

Practicing the Lesson

- Encourage the children to pretend to read a book to a baby doll or stuffed animal in the Dramatic Play Center. Have them move their fingers under the words of their book. Watch to see that they are moving their fingers from the top to the bottom of the pages.
- Give the children red, yellow, and blue blocks. Challenge them to stack the blocks with four blue blocks on the bottom, four yellow blocks in the middle, and four red blocks on the top.

Reflecting on the Lesson

Ask the children:
- *Which color is on the top of a traffic light? Which color is on the bottom?*
- *If you stand on your head, which part of your body is on the top and which part is on the bottom?*

Special Needs Adaptations

Special Need	Adaptation
Visual Impairments	■ Remember to select a book that has large enough print for the child to see, or give the child a copy of the book to place in front of him so he can easily distinguish between the top and the bottom of the page.
Hearing Impairments	■ When you show the child the top of the page or paragraph, use your finger or another pointer to demonstrate "top" and "bottom" for the child. Select another item in the room and ask the child to show you the top and the bottom.
Cognitive Challenges	■ Use a book with only a few words on the page. Point to the word at the top and say, "top." Then, point to the word at the bottom and say, "bottom." Even if the child can identify the top and bottom of a common object, such as the top of a box and the bottom of a box, he still may not understand concepts such as the top or the bottom of a page. Take the child's hand and place it on the word at the top of the page and say, "top." Do this again with the words at the bottom of the page. *Block play provides opportunities to develop an understanding of spatial relationships.*
Motor Delays	■ If the child cannot move well enough to do the movements in the song, encourage him to participate partially. Even if he approximates touching the right part, he will feel like he is part of the group.
Speech/ Language Delays	■ Make sure the child understands all the words used in this lesson, such as "top" and "bottom." If the child has a severe language delay, he may not understand the concepts of "top" and "bottom." Collect several common objects from around the room and place them with the book. Review the meanings of "top" and "bottom," using the book as well as the objects you have collected. Look for opportunities throughout the day to show the child "top" and "bottom."
Emotional/ Behavior Issues	■ If the child does not want to do the "Head, Shoulders, Knees, and Toes" song with the other children, let him stand apart from the group and watch. Some children become very anxious in a crowd.

Spatial relationships

Children will:

- understand that print moves from left to right.

Vocabulary

left
move
print
right

Materials

beanbag
children's favorite book,
    preferably a big book
magnetic letters
masking tape
red ribbon

Left to Right

Introducing and Developing the Lesson

❏ Tie a red ribbon around children's right arms. Dance the "Hokey Pokey."

❏ Tell the children that they will be learning about how to move from left to right when reading.

❏ Select one of the children's favorite story books, preferably a big book.

❏ Ask for a volunteer to show you the first word on the page. Say, "This is the left side of the page. When I read this story to you I will begin with this word and then I will move to the next word. The next word is to the right of this word. When you read you follow the words from left to right."

❏ Read the book, moving your hand under the words from left to right.

❏ Use masking tape to make large squares on the floor. Invite the children to hop around the squares, moving from left to right.

Practicing the Lesson

❏ Have the children sit on the floor in a row. Give them a beanbag to pass down the row from left to right.

❏ Provide magnetic letters and encourage the children to use the letters to spell their names. Point out that they are arranging the letters from left to right.

Reflecting on the Lesson

Ask the children:

❏ *When you spell your name with magnetic letters, how do you arrange the letters?*

❏ *Which hand is your left hand?*

Special Needs Adaptations

Special Need	Adaptation
Visual Impairments	<ul><li>Whether the child will ultimately learn to read independently or use adaptive devices such as page-readers or magnifiers, it is important that the child learn the concept of left to right.</li><li>Orient the child to the concept by standing behind him and gently touching his right hand or arm and saying "right." Repeat the process with his left hand.</li><li>Use brightly colored tape for the masking tape squares so the child can easily see where he is to move.</li></ul>
Hearing Impairments	<ul><li>Make sure the child can see you as you demonstrate the "Hokey Pokey." It may be necessary to have a "dress rehearsal" to help the child understand how to participate. It is easier for children with hearing impairments to participate when activities are presented in a small group.</li></ul>
Cognitive Challenges	<ul><li>Learning left and right is an important concept. However, it may not be a concept that the child learns easily. It is okay to teach him to make an "L" with the fingers of his left hand so he can easily identify left and right.</li><li>Another way to help the child practice is to write an L on the top of the child's left hand and an R on the top of his right hand.</li><li>Look for opportunities throughout the day for the child to practice identifying his left and his right.</li></ul>
Motor Delays	<ul><li>If the child cannot dance the "Hokey Pokey," let him be the "dance master" and turn the music on and off.</li></ul>
Speech/ Language Issues	<ul><li>Use the same techniques described above in cognitive challenges.</li></ul>
Emotional/ Behavior Delays	<ul><li>Invite the child to select the big book that you read. Research shows that using a preferred object or story holds a child's interest longer than using a story that is unfamiliar to the child.</li></ul>

Allowing a child to hold a preferred object, such as a blanket, relaxes the child so he will participate.

Following Print

Children will:

- understand that print is read from top to bottom and left to right.

Vocabulary

bottom	move	right
left	print	top

Materials

bulletin board paper

chart paper

flashlight

lamination machine or clear
    contact paper

marker

nursery rhyme or other favorite
    rhyme

paper (9" x 12" white)

recorded book for the Listening
    Center

Preparation

Print a nursery rhyme or other favorite rhyme (see suggestions in the Appendix on pages 261–265) on chart paper. Print each of the words in "I'm a Bouncing Ball" (on the right) on a separate sheet of 9" x 12" paper. Laminate each sheet of paper.

Introducing and Developing the Lesson

- ❑ Read the nursery rhyme to the children, moving your hand beneath the words as you read. Tell the children that they will learn about the direction in which to read print in a book.
- ❑ Put the words to "I'm a Bouncing Ball" in order on the floor.

I'm a Bouncing Ball (author unknown)
I'm bouncing, bouncing everywhere.
I bounce and bounce into the air.
I'm bouncing, bouncing like a ball.
I bounce and bounce until I fall.

- ❑ Have the children sit below the rhyme, and then read the rhyme to the children. Ask for a volunteer to "bounce" (walk one word at a time) along the rhyme, as you read the words. Point out that the volunteer is bouncing from left to right and from the top row to the bottom row.
- ❑ Print the first two lines of "This Little Light of Mine" (see page 260 in the Appendix) in large letters on bulletin board paper.
- ❑ Put the paper on the floor, turn off the lights, and shine a flashlight on the words as you read them to the class.

Practicing the Lesson

- ❑ Provide a recording and book in the Listening Center. Encourage the children to move their fingers under the words as they listen to the story.
- ❑ Sing "Reader's Wiggle" (see page 258 in the Appendix) to the tune of the "Hokey Pokey" with the children.

Reflecting on the Lesson

Ask the children:

- ❑ *What would happen if we read books from back to front? Would the story be mixed up? What if the author wrote the book backward?*
- ❑ *In which direction do we read words when we read a book? Show me.*

Special Needs Adaptations

Special Need	Adaptation
Visual Impairments	■ Make an additional copy of the nursery rhyme you select for the children. Enlarge the copy and place it directly in front of the child or on a desk easel (see page 249 in the Appendix—Desk Easel) where the child can see it as you talk about it with the other children.
Hearing Impairments	■ Provide a picture cue to go with the nursery rhyme so the child will know which rhyme you are talking about when you read it to the class.
Cognitive Challenges	■ Sudden changes scare some children. Before turning out the lights, show and describe for the child what will happen. ■ Invite him to be your helper and turn out the lights before starting the activity.
Motor Delays	■ Adapt "Reader's Wiggle" (see page 258 in the Appendix) to include movements the child can do. For example, if the child cannot wiggle his fingers, perhaps he can hold his hand open like he is reading. It may be necessary to help the child position his hands for this activity.
Speech/ Language Delays	■ Bounce a ball with the child before starting the activity. Make sure the child is familiar with the word "bounce."
Emotional/ Behavior Issues	■ The child may be overwhelmed by turning out the lights. Be sure to tell the child before turning out the lights. ■ Some children become too stimulated by lots of movement. It may be necessary to introduce each movement in stages, such as reading one verse in the morning and the second verse later in the day.

Sight words

Family Names

Children will:
- recognize familiar words.

Vocabulary
read
recognize
words

Materials
butcher paper
chart paper
crayons
4" x 6" index cards
magnetic letters
paper
sentence strips or sheets of
  drawing paper

Preparation
Make Word Cards (words printed on 4" x 6" index cards) for family members, such as Mommy, Daddy, brother, and sister. Depending on the configuration of the families in your class, add such family names as aunt, Grandma, Grandpa, and so on.

Introducing and Developing the Lesson
- ❏ Print the children's names on sentence strips or sheets of drawing paper. Display a few of the children's names that you know the children will recognize and ask them to "read" the names. Tell the children that words we see frequently, such as our names, are words that we can learn to recognize quickly just by looking at them. These words are called sight words.
- ❏ Tell the children that they will learn to read some words that they see all the time.
- ❏ Print the words "Mommy," "Daddy," "sister," and "brother" on chart paper. Words can be shortened to Mom and Dad, if appropriate for your class.
- ❏ Be sensitive to the family configurations of the children in your class and use appropriate names to represent the children's unique family configurations.
- ❏ Discuss each word with the children. Ask for volunteers to name the letters in each word.
- ❏ Invite volunteers to use magnetic letters to copy the words.

Practicing the Lesson
- ❏ Suggest that the children draw a family portrait. Challenge them to label each person in their picture. If they are not able to form the letters, allow them to dictate the identity of each person to you.
- ❏ Provide chart paper with sight words written on it. Give the children magnetic letters to use to copy the words.
- ❏ Print "I love my _____" on butcher paper and put the paper on the floor. Encourage the children to fill in the blank with word cards and then read the sentence to you.

Reflecting on the Lesson
Ask the children:
- ❏ *What letter does "Mommy" start with?*
- ❏ *Are you a brother or sister? If so, what letter does your brother's or sister's name start with?*

Special Needs Adaptations

Special Need	Adaptation
Visual Impairments	■ Make sure you take into consideration the child's visual working distance from the paper. Be sure to use large markers or brightly colored paint that he can easily see.
Hearing Impairments	■ If the child is using sign language, teach the whole class the sign for "Mommy," "Daddy," "sister," and any other appropriate family member. (See page 252 in the Appendix—Signs.)
Cognitive Challenges	■ Check with the child's family and find out what terms they use with the child for "Mommy," "Daddy," and so on. It will help if you use those same terms when you refer to members of the child's family.
Motor Delays	■ It may be easier for the child to draw his family picture independently if the paper is taped to a table. Use adapted crayons or markers (see page 248 in the Appendix—Art Supplies), so the child can easily pick them up.
Speech/ Language Delays	■ After the child has drawn his family picture, talk about it in detail with him. Ask him to tell you what each family member likes to eat, what they watch on TV, or what type of work they do.
Emotional/ Behavior Issues	■ If the child's emotional or behavior issues are a direct result of things the child has experienced at home, the child may not want to draw a picture of his family. If that is the case, suggest that he draw a picture of his "school family" (you and the class) or a picture of someone he likes to spend time with. ■ Children who are removed from their homes may be with grandparents or aunts and uncles. The child may want to draw a picture of the people he lives with.

Signing "mother" is one way to communicate the names of family members.

Color Words

Children will:
- recognize color words.

Vocabulary
black
blue
green
orange
purple
red
white
yellow

Materials
basket of colorful beads, buttons, or small blocks
chart paper
crayons or markers to match color words
I Love Colors by Margaret Miller or *Is It Red? Is It Yellow? Is It Blue?* by Tana Hoban
index cards—4" x 6"
margarine or ice cream tubs
tracing paper

Preparation
Make color word cards by printing color words on 4" x 6" index cards using the color of crayon or marker that represents the color word you are printing (print "red" using a red marker, and so on).

Introducing and Developing the Lesson

- Print the color words on chart paper using a matching marker to write the word. Read each word and discuss the letters in the words. What does the word start with? How many letters does it have? Which word has the least number of letters?
- Tell the children that they will be learning to read color names.
- Show the children the index cards with the color words written on them (see Preparation). Give the children crayons (to match the words) and tracing paper; encourage them to copy the words using the appropriate color.
- Provide a basket of colorful beads, buttons, or small blocks. Print color words on the sides of margarine or ice cream tubs. Invite the children to sort the beads, buttons, or blocks into the appropriate container.

Practicing the Lesson

- Have the children sort by color clothing items in the Dramatic Play Center and/or crayons in the Art Center.
- Place *I Love Colors* by Margaret Miller or *Is It Red? Is It Yellow? Is It Blue?* by Tana Hoban in the Library Center. Encourage the children to find the color words.

Reflecting on the Lesson

Ask the children:
- *Which color is your favorite? How do you spell it?*
- *Which color words start with the letter B? Which color words have two letters that are the same letter side by side in their names?*

Special Needs Adaptations

Special Need	Adaptation
Visual Impairments	■ To help the child focus on the index cards, begin with two cards. Make sure the color words are written boldly on each card. Hold the cards at an equal distance from the child's face. Say the name of the first color card, wiggle it slightly, and wait. Make sure the child has directed his focus toward that card and then say the name again. Repeat the same procedure with the second card.
Hearing Impairments	■ Go over each color word with the child. When you say the word, show him a piece of paper that is the same color as the word you are talking about.
Cognitive Challenges	■ Adapt the activity by selecting only two or three words for the child to work with. ■ It will be overwhelming if there are more than two or three colors represented in the basket of items you ask the child to sort.
Motor Delays	■ Select items to sort that are easily picked up by the child. Make sure he sorts the items into containers such as a box or industrial-size food can that have large openings.
Speech/ Language Delays	■ Go on a color walk with the child. Select a color, walk around the room with the child, and ask him to show you an object in that color. If the child is able, ask him to use the name of the object in a sentence. If he does not have enough language, help him by making up the sentence and then asking him to repeat each word after you say it.
Emotional/ Behavior Issues	■ Select the child's favorite color and ask him to show you some things in the classroom that are that color. Next, try a color he is less familiar with and repeat the activity. ■ If the child is hesitant to participate in the color-sorting activity with a group, ask him to try it by himself. Many children with autism prefer to work alone. While this may not be possible all the time, try to vary some activities to allow the child opportunities to work by himself.

Labels

Children will:

- understand that the names of all items have a written form.

Vocabulary

letters
names
words
written

Materials

box to hold index cards
cards—three small (the size of
    business cards) for each child
4" x 6" index cards
poster board, tag board, or
    cardstock
school supply catalogs

Preparation

Create a box of cards that are labels for classroom items, such as *door, window, table, chair,* and so on (4" x 6" index cards work well). Make business-size cards by cutting poster board, tag board, or cardstock to the size of business cards. Make enough to give each child three cards.

Introducing and Developing the Lesson

❏ Point out some of the labels that occur naturally in the classroom, such as the exit sign by the door, the letters that mark the faucets in the sink, or center signs. Explain that everything has a written form that identifies it. Tell the children that they will be labeling items in the classroom.

❏ Show the children the box of classroom labels. Explain that there are labels (or signs) in the box that can be used to identify things in the classroom. Pull out a few labels and read them to the children. Explain that everything has a written form that names or describes it. Show the children where to place the labels in the classroom that you are using as examples.

❏ Ask the children what thing in the room they would like to have a written label, and, with the help of the children, label three things in the classroom. **Note:** Do not label more than three things because there will be too many labels and children will be overwhelmed. After a few days, remove the labels and, with the help of the children, label three new things in the room.

❏ Give each child three small business-card-size cards. Help them print their name on the cards. Allow the children to use the cards to label their cubby and their seat in the circle. Have them place the third card in a box in the Writing Center so other children can use the card as a model when writing.

Practicing the Lesson

❏ Invite the children to help you label the block shelf by tracing block shapes onto tag board and then placing the tracing on the block shelf to indicate where the blocks go on the shelf.

❏ Suggest that the children look through school supply catalogs for pictures of items in the Manipulatives Center. Have the children cut the photos out of the catalog and glue them on index cards to label the shelves in the Manipulatives Center.

Reflecting on the Lesson

Ask the children:

❏ *Is there a written word for "door"?*

❏ *Is there a written word for you? What is it?*

Special Needs Adaptations

Special Need	Adaptation
Visual Impairments	■ Provide extra information about things that are to be labeled. For example, if you hold up the word label for *door* you might say, "We open and close the *door* (hold up label) when we go outside."
Hearing Impairments	■ Provide a picture clue to go with some of the labels, such as a picture of a block on the label that says "Block Center."
Cognitive Challenges	■ Children with cognitive challenges need consistency in the words they hear. Make sure you use the same word each time. For example, do not use "bathroom," "restroom," and "potty" interchangeably. Use the same word each time you refer to the Book Center. Calling it the "Book Center," "Library Center," and "Reading Center" will be confusing to the child.
Motor Delays	■ As you and the children label the three items in the class, use this opportunity to do an environmental check for children with motor delays. Are materials easy to reach even if the child is in a wheelchair? Is the environment arranged so there is enough room for a child on a walker to move from place to place? Are the labels you are using placed in a position so all children can see them?
Speech/ Language Delays	■ When the child labels his cubby with his name card, see if he can name the objects in his cubby. Invite him to use the object names in a sentence. ■ If he can't name the items, ask him questions such as, "What do you wear when it's cold outside?" Look at or point to the child's coat.
Emotional/ Behavior Issues	■ Let the child select the color marker he will use to make his name labels. Remember some children are highly sensitive to smells. Markers that have an odor such as lemon or grape may be irritating to him.

Word Banks

Children will:
- recognize favorite words.

Vocabulary

cards
favorite
names
word bank
words

Materials

chart paper
crayons
hole punch
index cards, five 3" x 5" cards for
    each child
loose-leaf book rings
magnetic letters
markers
paper
word box

Preparation

Make a Word Bank for each child. Punch a hole in five 3" x 5" index cards. Put each five-card set on a loose-leaf book ring and write one child's name on the first card of a set. Punch holes in additional blank cards and store them in a word box. Over time, the children will add many words to their Word Banks.

Introducing and Developing the Lesson

- ❑ Ask for a volunteer to provide a word that he would like to see written. Write the word on chart paper. Ask a second and third volunteer to suggest words. Remind the children that all things have a written form—any word that we say can also be written. Tell the children that they will be learning to recognize important words.
- ❑ Give each child their Word Bank. Tell the children that the words in their Word Banks will be words that are of interest to them. Ask a volunteer to suggest a word he would like to learn how to read. Print the word with a marker on a card in his ring. After you write the word on one of his cards, show the word to all the children. Do the same for a couple of other children.
- ❑ Tell the children that you will help each one write a word for their Word Banks during center time.
- ❑ Explain that you will add a new word to each child's bank each day, so each day the children should think about a word they would like to learn to read. Tell the children that they will soon have many words in their Word Banks. Suggest that the children illustrate the words they have selected for their Word Banks.

Practicing the Lesson

- ❑ Provide magnetic letters. Have the children use the letters to copy the word(s) in their Word Banks. As time goes by, the words will accumulate and the children will have many words they can copy.
- ❑ Play games with the cards in the Word Banks. When the children have a few words on their rings (in their banks), encourage them to try to make sentences using their words. This will be easier to do when the children begin to add verbs, such as "like" and "is."

Reflecting on the Lesson

Ask the children:
- ❑ *Which word did you add to your Word Bank today? Are you thinking about a word for tomorrow?*
- ❑ *How are Word Banks like real banks?*

Special Needs Adaptations

Special Need	Adaptation
Visual Impairments	■ If the child has residual or partial vision, remember to provide information that involves other senses as well (touch, smell, hearing). As you add a word to his word bank, invite him to say the word with you. Provide magnetic letters so he can feel each letter as you write the word.
Hearing Impairments	■ If the child is using sign language, add a picture of how to make the sign on each of his cards. Use both the spoken and sign language word when using the words in the bank. The picture will remind you how to make the sign when you are working with the child.
Cognitive Challenges	■ Select words for the child's word bank that will be functional (useful) for the child. It is very hard for a child with cognitive challenges to learn to identify words, and often it takes a lot of time and practice. So, it is important that the words on his cards are words he will use throughout his life such as "on" "off," "stop," "exit," "restroom," "food," and so on.
Motor Delays	■ Use larger cards made of heavy cardstock material, because they will be easier for the child to manipulate and hold. If necessary, separate the cards by placing a dot of hot glue at the top right hand corner of each card. Allow the dot to cool before adding a dot to the next card. This separates the cards slightly, making it easier for the child to turn them.
Speech/ Challenges Delays	■ When the child adds a new word to his word bank, invite him to use it in a sentence. Continue to work with the child to encourage him to add descriptive words and make longer sentences.
Emotional/ Behavior Issues	■ Children with emotional/behavioral issues, especially those with autism spectrum disorder, will be more likely to participate in activities that are of interest to them personally. Even if the words the child wants written in his word bank don't make sense to you, they may have meaning to him. Remember, the focus of the activity is to help the child learn to recognize his favorite words.

Sight words

Environmental Print

Children will:

- recognize familiar words in the environment.

Vocabulary

environment
familiar
labels
logs
read
sight
signs

Materials

cups, napkins, and food
    containers from several fast
    food restaurants
familiar logos
glue
index cards, small
labels from food products or
    other items
picture of a stop sign

Preparation

Ask each child to bring a label
from something at home, such as
a fast food cup, a label from a
cereal box, or a candy wrapper.

Introducing and Developing the Lesson

- ❑ Show the children a picture of a stop sign. Ask what the sign says. When someone says "Stop," ask that child how he knows.
- ❑ Tell the children that they will be looking at print that is around all the time—words that we read by sight because we recognize their color, shape, pictures, and so on. Explain that this print is called environmental print.
- ❑ Explain that environmental print is all around us. It is on cereal boxes, fast food restaurants, candy wrappers, highway signs, building signs, and cans of food. Ask the children to think of similar examples inside the school, such as exit signs, the name of the school, words that label a fire extinguisher, and so on.
- ❑ Have each child show the label or wrapper he brought from home without saying what it is. Challenge the other children to read the label. How many items can they read without help?

Practicing the Lesson

- ❑ Make environmental print books. For example, a book of places the children like to eat, places they like to shop, food they enjoy, and so on. Invite children to look at the books in a small group or with a friend.
- ❑ Provide cups, napkins, and food containers from several fast food restaurants. Suggest that the children sort the items.

Reflecting on the Lesson

Ask the children:

- ❑ *Which restaurant is your favorite place to eat? What does the sign look like at this restaurant?*
- ❑ *What does a stop sign look like? When you see a stop sign, do you know what it says?*

Special Needs Adaptations

Special Need	Adaptation
Visual Impairments	■ Make sure that the pictures in the environmental print book the child uses are not too detailed. Do not be surprised if the child is not familiar with environmental print that other children easily recognize. Provide a magnifying glass or adaptive magnifier if the child needs one (see page 249 in the Appendix—Low-Vision Aids).
Hearing Impairments	■ Make sure the child is seated so he can see the environmental print wrappers that the other children show. Children with hearing impairments learn to depend on other senses for information, so it is important that they be able to see and touch items in the environment.
Cognitive Challenges	■ Help the child select words for his environmental print book that are useful and meaningful to him. Allow the child to take one of the environmental print books home so his family can refer to the book too.
Motor Delays	■ Make page turners (see page 251 in the Appendix—Motor Adaptations) for the environmental print books so the child can easily turn the pages.
Speech/ Language Delays	■ Ask the child's family to tell you where they like to eat or shop and use the information as you plan for the environmental print books or other environmental print activities.
Emotional/ Behavior Issues	■ Make sure parents or family members know that the child will be asked to bring a label from home. Invite them to help him select a label from a favorite food or restaurant.

Rebus Support

Children will:
- recognize that pictures can substitute for words when reading.

Vocabulary

pictures

read

rebus

substitute

words

Materials

chart paper

easel

ingredients for trail mix

marker

paint

paintbrushes

paper

rebus card for "Head, Shoulders, Knees, and Toes"

The Bag I'm Taking to Grandma's or *Our Class Took a Trip to the Zoo* by Shirley Neitzel

Preparation

Use the rebus art (see page 271 in the Appendix) to make a rebus chart of "Jack and Jill" on chart paper. Print the rhyme on another piece of chart paper. Use the rebus art with the print.

Introducing and Developing the Lesson

❏ Use the "Head, Shoulders, Knees, and Toes" rebus cards (see pages 269–270 in the Appendix) to help children sing the song. Explain to the children that they have just read—they read pictures, instead of words. When pictures substitute for words, it is called rebus.

❏ Tell the children that they will be using rebus pictures to help them read.

❏ Invite the children to help you read the rebus "Jack and Jill."

❏ Read the rhyme with the children. Remind them that the pictures are replacing words in the rhyme. Celebrate their reading of the rhyme.

❏ Read *The Bag I'm Taking to Grandma's* or *Our Class Took a Trip to the Zoo* by Shirley Neitzel with the children. They will be able to use the rebus clues to help you read the book.

Practicing the Lesson

❏ Provide a trail mix rebus recipe (see page 273 in the Appendix) and invite the children to use it to make their snack.

❏ Tell the children to use easel painting rebus directions (see page 272 in the Appendix) to create an easel painting.

Reflecting on the Lesson

Ask the children:

❏ *Do the pictures help you read the book?*

❏ *Someday, we will be able to take the pictures away and you will still be able to read the book. How will you read the book when the pictures are gone?*

Special Needs Adaptations

Special Need	Adaptation
Visual Impairments	■ Rebus cards can be great visual cues. Remember to enlarge and mount them so the child can easily see the cards.
Hearing Impairments	■ Using the visual cues provided by rebus cards can be very helpful for a child who has a hearing impairment. ■ If the child is using sign language, combine it with the rebus card while you say the rhyme.
Cognitive Challenges	■ Try making a rebus picture schedule (see directions for making a rebus picture schedule on page 251 in the Appendix—Picture Schedule) to use with the child throughout the day. This helps the child know what will happen next and makes it easier for him to make transitions.
Motor Delays	■ Children in a wheelchair, or those who use a walker, will need the rebus directions posted at eye level, which may be different from where you place it for children who are more mobile.
Speech/ Language Delays	■ Select a few of the rebus cards and ask the child questions about the object or item represented by the picture. See if the child will help you use that word in a sentence. If you can't understand what he is saying, try to interpret it and encourage him to keep trying. Turning away or finishing the word or sentence for the child reinforces his frustration and may decrease the likelihood of him speaking or participating in language activities.
Emotional/ Behavior Issues	■ Use this as an opportunity to practice "reading" as well as learning social skills. Make a few rebus cards depicting an important social skill, such as sharing with friends or waiting for your turn.

Sharing and cooperative play are important life skills for all children to learn.

Journals

Children will:
- understand that thoughts can be written.

Vocabulary
daily
date
illustrate
journals
thoughts
write

Materials
chart paper
crayons
markers
small notebooks, provided by
    families, if possible
pencils

Preparation
Ask families to provide a small
notebook for their child.

Introducing and Developing the Lesson

- ❏ Ask children to describe or talk about something that they did last night. Write their statements on chart paper. Tell the children that many people write their thoughts down every day. Some people write their thoughts in a book called a *journal* and others write their thoughts in a book called a *diary*.
- ❏ Tell the children that they are going to begin using a journal. Give each child a small notebook. Help the children print their names inside and on the outside of their books. Print the date on chart paper. Show the children where they are to copy the date into their journals. (If necessary, help children write the date.) Tell them that each day before they write, they will copy the date.
- ❏ Provide markers, crayons, and pencils. Now, have the children make an entry in their journals. If they are not yet writing, have them draw a picture of something that happened yesterday or something they are looking forward to today.
- ❏ Encourage the children to share their journal entries with each other.

Practicing the Lesson

- ❏ Suggest that the children decorate the covers of their journals.
- ❏ On occasion, allow children to take their journals home to share with their families. Suggest that families write in a family journal at home. Make a copy of the Writing Continuum (see page 286 in the Appendix) to send home along with the child's journal.

Reflecting on the Lesson

Ask the children:
- ❏ *What did you write in your journal today?*
- ❏ *Does anyone in your family write in a journal?*

Special Needs Adaptations

Special Need	Adaptation
Visual Impairments	■ The child may need a large notebook for his journal. If the child is unable to write the date, print it for him.
Hearing Impairments	■ Send a note home before beginning the journal activity. Ask the child's family specific questions about what the child does at home, where he goes, and who he plays with. ■ Ask the families if the child has a favorite book or game at home that he enjoys. This will help you encourage the child as he begins to learn about writing or drawing in a journal.
Cognitive Challenges	■ Print the date for the child at the top of the page. After the child draws a picture or tries to write in his journal, tell him "good job." Until the child begins to understand what you want him to do, it may be necessary to prompt him, such as saying, "Draw a picture of what you ate last night," or "Draw a picture of what you did when you got up this morning." ■ Ask parents and family members to help you identify some things the child enjoys so you can prompt him as he begins to write or draw in his journal. Later, he may be able to decide what to do without a prompt, but initially it is important that he begin to understand the concept and purpose behind writing in a journal.
Motor Delays	■ Give the child a desk or tabletop easel (see page 249 in the Appendix—Desk or Tabletop Easel) to use when writing or drawing in his journal. ■ Attach paper clips or clothespins to the paper in the journal to make it easier for a child with motor delays to participate in journal writing.
Speech/ Language Delays	■ After the child makes an entry in his journal, encourage him to tell you about it or describe it in more detail. When sharing an entry with a friend, be sure to use a peer buddy who will be patient with the child (see page 29 in the Introduction).
Emotional/ Behavior Issues	■ Because you want journal writing to be a pleasant experience for the child, allow him to write in his journal in a place in the room that is comfortable for him. Do not be surprised if the child crawls under a table or goes to the Quiet Center. It is very important that there be at least one place in the room where the lighting is indirect and noise is minimal.

Picture Dictionaries

Children will:
- increase sight word recognition.

Vocabulary
definitions
dictionary
pictures

Materials
crayons
drawing paper
picture dictionary
Word Cards

Preparation
Make several Word Cards for concrete objects in the classroom, such as blocks, crayons, beads, and books.

Introducing and Developing the Lesson

- ❏ Show children a picture dictionary. Point out how words and pictures go together. Tell the children that they will be making picture dictionaries.
- ❏ Create a three-dimensional picture dictionary. Place the Word Cards on the floor in a column. Place a corresponding concrete item beside each Word Card.
- ❏ Point out that the words can be easily read by looking at the picture beside them.
- ❏ Give each child a sheet of drawing paper. Have them fold their paper in half the long way—"hot dog bun" style.
- ❏ Ask each child to tell you five or six of their favorite words. Write each child's words in a column down the left side of their paper. Provide crayons and challenge the children to illustrate their favorite words on the right side of their paper, creating a picture dictionary of their favorite words.

Practicing the Lesson

- ❏ Suggest that the children use their picture dictionaries to practice copying some of their favorite words.
- ❏ Give the children the Word Cards and concrete objects and challenge them to match the words to the objects.
- ❏ Encourage the children to add new words to their picture dictionaries.

Reflecting on the Lesson

Ask the children:
- ❏ *How can you use your dictionary to help you write?*
- ❏ *Which word in your dictionary is your favorite?*

Special Needs Adaptations

Special Need	Adaptation
Visual Impairments	■ Rather than on the floor, place the items on a table. Write the word on the bottom half of the card and fold each card into a "tent card" that stands up. Place the item beside it or slightly to the right or left of the card. ■ When you say the word, hold up the word card and then hand the object to the child so he can touch it or hold it while you say the word.
Hearing Impairments	■ Use the same procedure listed above. Ask the child to repeat each word after you. If the child has severe hearing impairments, learn the sign language for each object and its word. Sign the word, and then hold up the object or hand the object to the child.
Cognitive Challenges	■ Select words that are functional and commonly used by the child such as "plate," "cup," "book," "ball," and "marker." ■ Hold the word card in one hand and the object in the other then put them down side by side.
Motor Delays	■ Fold the word cards in half and make them stand up to make the cards easier for the child to grasp and use.
Speech/ Language Delays	■ To build vocabulary, use a few words and items that the child is familiar with and one or two that will be new or novel for him. Invite him to repeat each word when you say it. Hand him the object, and then say the word again. Continue until you feel that he understands that the object name is written on the card.
Emotional/ Behavior Issues	■ Most children learn best with real objects rather than pictures. Encourage the child to hold the object as you show him the card with the name written on it. If he is willing, ask him to tell you the letter name of the first letter in the word.

Real objects, rather than pictures or photographs, help some children learn new words.

Written expression

Punctuation

Children will:

- recognize nonletter symbols in text.

Vocabulary

comma
exclamation mark
period
punctuation
question mark

Materials

big book
books
chart paper
enlarged copy from magazine ad
index cards—4" x 6"
lamination process
Letter Finder
marker
tray of sand
Wikki Stix™ or chenille wires
writing tools

Preparation

Photocopy, cut out, and laminate the Letter Finder (see page 274 in the Appendix). Print punctuation marks (comma, period, exclamation mark, and question mark) on 4" x 6" index cards.

Introducing and Developing the Lesson

- ❏ Write "What is today?" on chart paper. Circle the question mark. Ask the children if they know what the symbol means. Explain that there are several marks that appear in print that are not letters. Make an exclamation mark, comma, and period on the chart paper. Identify each mark as you make it. Tell the children that these marks are called *punctuation marks*. Tell the children that they will be learning about punctuation marks.
- ❏ Read a big book to the children. As punctuation marks appear in the text, show the children the corresponding punctuation mark on the cards you made. Ask for a volunteer to come to the book and show you the mark in the text, using the Letter Finder.
  Note: Do not stop for every period or every punctuation mark.
- ❏ Discuss the role of each punctuation mark as you come to them in the text. For example, a question mark signals a question. A comma divides text. A period signals the end of a sentence. An exclamation mark means that this word is said with excitement and emphasis.
- ❏ Place the chart paper with the punctuation marks in the Writing Center. Provide writing tools and suggest that the children copy the marks. For children who are not yet ready to hold a pen or pencil, provide a tray of sand and allow them to make the marks in the sand.
- ❏ Provide Wikki Stix or chenille wires for the children to use to make punctuation marks.

Practicing the Lesson

- ❏ Give the children Letter Finders and allow them to look through books searching for commas, periods, question marks, and exclamation marks.
- ❏ Provide enlarged copy from a magazine ad and challenge children to use a marker to circle punctuation marks.

Reflecting on the Lesson

Ask the children:

- ❏ *How do we know that a sentence has ended?*
- ❏ *How do we know that a sentence is a question?*

Special Needs Adaptations

Special Need	Adaptation
Visual Impairments	■ Provide the child with his own set of tactile punctuation cards. Encourage him to touch the comma when you talk about a comma or touch the question mark when you ask a question. If possible, use some craft foam to make punctuation mark cutouts for the child.
Hearing Impairments	■ Make sure the child understands the directions for using the Letter Finders or for circling punctuation marks. Model for him what to do before asking him to do it.
Cognitive Challenges	■ Begin by trying to teach the child to recognize and identify a question mark. It is important that children understand that a question mark comes at the end of question, and that when someone asks a question they usually want a response. ■ Ask the child simple questions, such as, "What is your name?" Hold up a cutout of a question mark when you ask him. Repeat using several other questions that you know he can answer. Hand the question mark to the child and see if he will ask you a question. Practice this activity frequently.
Motor Delays	■ Write "What is today?" on a piece of cardstock and place it on a cookie sheet in front of the child. ■ Use the uppercase letter O in your magnetic numbers and place it on the question mark to circle it while you describe it for the child. Help the child circle other punctuation marks as well.
Speech/ Language Delays	■ Use the same procedure described above under cognitive challenges. Start by asking the child easy questions and then ask a question that might be more difficult to answer. Encourage the child to ask his friends a question and remind him to wait for a response.
Emotional/ Behavior Issues	■ Participating in a conversation is an important social skill. Cut out a question mark and a period and paste each one on an index card. Select a peer buddy (see page 29 in the Introduction) and tell the child and his peer buddy that you are going to play a question-and-answer game with them. Explain that the child holding the question mark will ask a question, and the child holding the period will answer it. Model for them what you want them to do. Hold up the question mark and ask a question. Hand the period to the peer buddy. Invite the children to take turns asking and answering questions. Look for signs, such as body language, that tell you the child with emotional issues is tired of playing the game. Thank the child and the peer buddy for participating in the game.

Wordless Books

Children will:

- dictate text that accompanies pictures.

Vocabulary

pictures
sentences
story
words

Materials

book
crayons, markers, or pencils
drawing paper
glue
paper
photos from magazines
stick-on notes
wordless books, such as *Pancakes for Breakfast* by Tomie dePaola; or *Good Dog, Carl* by Alexandra Day

Introducing and Developing the Lesson

- ❑ Show the children the cover to a favorite book. Point out the title, author, and illustrator. Discuss the role of the author and the illustrator. Tell the children that they will be authors.
- ❑ Select a wordless book, such as *Pancakes for Breakfast* by Tomie dePaola, *Good Dog, Carl* by Alexandra Day, or *One Frog Too Many* by Mercer Mayer. Use stick-on notes at the bottom of book pages to create a space to write text to accompany the pictures in the book.
- ❑ If you don't have access to a wordless book, you can cover the text of a regular book with stick-on notes. Make sure that the book you select has simple and uncluttered illustrations.
- ❑ Turn to the first page of the book and invite the children to describe what is happening in the illustrations. Help them summarize their ideas to create text for the book. Print their text on the stick-on notes at the bottom of the page.
- ❑ Continue until every page has accompanying text. Read the book back to the children.

Practicing the Lesson

- ❑ Suggest that the children draw pictures of things they like to do and then have them dictate stories about their pictures. Gather all the children's pictures and stories into a class book. Place the class book in the Library Center so the children can "read" their stories. Fill the library with other wordless books and invite the children to create a stories to accompany the illustrations.
- ❑ Provide interesting photos from magazines. Encourage the children to select a photo, glue it to a sheet of drawing paper, and dictate a story about the photo for you to transcribe.
- ❑ Encourage children to bring a favorite photo from home. Ask them to tell you a story about their picture.

Reflecting on the Lesson

Ask the children:

- ❑ *How did you know which words to write on each page of your book?*
- ❑ *Do you like the book better with or without words?*

Special Needs Adaptations

Special Need	Adaptation
Visual Impairments	■ Make sure the wordless books you create or use are large enough to for the child to see and that they are placed at an angle optimal for his field of vision. Remember to use a book light or adaptive magnification device if it will help the child see the book more easily (see page 249 in the Appendix—Low-Vision Aids).
Hearing Impairments	■ When you read the wordless book back to the child, make sure the child is seated so he can see your face as you read. ■ Pointing to the pictures in the story may serve as a clue to the child about what is happening.
Cognitive Challenges	■ Use this activity as an opportunity to make a functional self-help book for the child to follow. Select a self-help skill, (sometimes referred to as functional skill) that the child is just learning, for example, washing hands, going to the bathroom, participating in a group activity, and so on.
Motor Delays	■ Provide the child with his own copy of the wordless book. Make sure it placed at an angle that is easy for him to see.
Speech/ Language Delays	■ Talk about what the children write for the wordless book texts. Ask the child to name objects on the page and use each one in a sentence. Remember to model sentences with descriptive words such as color names, "size," "shape," and so on.
Emotional/ Behavior Issues	■ Select a picture that depicts a social skill you want the child to learn, such as a picture of a child sharing a toy with another child.

Books That Support Print Awareness

Dear Mr. Blueberry by Simon James

Don't Let the Pigeon Drive the Bus! by Mo Willems

Extraordinary Friends by Fred Rogers *

Flop Ear by Guido Van Genechten *

Hey Pancakes! by Tamson Weston

Hurray for Pre-k by Ellen B. Senisi

I Love You: A Rebus Poem by Jean Marzollo

Mama Zooms by Janice Corwin Fletcher *

Nonsense! by Sally Kahler Phillips

The Pigeon Has Feelings Too by Mo Willems

Books About Spatial Relationships

The Cat in the Hat by Dr. Seuss

A Fish Out of Water by Helen Palmer

Flower Garden by Eve Bunting

Green Eggs and Ham by Dr. Seuss

Inside, Outside, Upside Down by Jan and Stan
    Berenstain

On Top of Spaghetti by Paul Brett Johnson

Rolling Along with Goldilocks and the Three Bears by
    Cindy Meyers *

Rosie's Walk by Pat Hutchins

Wacky Wednesday by Dr. Seuss

We Go in a Circle by Peggy Perry Anderson *

Where's Chimpy? by Berniece Rabe *

* Denotes books featuring children with special
    needs

Chapter 6

Comprehension

Overview

Comprehension is the internalization of story. It occurs when children have an opportunity to retell stories in their own words, act out stories, and listen to stories that are not accompanied by illustrations. Comprehension occurs as children make the story their own.

Comprehension is enhanced when children use higher-level thinking skills; make applications, conduct analyses, experiment with synthesis, and make evaluations. Activities and questions should encourage these skills.

Children who understand concepts authors use to create stories will use their story language to predict story events and cognitively organize story ideas while listening to stories and involving themselves in the storyline. This strengthens their comprehension of stories while listening. In addition, understanding how authors describe settings, develop characters, and organize the storyline helps young children craft their own stories.

Because children with special needs often do not have the same internalization skills as their peers, it is important that teachers look for ways to help them involve themselves in the storyline. Short attention-spans often interfere with developing critical listening skills. In addition, a child with limited language repertoire will need implicit instructions and will need multiple opportunities to understand what words mean and how they are used in context. Because comprehension involves both seeing pictures and words and hearing what they are, it is especially important that children with vision or hearing loss receive specialized instruction. Stories and activities should be adapted in a way that these children can understand, so that they have the same opportunities to learn comprehension.

Comprehension

Story Sequence

Children will:

- retell a story in own words.

Vocabulary

retell
sequence
story
words

Materials

chart paper
crayons
drawing paper
lamination process
scissors
sequence cards to other stories or
    activities

Preparation

Photocopy the Three Bears
Sequence Cards (see pages
275–276 in the Appendix). Color
them, cut them out, and laminate
them.

Introducing and Developing the Lesson

- ❑ Sing "Itsy Bitsy Spider" (see page 258 in the Appendix) with the children. Discuss the events in the song. What happens first, next, and last? What is the sequence of the story in the song?
- ❑ Tell the children that they will be practicing telling stories in their own words.
- ❑ Read or tell the children the story of "The Three Bears." Discuss the sequence of the story. List the major events on chart paper as the children relate them.
- ❑ Point out that the events of the story are what hold the story together. The sequence of events in a story allows us to retell the story accurately.
- ❑ Give the children the Three Bears Sequence Cards (see pages 275–276 in the Appendix). Have them place the cards in the correct sequence and use the cards to retell the story.

Practicing the Lesson

- ❑ Fold a sheet of drawing paper to create a six-square grid. Invite the children to draw pictures of things that happened in the story, starting at the square at the top left of their paper and working down to the last square on the bottom right. Have the children use their drawings to retell the story.
- ❑ Provide sequence cards to other stories or activities and ask the children to place the story or event in the correct sequence. Ask children to use the cards to retell the story or event.

Reflecting on the Lesson

Ask the children:

- ❑ *What is the first thing that happened in the story of the three bears?*
- ❑ *What happened after Goldilocks fell asleep?*

Special Needs Adaptations

Choosing when and where to retell a story can help children participate in storytelling.

Special Need	Adaptation
Visual Impairments	■ To help the child understand the activity more fully, read or tell her the story of "The Three Bears" before starting this activity.
Hearing Impairments	■ Put a Velcro strip on the back of each sequence card and attach them, in order, on a carpet square in front of the child. She can refer to the cards as you tell or read the story.
Cognitive Challenges	■ Work with the child when she tries to place the sequence cards in order. Place one, and then ask her to place the second card. Repeat this process until they are sequenced correctly. Remember to reinforce the concepts of first, next, and last.
Motor Delays	■ Instead of the traditional story of "The Three Bears," read *Rolling Along With Goldilocks and the Three Bears* by Cindy Meyers. It is the same story, but baby bear is in a wheelchair and goes to physical therapy.
Speech/ Language Delays	■ After the child has placed the sequence cards in the correct order, ask her to tell you about each one. Encourage her to retell the story using the sequence cards as a guide.
Emotional/ Behavior Issues	■ Use the story of "The Three Bears" to talk about the concept of respecting the property of others. Talk about the importance of never going into someone's home when they are not there. Ask the child if she can think of other things that Goldilocks did in the story that children should not do.

Thinking Questions

Children will:

- answer questions that require higher-level thinking skills.

Vocabulary

part
questions
thinking

Materials

another story version of "The Little Red Hen"
crayons
drawing paper
pencils
writing paper

Introducing and Developing the Lesson

- ❏ Sing "The Little Red Hen" (see page 258 in the Appendix) with the children. Tell the children that they will be practicing answering questions that make them think.

- ❏ Read the story of "The Little Red Hen" (many versions available). After the story, ask the children questions that require higher-level thinking. Do not ask more than one question after each reading. Each time you read the story, ask questions from a different level of thinking. Asking too many questions at the end of a story can squelch the joy of the story.

  - **Analysis** (taking information apart): The story has several parts. The first part is about the little hen finding a few grains of wheat. Let's talk about some of the other parts of the story.
    - How is the part of the story about the hen baking the bread different from the part about the hen eating the bread?

  - **Synthesis** (putting information together in a new way): Let's see how changing one part of the story might make the story different.
    - What if the dog said, "I am happy to help you"? How would the story be different?

  - **Evaluation** (critical judgment): Let's see what you thought about the story.
    - If you could choose to be any character in the story, who would you choose? Why?

Practicing the Lesson

- ❏ Encourage each child to draw her favorite character in the story. Ask her why she liked this character best.

- ❏ Read another version of the story. Compare the characters, setting, and plot. Which things are alike in both stories? Which things are different?

Reflecting on the Lesson

Ask the children:

- ❏ *Why did the hen decide not to share her bread? What would you have done?*

- ❏ *Why do you think the animals refused to help?*

Special Needs Adaptations

Special Need	Adaptation
Visual Impairments	■ Read the story to the child before you introduce the song, because this will help her understand why you are singing about a clever hen.
Hearing Impairments	■ Draw a circle and place a question mark inside the circle. Cut out the circle. Explain to the child that when you hold up the question mark you will be asking a question. This gives the child cues about what you will be asking her.
Cognitive Challenges	■ Ask the child questions about the story itself. For example, "What did the hen do first?" and so on.
Motor Delays	■ The child should be able to participate without special adaptations as long as the child is seated comfortably and can see you as you read the story and ask the questions.
Speech/ Language Delays	■ There may be words in the song, such as "wheat," "clever," and "barnyard," that the child does not know. Go over these words and talk about what they mean before introducing the song.
Emotional/ Behavior Issues	■ Talk to the child about why it is important to share, even if we don't want to. ■ Ask the child how the animals might feel if the hen had shared the bread.

Comprehension

Retelling Stories

Children will:

- retell stories in their own words.

Vocabulary

puppets
retell
story

Materials

craft sticks
crayons
lamination process
paper
scissors
story props (a basket of goodies, a red cap, and so on)

Preparation

Make Stick Puppets. Photocopy Little Red Riding Hood characters (Red Riding Hood, Wolf, and Grandmother) from patterns (see page 279 in the Appendix). Color the characters, cut them out, and laminate them. Attach the characters to craft sticks to create stick puppets.

Introducing and Developing the Lesson

- ❑ Ask children to tell about something that happened to them yesterday after school. If they cannot think of a story, tell them one of yours. Discuss telling stories in our own words. Tell the children that they will practice telling stories in their own words.
- ❑ Use the Little Red Riding Hood Stick Puppets to tell the story of "Little Red Riding Hood" (many versions available). Ask questions at the end of the story:
  - ▪ Where was Little Red Riding Hood going?
  - ▪ Which parts of the story could really happen?
  - ▪ Which parts of the story are make-believe?
  - ▪ How would the story be different if the wolf had gotten lost on the way to Grandmother's house?
  - ▪ How would the story be different if Little Red Riding Hood had not talked to a stranger?
- ❑ Reinforce the concepts of *first, next,* and *last* by talking about the sequence of events in the story. For children who are having trouble talking about the story, ask directed questions, such as "After Goldilocks left home, where did she walk?" "Who did she talk to?"

Practicing the Lesson

- ❑ Place the props in the Language Center. Encourage the children to use the props to retell the story.
- ❑ Invite the children to retell the story using the Little Red Riding Hood Stick Puppets.

Reflecting on the Lesson

Ask the children:
- ❑ *What rule should Little Red Riding Hood have followed?*
- ❑ *Why was the wolf not able to catch Little Red Riding Hood?*

Special Needs Adaptations

Special Need	Adaptation
Visual Impairments	■ Make sure the stick puppets are brightly colored but do not have too much detail. Because children with special needs are easy victims for strangers, reinforce the rules about Stranger Danger (see page 253 in the Appendix).
Hearing Impairments	■ Hold each flannel board piece up so the child can see it as you tell the story.
Cognitive Challenges	■ Talk to the child about the importance of following rules. Review with the child what to do if she is lost. If the child does not already have an identification card, make one for her (see page 249 in the Appendix). Practice using the card with the child when someone asks her name. ■ Discuss Stranger Danger (see page 253 in the Appendix). Remind the child what to do if she is concerned.
Motor Delays	■ A child with limited motor skills will need extra time to tell about a story or event. If the child has significant motor delays, ask her family to send an object to school that represents a favorite family activity, such as a picture from a family trip or a family birthday party. Invite the child to hold the picture while you describe what is happening.
Speech/ Language Delays	■ Ask the child to describe for you some of the details from the story, such as "What did Red Riding Hood wear?" or "Where was she going?" Wait, and give the child an opportunity to answer. If the child can't answer the question, provide a cue to help her.
Emotional/ Behavior Issues	■ Invite the child to tell you her favorite story in her own words. If the child is hesitant, ask her to tell you about her favorite TV show or movie. Remind the child about talking to strangers and about respecting the property of others (see page 253 in the Appendix—Stranger Danger).

Actor's Theater

Children will:
- retell the story.

Vocabulary

characters

props

re-enact

role play

traipsing

Materials

blocks

crayons

glue

scissors

"The Three Billy Goats Gruff"
    (many versions available)

tongue depressors or craft sticks

Preparation

Make Three Billy Goats Gruff Puppets (see page 277 in the Appendix). Photocopy the patterns. Color them, cut them out, and glue them to tongue depressors or craft sticks, to make stick puppets.

Introducing and Developing the Lesson

❏ Explain to the children that they will be learning how to be actors in a play about the Three Billy Goats Gruff.

❏ Read or tell the children the story of "The Three Billy Goats Gruff" (many versions available). Invite the children to re-enact the story. Ask for volunteers to play the roles of each character in the story.

❏ Suggest that the children to use Three Billy Goats Gruff Puppets (see page 277 in the Appendix) to re-enact the story.

Practicing the Lesson

❏ Suggest that the children build a bridge with the large blocks in the Block Center and use it to re-enact the story.

❏ After the children have re-enacted the story, encourage them to play Who Is Traipsing on My Bridge? using the same block bridge. Select one child to be the troll. Have the troll sit with her back to the bridge and her eyes closed. Select a child to walk across the bridge and say, "Trip, trap, trip, trap" as she walks. Have the troll respond with the verse shown below and then name the child who is traipsing, just by listening to the voice. Give the troll three chances to name the correct child. If she names the trespasser, she becomes one of the group and the trespasser child will take her place. If she fails to name the trespasser, she will play the part of the troll again.

Who Is Traipsing on My Bridge? by Pam Schiller

Who is traipsing on my bridge?
Trip, trap, trip, trap! Get off my bridge!
No one should be traipsing there.
Get off! Get off! Don't you dare.

Reflecting on the Lesson

Ask the children:

❏ *Do you think it is okay that the small Billy Goat and the middle-sized Billy Goat told the troll to wait for their brother? Why, or why not?*

❏ *How would the story of "The Three Billy Goats Gruff" be different if the troll had said, "Glad to see you! Come on across my bridge"?*

Special Needs Adaptations

Special Need	Adaptation
Visual Impairments	■ Review the story with the child. Tell her the story one-on-one.
Hearing Impairments	■ Use the goat puppets when you tell the story, because the puppets will help the child know more about what is happening in the story.
Cognitive Challenges	■ Give the child one of the goat puppets and ask her to use it to make a sentence about a goat.
Motor Delays	■ If the child cannot participate in the making a bridge in the Block Center, invite her to be the construction foreman who supervises the workers as they build the bridge.
Speech/ Language Delays	■ "Role play," "re-enact," "props," and "traipsing" are words that the child may not know. Talk about each one with the child and demonstrate the meaning of each word with an action, such as walking when you talk about the word "traipsing." Say a word and ask the child to tell you, in her own words, what it means.
Emotional/ Behavior Issues	■ Many children have difficulty talking about their feelings. Use this activity to ask the child how she thinks the characters might have felt. For example, "Do you think the smallest goat was scared?" "How do you think the troll felt when she was telling the goats they couldn't cross?"

Writes, Rewrites, and Continued Stories

Introducing and Developing the Lesson

❏ Sing "Down by the Bay" (see page 256 in the Appendix). Ask the children to help write a new verse for the song.

❏ Tell the children that they will be writing a story.

❏ Read a story that has a predictable format, such as *Brown Bear, Brown Bear, What Do You See?* by Bill Martin, Jr., or one with an ending that suggests a follow-up story, such as *Imogene's Antlers* by David Small.

❏ After finishing the story, discuss the story framework. Help the children write a group story that has the same predictable pattern *(Brown Bear)* as the original story or is a continuation of the original story *(Imogene's Antlers*—what will it be like to work and play with a peacock tail).

❏ Encourage the children to draw a picture that illustrates a continuation of the story or a new ending for the story.

Practicing the Lesson

❏ Give the children a topic and invite them to write a group story. Some possible titles include "The Frog on our Playground," "The Best Toy in our Room," and "Our Favorite Snack."

❏ Suggest that the children write or dictate a note to a character in the story.

Reflecting on the Lesson

Ask the children:

❏ *Did you like the story we wrote? Which part is your favorite?*

❏ *If you were going to write a second book about* Goldilocks and the Three Bears, *what would it be about?*

Children will:

■ understand story format.

Vocabulary

bay
dare not
jig
new
polka dot
rewrite
story

Materials

Brown Bear, Brown Bear, What Do You See? by Bill Martin, Jr. or *Imogene's Antlers* by David Small
crayons
drawing paper
pencils
writing paper

Special Needs Adaptations

Special Need	Adaptation
Visual Impairments	■ Select a topic for the group story that is easy to identify. For example, if the children write a story about a frog, show the child a picture of a frog. If possible, hand the child a stuffed frog so she understands the story is about a frog.
Hearing Impairments	■ Give the child a copy of the book you chose to read to the class. Encourage the child to follow along as you read, looking at the pictures as you tell the story.
Cognitive Challenges	■ Select one of the child's favorite stories, read it to her, and then ask her questions about the story. When the class begins to write a group story, invite the child to work with a friend when it is her turn.
Motor Delays	■ Instead of drawing a picture that is a continuation of the story, ask the child to tell you aloud how she thinks the story should continue. Ask a peer buddy to help her draw a picture for the class story.
Speech/ Language Delays	■ Look for words in the song that may be unfamiliar to the child, such as "bay," "jig," and "polka dot." Try to find a picture that goes with each word. Show the child the picture and talk about these rare words, before introducing the song.
Emotional/ Behavior Issues	■ The child may be more likely to want to add to a story that is a personal favorite. When writing a class story on a teacher-selected topic, remember that many children will respond better to concrete topics, such as *The Case of the Missing Cookies in the Lunch Room* by Connie Gatlin rather than magic or pretend stories, such as *The Cat in the Hat* by Dr. Seuss.

Venn Diagram

Children will:
- make comparisons.

Vocabulary

alike
author
characters
differences
different
illustrator
similarities
title

Materials

The Mitten; one version by Alvin Tresselt and a second version by Jan Brett

clothes for sorting (boys, girls, and both; or winter, summer, and so on)

glove

Hula Hoops™, masking tape, or yarn

mitten

sentence strips

marker

Introducing and Developing the Lesson

- ❑ Show the children a mitten and a glove. Ask them how the two things are alike and how they are different. Tell the children that you will be practicing making comparisons.
- ❑ Read two versions of *The Mitten*. There are many versions available, including two excellent variations, one by Alvin Tresselt and another by Jan Brett.
- ❑ Help the children make comparisons between the two books. Use Hula Hoops to create a Venn diagram, to represent similarities and differences (a sample Venn diagram is on page 283). **Note:** If Hula Hoops are not available, use masking tape or yarn to create the overlapping circles.
- ❑ Place one book in the left section of the diagram and one in the right. Print "Alike" on a sentence strip and place it in the center section. Print facts specific to Brett's book on sentence strips and place the strips in the section of the diagram that belongs to her book. Print facts specific to Tresselt's version on sentence strips and place them in the section of the diagram designated for her book. Print things common to both books on sentence strips and place them in the overlapping area of the diagram labeled "Alike."

Practicing the Lesson

- ❑ Create a Venn diagram on the floor with masking tape. Make the circles large enough for two children to stand inside. Ask for the children three questions: 1) Who likes both peanut butter and jelly on your sandwich?; 2) Who likes only jelly on your sandwich?; and 3) Who likes only peanut butter on your sandwich? As the children answer the questions, have a few of them take their position in the Venn diagram. Jelly will be on one side, peanut butter on the other side, and peanut butter and jelly in the middle.

Reflecting on the Lesson

Ask the children:

- ❑ *Who is your best friend? What things do you and your best friend both like? Can you think of something that you like but your friend doesn't like? What is it?*
- ❑ *Which version of* The Mitten *do you like best? Why?*

Special Needs Adaptations

Special Need	Adaptation
Visual Impairments	■ Draw a Venn diagram on white paper. Use thick lines for the circles in the diagram. Place the diagram in front of the child and demonstrate the concept with her before introducing it to the rest of the class.
Hearing Impairments	■ Add additional adaptations by asking the child questions such as, "Do you like to watch TV?" "Do you like to eat spinach?" and so on. Write the child's answers and place them in the correct area on the paper diagram.
Cognitive Challenges	■ A child with cognitive challenges will not be able to understand the abstract concept of a Venn diagram. Therefore, the goal for her in this activity may include answering questions when asked. ■ When it is her turn to go stand in the diagram, praise her for answering the question and participating, even if she does not participate to the same degree as her classmates.
Motor Delays	■ Instead of standing in the circle that matches her answers, allow the child to sit on a beanbag chair.
Speech/ Language Delays	■ Use the paper Venn diagram described in the visual impairments adaptation to practice with the child until she understands the concept behind the diagram. Ask her questions that she can answer and praise her for responding.
Emotional/ Behavior Issues	■ Use the reflection piece of this lesson to review with the child how to treat a friend. Talk about the importance of sharing, talking, taking turns, and using soft touches rather than hitting. Talk about how sometimes friends do not want to play with each other and that when they do not want to play with each other it is okay.

Comprehension

Story Map

Children will:
- analyze story parts.

Vocabulary

author
characters
illustrator
plot
setting
story
title

Materials

butcher paper
crayons
large puzzle
markers
props to represent houses
sentence strips
Story Map (see samples on pages 284–285 in the Appendix)

Preparation

Print story map components on sentence strips.

Introducing and Developing the Lesson

❑ Show the children a large puzzle with all its pieces. Point out that the puzzle is made up of many parts. It takes all the pieces to make the puzzle complete. Tell the children that a story is like a puzzle. It takes many pieces to make it complete. Allow the children to help you put the puzzle together.

❑ Tell the children that they will be learning how to examine the pieces of a story.

❑ Read or tell the story "The Three Little Pigs" (many versions available).

❑ Select one of the Story Maps (see pages 284–285 in the Appendix). Ask the children to help you fill in the information on the map.

❑ Tell the children that authors often use a story map when they are writing a story. A story map shows the structure of the story and all the parts that make up the story.

❑ Use other story maps to examine other stories.

Practicing the Lesson

❑ Invite the children to re-enact the story of "The Three Little Pigs." After they have finished the re-enactment, arrange them into a concrete story map. Print story map components on sentence strips and place the strips on the floor. Have the characters stand beside the sentence strip that says "characters."

❑ Use props to represent the "events" in the story—two houses that are blown away and the house that stays put. Place the book or a sentence strip with the story title at the top of the concrete map.

❑ Encourage the children to draw characters or events from the story. Use their drawings to fill in a large story map. Select a format from the suggested Story Maps (see pages 284–285 in the Appendix) and enlarge it by drawing it onto butcher paper.

Reflecting on the Lesson

Ask the children:

❑ *How many characters are in the story of "The Three Little Pigs"?*
❑ *What is the first thing that happens in the story of "The Three Little Pigs"?*

Special Needs Adaptations

Special Need	Adaptation
Visual Impairments	■ After you have made the story map with the large group, review the story map one-on-one with the child. This will help you know if she understands what happens in the story.
Hearing Impairments	■ Use pictures or puppets to tell the story. Make sure the child is seated where she can see you as you tell or read the story.
Cognitive Challenges	■ Provide "The Three Little Pigs" sequence cards (see pages 278 in the Appendix) and help the child place them in order. It may be necessary to model for her how to place the cards. What is important is that she begins to recognize the concepts of first, second, next, and last.
Motor Delays	■ If the child cannot participate in the re-enactment due to her motor limitations, make her the stage director or the producer. Make a sign that says "director" and place it on a chair or on her wheelchair. Explain that the director helps lead the re-enactment.
Speech/ Language Delays	■ Use the same sequence cards described above (cognitive challenges). Encourage the child to explain the order in which the story happens. Look for opportunities throughout the day to reinforce the concepts of first, second, next, and last.
Emotional/ Behavior Issues	■ Invite the child to participate in the re-enactment. Let the child select what role she will play. Tell the child before the activity begins that her job is to play her part, not to direct others. Remind the child that the group re-enactment may be different from the book.

K-W-L Chart

Introducing and Developing the Lesson

❑ Invite the children to do the action rhyme "The Elephant Goes" (see page 263 in the Appendix). Ask the children, "What do you know about elephants?"

❑ Provide photos of elephants. Use the photos as a springboard to a discussion about elephants. Tell the children that learning is a matter of thinking about what is already known and deciding what things you would like to know. Tell them that you will show them a way to organize what they learn. Tell them that they will also be learning some new things about elephants.

❑ Make a K-W-L Chart (see page 282 in the Appendix) on butcher paper. Ask the children what they know about elephants and write their responses under the "What We Know" section of the chart.

❑ Ask the children what they would like to know and write the responses under the "What We Would Like to Know" section of the chart.

❑ Use the children's responses to "What I Would Like to Know" to develop activities for the day. At the end of the day, or after a few days, fill in the last section of the chart—"What We Learned."

Children will:
- organize information.

Vocabulary
know
learn
organize

Materials
chart paper or butcher paper
marker
photos of elephants
The Saggy Baggy Elephant by
   Kathryn and Byron Jackson;
   *"Stand Back," Said the
   Elephant, "I'm Going to
   Sneeze!"* by Patricia Thomas;
   or *Ellison the Elephant* by
   Eric Drachman

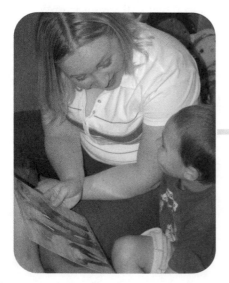

Practicing the Lesson

❑ Read books about elephants, such as, *The Saggy Baggy Elephant* by Kathryn and Byron Jackson; *"Stand Back," Said the Elephant, "I'm Going to Sneeze!"* by Patricia Thomas; and *Ellison the Elephant* by Eric Drachman.

❑ Take a trip to the zoo to see the elephants.

Pictures help reinforce concepts and word knowledge for children with a limited vocabulary.

Reflecting on the Lesson

Ask the children:

❑ *What did you learn about elephants today?*

❑ *What would you still like to know about elephants?*

Special Needs Adaptations

Special Need	Adaptation
Visual Impairments	■ Before beginning the activity, show the child a picture of an elephant. Talk about the elephant's physical characteristics with the child. Place the photo in front of her, so the child can see it as you begin the activity with the large group.
Hearing Impairments	■ If the child depends on sign language to communicate, teach the entire class the sign for elephant (scc page 252 in the Appendix—Signs Used in Lessons).
Cognitive Challenges	■ Show the child a picture of an elephant. Ask the child if she knows what animal is in the picture? Talk about the picture with the child and invite her to point to the elephant's leg, nose, head, and so on.
Motor Delays	■ If the child cannot move around on all fours, tell her to move her body back and forth (elephants often sway from side to side).
Speech/ Language Delays	■ Show the child a picture of an elephant and talk about what elephants eat, where they live, and how big they are. Ask the child to use these attributes in a sentence.
Emotional/ Behavior Issues	■ Use this lesson as an opportunity to make a K-W-L Chart about social skill you want the child to learn. Social skills are fundamental life skills that she will need to function in a social situation. For example, you may do a K-W-L Chart with the child about being a friend, starting a conversation, asking to play with someone, and so on. Send the chart home with a note to the child's family so they can help her as she learns her new social skill.

Books That Support Comprehension

Traditional Tales (many versions available)
"The Gingerbread Man"
"Henny Penny"
"Jack and the Beanstalk"
"The Little Red Hen"
"Little Red Riding Hood"
"The Three Bears"
"The Three Billy Goats Gruff"
"The Three Little Pigs"

Predictable Text
Repetitive
"The Gingerbread Man" (many versions available)
Here Are My Hands by Bill Martin, Jr.
I Can, Can You? by Marjorie W. Pitzer *
Rolling Along With Goldilocks and Three Bears by Cindy Mayer *
"The Three Little Pigs" (many versions available)

Rhyming
Down by the Bay by Raffi
Fire! Fire! Said Mrs. McGuire by Bill Martin, Jr.

Cumulative
My Friend with Autism by Beverly Bishop *
There Was an Old Lady Who Swallowed a Fly by Simms Taback
This Is the House That Jack Built (many versions available)

Cultural—Familiar (A repetition that is familiar within a culture, such as days of the week, numbers, months, and so on.)
Tuesday by David Wiesner
The Very Hungry Caterpillar by Eric Carle

Interlocking
Brown Bear, Brown Bear, What Do You See? by Bill Martin, Jr.
Who Took the Cookies from the Cookie Jar? by Bonnie Lass & Philemon Sturges

General Titles
Guess Who? by Margaret Miller
The Jolly Postman by Janet and Allan Ahlberg
My Friend Isabelle by Eliza Woloson *
Signs on the Road (Welcome Books: Signs in My World) by Mary Hill *
We'll Paint the Octopus Red by Stephanie Stuve-Bodeen *
Who Is the Beast? by Keith Baker

* Denotes books featuring children with special needs

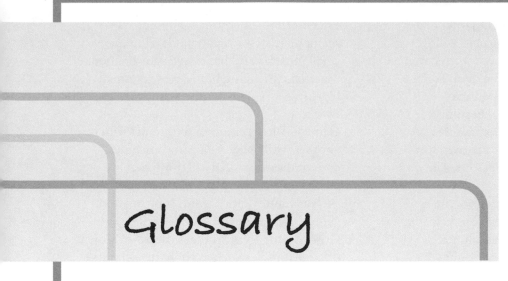

Glossary

Alliteration—A series of words that all begin with the same consonant sound, such as "Peter Piper Picked a Pail of Pickled Peppers."

Articulation disorder—When a sound is pronounced incorrectly such as saying "tuptake" instead of "cupcake".

Assessment—Systematic evaluation of the progress children make on their learning journey.

Attributes—Characteristics of an item or individual, such as *large, small, round, tall, short,* and so forth.

Autism spectrum disorder—A term used to describe all types of autism. It is called a spectrum disorder because the characteristics range from mild in some areas to quite severe in other areas.

Bilingual instruction—Instruction intended to help second-language learners acquire a language other than their native language.

Brain research—A body of scientific data that emerged in the 1980s with the advent of technology that allows scientists to view the brain while an individual is still living.

Classification—Sorting and grouping items according to similarities and differences of the attributes of those objects.

Cortical vision impairment—A type of vision impairment that results in damage to the visual cortex of the brain and not the structure of the eye itself.

Dual-language instruction—Instruction that attempts to help all children become fluent in two languages.

Environmental print—Print of everyday life: The symbols, signs, numbers, and colors found in traffic signs, stores and restaurants, such as McDonald's and Pizza Hut, and so on.

ESL—(English as a second language) Refers to children whose primary language is a language other than English. Some areas of the country use the term SLL (second language learners) instead of ESL.

Fine motor development—The development of small muscles, such as fingers and toes.

Functional skills—Skills that a child will use every day, such as brushing teeth or dressing. These are also referred to as life skills or self-help skills.

Generalization—Being able to perform the same task, skill, or activity in a variety of settings or with a variety of people and/or objects.

Gross motor development—The development of large muscles, such as arms and legs.

Higher-level thinking skills—The use of activities and questions that encourage divergent thinking. Skill include application, analysis, synthesis, and evaluation.

Learning centers—Small-group activities intended to help children develop skills and concepts as they work with concrete materials. Most classrooms have at least six centers operating at one time. Some classrooms with larger groups of children may operate 10–12 centers simultaneously. Learning centers should, ideally, represent approximately 70% of instructional time. Learning centers are used to practice skills and concepts taught in lessons. The following are 17 typical centers:

Art—Offers opportunities for children to explore their creativity and develop their fine motor control. Materials: easels, paints, crayons, markers, stencils, scissors, glue, paste, and collage materials.

Blocks—Encourages children to play creatively and develop their sense of balance and spatial relationships. Materials: building blocks (large and small) and an assortment of rubber animals, cars, trucks, and buildings.

Construction—Offers opportunities for children to develop hand–eye coordination, spatial concepts, and creativity. Materials: glue, paste, cardboard boxes, small pieces of wood, and tools (screwdrivers, safe-edge saws, hammers, pliers, wrenches, and so on).

Cooking—Encourages children to participate in cooking activities. Develops the understanding of sequence, written communication, whole–part relationships, and change of state. Cooking also allows for fine motor development and hand–eye coordination. Materials: pots and pans, empty boxes of cooking ingredients, such as flour, salt, baking soda, rice, and so on.

Discovery—Allows children to investigate items, to discover what's inside, what happens when one item is mixed with another, or what happens when an item is manipulated in a certain way. Materials: magnifying glasses, magnets, scales, and so forth.

Dramatic play—Provides opportunities for children to act out different roles, such as those of a mother, father, police officer, or office worker. Develops imagination and creativity and encourages children to practice social skills. Materials: props that encourage children to play dramatically, dress-up clothing, puppets, mirror, kitchen furniture, and so on.

Fine motor—Encourages children to manipulate items that help develop their small muscles and hand–eye coordination. Materials: stringing beads, puzzles, small blocks, scissors, buttons, eyedroppers, and tweezers.

Game—Allows children to interact with one another while playing a game. Includes counting games, such as Hi-Ho the Cherry-O™; color identification games, such as Candy Land™; and coordination games, such as Barrel of Monkeys™.

Gross motor—Encourages the development of large muscles such as those in the arms and legs. Materials: bean bags, balance beams, and balls.

Language—Encourages all of the aspects of language development. Materials: books, posters, magnetic letters, chalkboards, markers, paper, and puzzles.

Library—Provides a wealth of books for the children to browse. Typically, these books are changed weekly and generally tie to themes or concepts being taught.

Listening—Provides for children to listen independently to a story and to turn the pages of a book as the story progresses. Materials: audio recorder/player, recording media (tapes, CDs), headphones, listening post, and books.

Math—Encourages children to explore patterning, one-to-one correspondence, and counting activities. Materials: counters, puzzles, games, stringing beads, small blocks, and numerical patterns and stencils.

Music and movement—Provides opportunities for the children to dance, sing, and explore musical instruments. Materials: rhythm band instruments, a tuning fork, tapes/CD, tape/CD player, and tone bottles.

Sand/water—Encourages children to explore tactile items, such as sand and water. May also include sawdust, pebbles, and Styrofoam packing chips. Offers opportunities for children to develop eye–hand coordination, and an understanding of weight, volume, and change of state. Materials: measuring and pouring equipment.

Science—Encourages children to observe insects, animals, and plant life. Materials: live animals, plants, magnifying glasses, scales, magnets, prisms, and so forth.
Writing—Offers opportunities for children to experiment with letters and writing materials. Materials: magnetic letters, chalk and chalkboard, markers and paper.

Music and movement—A short part of the preschool daily schedule when children are invited to dance, sing, and move to music. This provides opportunities for children to develop listening skills, balance, coordination, and rhythm.

Onomatopoeia—Words that sound like the item that they are describing. For example, *splish-splash* or *pitter-patter* used to describe the sound of rain.

Orientation and mobility specialist—Develops and trains individuals to restore orientation and mobility skills to the legally blind. The goal of orientation and mobility is to help a person with visual challenges move independently in the environment.

Partial participation—The idea that children with special needs can participate in an activity to the degree that their abilities allow them to participate.

Pattern—The repetition of a designated item (color, block, crayon, or book) or group of items. Patterns occur naturally everywhere in the environment.

People-first language—Reference to a child first and the special need or limitation second, for example, "a child with autism" rather than "an autistic child."

Peripheral vision—The ability to see objects and movement outside of the direct line of vision.

Phonological awareness—The sound of language, beginning with babbling and cooing and moving along to the sound and symbol relationships that are decoded for reading.

Pragmatic language—How language is used in a social setting, including understanding that the speaker speaks and the listener listens until it is his or her turn to speak.

Prompts—Specific cues or clues that the teacher uses to help the child know what to do.

Punctuation marks—The use of standard marks (exclamation, question, quotation, commas, periods and so on) and signs in writing and printing to separate words into sentences, clauses, and phrases in order to clarify meaning.

Sight word—Words that become so familiar that they can be recognized by sight. Beginning sight words usually include the child's name, the pronouns *I* and *you* and the articles *the*, *a*, and *an*.

Slotting—A technique to encourage a child to fill in the blank with a word he or she knows. The teacher uses clues in the sentence to help the child select the correct word.

Story maps—A graphic organizer that can be useful in helping a student analyze or write a story. This type of analysis is especially good for examining fables and folktales.

Telegraphic speech—Speaking in one- or two-word sentences, consisting of a noun and sometimes a verb.

Venn diagram—A visual representation of the similarities and differences between concepts.

Visual impairment—The functional loss of vision.

Appendix

Special Needs Resources

Supplies

Ball Dynamics International, LLC
14215 Mead Street
Longmont, CO 80504
Phone: 1–800–752–2255 (toll-free)
Fax: 1–877–223–2962 (toll-free)
Website: http://balldynamics.com
E-mail: orders@balldynamics.com

Battat Inc.
44 Martina Circle
Plattsburgh, NY 12901-0149
Phone: 518–562–2200
Fax: 518–562–2203
Website: http://www.battattoys.com
E-mail: sales@battat-toys.com

FlagHouse Inc.
601 FlagHouse Drive
Hasbrouck Heights, NJ 07604–3116
Phone: 1–800–793–7900
Fax: 1-800–793–7922
Website: http://www.flaghouse.com

Communicative Replacement

A communicative replacement is used when a teacher chooses to replace a child's challenging behavior (hitting, spitting, yelling, throwing things) with a more acceptable alternative. For example, teaching the child to raise his hand when he feels frustrated rather than yelling out. For this strategy to work, it is important that the teacher determine the function (reason) behind the child's behavior and

look for an alternative that the child can learn to use. The following guidelines help a teacher decide when to teach a communicative replacement:

❏ If the teacher chooses to teach a communicative replacement, he/she must ensure that the communicative replacement serves the same function (reason) as the challenging behavior. In other words, the replacement used must get the same result that the child got when he used an unacceptable behavior.

❏ The goal of this procedure is to teach the child to regulate his own behavior and to avoid using behaviors that are disruptive or hurt others.

Desk or Tabletop Easel

This can be used with a child with visual or motor issues. The table-top easel is used to help the child see a book or a written activity.

1. Get a sturdy cardboard box.
2. Cut the top of the box. Then, cut the box in half, along the diagonal shown in the illustration.
3. Place each half of the box on its open end, creating two tabletop easels.
4. Cut two slits along the peak, where you can insert clothespins to secure paper to the easel.
5. If the easel slides around too much, place a book or other heavy object in the bottom section or place it on a piece of non-slip material, such as scatter-rug backing.

Identification Card

Use a 5" x 7" index card. If possible, place the child's picture on the front of the card. Write the child's name, address, phone number, and parent's names on the card on the back of the card. Laminate the card. Encourage the child to carry the card with him at all times. Look for opportunities throughout the day to ask him to show you his identification card. Ask other people around the school to help you; invite them to ask him for his identification. The more he practices using it, the easier it will be for him to remember to use it when he needs to.

Low Vision Aids

General Information about Low Vision Aids— website: http://www.lowvision.org

Low Vision Aid Companies

EnableMart Sales Office
4210 E 4th Plain Blvd
Vancouver, WA 98661
Phone: 888–640–1999
Website: http://enablemart.com

Enhanced Vision Headquarters
5882 Machine Drive
Huntington Beach, CA 92649
Phone: 714–374–1829
Website: http://enhancedvision.com

Independent Living Aids, Inc.
200 Robbins Lane
Jericho, NY 11753
Phone: 800–537–2118
Website: http://independentliving.com

Books on Tape/Large Print Books
National Association for Visually Handicapped
22 West 21st Street
New York, NY 10010
Phone: 888–205–5951
Phone: 212–889–3141
Fax: 212–727–2931
E-mail: staff@navh.org
Website: http://www.navh.org

National Library Service for the Blind and Physically Handicapped
Library of Congress
1291 Taylor Street, NW
Washington, DC 20011
Phone: 888–657–7323 & 800–424–8567
Phone: 202–707–5100
TDD: 202–707–0744
Fax: 202–707–0712
E-mail: nls@loc.gov
Website: www.loc.gov/nls

Braille Books/Materials
National Braille Press—Website:
http://www.nbp.org/
Seedlings Braille Books—Website:
http://seedlings.org
American Foundation for the Blind—Website:
http://www.afb.org/
American Printing House for the Blind—Website:
http://www.APH.org/

Customized Large Print Books
Huge Print Press
North Central Plaza I
12655 N Central Expressway, Suite 416
Dallas, TX 75243
Phone: 866–484–3774
Phone: 972–701–8288
Fax: 972–701–8088
E-mail: info@hugeprint.com
Website: www.hugeprint.com

Motor Adaptations
Adaptive Switches
Most battery-operated toys, as well as computer keyboards, are not accessible (user friendly) for children with certain types of physical special needs. Adaptive switches provide an alternate means for children to use toys. Basic switches are used to control the on and off functions of devices, such as tape recorders and battery toys. More sophisticated switches are used to help a child access a computer. The switch can be used either with a device that has been adapted for switch access (such as a special toy) or with an interface (such as a pig-tail adapter) that links the switch to a non-adapted device. Interfaces are inexpensive and are placed next to the battery in the toy and provide a connection to plug the adaptive switch into the toy or recorder.

Types of Adaptive Switches
❑ Pressure-sensitive switches that require a press, push, or pull action.
❑ Touch-sensitive switches that respond to a very light touch.
❑ Air-pressure switches, such as a pneumatic grip switch or a sip-and-puff switch.
❑ Small muscle sensors that can sense the voluntary movement of a finger, eyebrow, cheek, or other small muscles.
❑ Infrared beam switches that respond to movement within their "field of vision."
❑ Sound-sensitive switches.

Vendors who carry adaptive switches and battery interrupters
Ablenet—www.ablenetinc.com
Don Johnston, Inc.—www.donjohnston.com
Enabling Devices—www.enablingdevices.com
TASH, Inc.—www.tashint.com

Adaptive Handles

Adaptive handles are used to help a child pick up an object. Suggestions of how to adapt handles include:

1. Attach foam hair rollers, like those used to curl hair, to the handle of objects creating handles that are easier to grasp.
2. Securing a few crayons together with rubber bands creates a "crayon" that is easier for some children to use.
3. Wrap a few rubber bands around an object, including a single crayon or marker, making the object easier to grasp and handle.
4. Tape metal nuts to a pencil to give it more weight.

Page Turners

Page turners are used to help a child more easily turn a page in a book.

1. Attach a wooden clothespin to each page. This gives the child a handle to hold when turning the pages.
2. Place a dot of hot glue on the upper left-hand corner of each page. Wait for each dot to cool, before going to the next page.
3. Attach a metal paperclip to the top left-hand corner of each page. This provides something for the child to grasp.

Picture Schedules

Picture schedules are used to help the child know what is going to happen in his daily routine. The following are guidelines for making a simple picture schedule:

1. Draw or cut out simple pictures showing daily activities.
2. Glue pictures onto construction paper.
3. Laminate or cover with clear contact paper.
4. Attach with Velcro or tape.
5. Create a picture schedule.

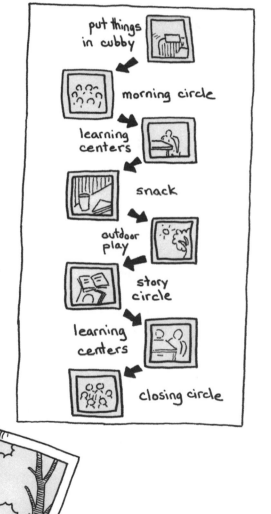

Signs Used in Lessons

around

elephant

out

brother

family

over

cookie

in

same

different

mom

sister

dad

off

spider

down

on

star

thank you

under

up

Stranger Danger

Most adults care about what happens to young children and want to help them grow and develop. However, there are grown-ups who may try to touch a child in a way that is not appropriate. It could be a person the child knows and trusts, like a relative, or neighbor. Unfortunately, sexual assault is 10 times more likely if the child has a special need. There are a few things adults can do to help children with special needs take care of themselves:

1. Your body belongs to you. Teach children that there are places on their body that are private—like the places a swimsuit covers—that an adult should not try to touch, unless it is the doctor and a parent or guardian is in the room.

2. Adults should never ask a child to keep a secret. Tell them to find someone they trust and tell what happened, even if the person said it was a secret or that they, or someone else, would be hurt if they told.

3. Adults should never ask a child to take off their clothes. Never allow someone to take a picture without your clothes.

4. If something feels wrong, it usually is wrong!

5. The first number every child should know and practice dialing is "911."

6. Never—ever—get into a car with anyone whom you do not know. Adults do not need to ask children for directions.

7. If someone grabs you, it is okay to scream, yell, and kick.

8. Encourage children to always play with a friend and never to play in a secluded place or an abandoned building.

Songs

The Alphabet March by Pam Schiller

Tune: "The Ants Go Marching"

The ants go marching one by one,
Hurrah, hurrah.
The ants go marching one by one,
Hurrah, hurrah.
The ants go marching one by one,
The little one stops for alphabet fun,
And they all go marching down
To the ground
To get out of the rain.
Zoom! Zoom! Zoom! Zoom!
Zoom! Zoom! Zoom! Zoom!

The alphabet letters are on the floor,
Hurrah, hurrah.
The alphabet letters are on the floor,
Hurrah, hurrah.
The children carry a letter in their hand
And by their match on the floor they stand.
And they all go switching letters
With a friend
To begin…again
Zoom! Zoom! Zoom! Zoom!
Zoom! Zoom! Zoom! Zoom!

The children march around the room,
Hurrah, hurrah.
The children march around the room,
Hurrah, hurrah.
The children march around the room
And stand by their match with a zoom, zoom, zoom.
And they all go switching letters
With a friend
To begin…again.

Zoom! Zoom! Zoom! Zoom!
Zoom! Zoom! Zoom! Zoom!

(Repeat!)

The children march around the room…
And they all go marching around
With a friend.
This is the end
Of the game,
Zoom! Zoom! Zoom! Zoom!
Zoom! Zoom! Zoom! Zoom! Zoom!

The Alphabet Song (Traditional)

A-B-C-D-E-F-G,
H-I-J-K-L-M-N-O-P,
Q-R-S-T-U and V
W-X-Y and Z.
Now I know my ABCs.
Next time won't you sing with me?

The Alphabet Song Forward and Backward
(Traditional)

A-B-C-D-E-F-G, H-I-J-K-L-M-N-O-P,
Q-R-S, T-U-V, W-X-Y-Z
Now I know my ABCs.
Next time sing them backwards with me.
Z-Y-X-W-V-U-T, S-R-Q-P-O-N-M,
L-K-J, I-H-G, F-E-D, C-B-A.
Now I've said my ZYXs.
Bet that's not what you expected!

Billy Boy (Traditional, adapted)

Oh, where have you been, Billy Boy, Billy Boy?
Oh, where have you been, charming Billy?
"I have gone to seek a wife; she's the joy of my life.
She's a young thing and cannot leave her mother."
Are her eyes blue and bright, Billy Boy, Billy Boy?
Are her eyes blue and bright, charming Billy?
"Yes, her eyes are blue and bright, and they sparkle in
    the light.
She's a young thing and cannot leave her mother."

Bingo (Traditional)

There was a farmer had a dog,
And Bingo was his name-o.
B-I-N-G-O!
B-I-N-G-O!
B-I-N-G-O!
And Bingo was his name-o!

Can You Move with Me? (author unknown)

Tune: "Do Your Ears Hang Low?"
Can you wiggle like a worm?
Can you squiggle? Can you squirm?
Can you flutter? Can you fly like a gentle butterfly?
Can you crawl upon the ground
Like a beetle that is round?
Can you move with me?

I can wiggle like a worm.
I can squiggle. I can squirm.
I can flutter. I can fly like a gentle butterfly.
I can crawl upon the ground
Like a beetle that is round.
I can move with you.

Can you flip? Can you flop?
Can you give a little hop?
Can you slither like a snake?
Can you give a little shake?
Can you dance like a bee
That is buzzing 'round a tree?
Can you move with me?

I can flip. I can flop.
I can give a little hop.
I can slither like a snake.
I can give a little shake.
I can dance like a bee
That is buzzing 'round a tree.
I can move with you.

Catalina Magnalina (Traditional)

She had a peculiar name but she wasn't to blame.
She got it from her mother, who's the same, same, same.

Chorus:

Catalina Magnalina, Hootensteiner Bogentwiner
Hogan Logan Bogan was her name.

She had two peculiar teeth in her mouth,
One pointed north and the other pointed south.

(Chorus)

She had two peculiar eyes in her head,
One was purple and the other was red.

(Chorus)

She had two peculiar hairs on her chin,
One stuck out and the other stuck in.

(Chorus)

Her feet were as flat as a bathroom mat,
I forgot to ask her how they got like that.

(Chorus)

Chew! Slurp! Crunch! by Pam Schiller

Tune: "She'll Be Comin' 'Round the Mountain"
Oh, the kids are happy chewing chocolate chips.
    Chomp! Chomp!
Oh, the kids are happy chewing chocolate chips.
    Chomp, Chomp!
See them chewing crumbs and cookies, these kids aren't
    cookie rookies!
Oh, the kids are happy chewing chocolate chips.
    Chomp, Chomp!

Oh, the kids are busy slurping chocolate shakes. Slurp!
    Slurp!
Oh, the kids are busy slurping chocolate shakes. Slurp!
    Slurp!
See them slurping up their shakes, slow down for
    goodness sakes!
Oh, the kids are busy slurping chocolate shakes. Slurp!
    Slurp!

Oh, the kids are crunching Cracker Jacks. Crunch!
    Crunch!
Oh, the kids are crunching Cracker Jacks. Crunch!
    Crunch!

See them crunching corn like candy, oh the popcorn is
    so dandy!
Oh, the kids are busy crunching Cracker Jacks.
    Crunch! Crunch!

Oh, my tummy is so funny, yes it is! Sure is!
Oh, my tummy is so funny, yes it is! Sure is!
Oh, my tummy is so funny, full of cookies, shakes, and
    honey,
Oh, my tummy is so funny, yes it is! Sure is!

Chocolate Chip Cookies by Pam Schiller

Tune: "Mary Had a Little Lamb"
Chorus:
Chocolate chip cookies, you gotta have more.
You can bake 'em in the oven, or buy 'em at the store.
But whatever you do, have 'em ready at my door
And I'll love ya 'til I die.

They're made out of sugar and butter and flour.
You put 'em in the oven about a quarter hour.
But the thing that gives them their magic power
Is the chocolate chips inside.

(Chorus)

You can't eat one, you can't eat two.
Once you start chewing, there's nothing to do.
But clean your plate, and eat the crumbs too.
Then go and find some more.

(Chorus)

Now when I die, I don't want wings
A golden halo or a harp that sings.
Give me a book, and someone that brings me
Chocolate chip cookies all day.

(Chorus)

The Color Song by Pam Schiller

Tune: "I've Been Workin' on the Railroad"
Red is the color for an apple to eat.
Red is the color for cherries, too.
Red is the color for strawberries.
I like red, don't you?

Blue is the color for the big blue sky.
Blue is the color for baby things, too.
Blue is the color of my sister's eyes.
I like blue, don't you?

Yellow is the color for the great big sun.
Yellow is the color for lemonade, too.
Yellow is the color of a baby chick.
I like yellow, don't you?

Green is the color for the leaves on the trees.
Green is the color for green peas, too.
Green is the color of a watermelon.
I like green, don't you?

Orange is the color for oranges.
Orange is the color for carrots, too.
Orange is the color of a jack-o-lantern.
I like orange, don't you?

Purple is the color for a bunch of grapes.
Purple is the color for grape juice, too.
Purple is the color for a violet.
I like purple, don't you?

Down by the Bay (Traditional)

Down by the bay here the watermelons grow,
Back to my home I dare not go,
For if I do my mother will say,
"Did you ever see a pig dancing the jig?"
Down by the bay.

Additional verses:
"Did you ever see a goose kissing a moose?"
"Did you ever see a bear combing his hair?"
"Did you ever see a whale with a polka dot tail?"

Make up your own verses.

Fiddle-i-Fee (Traditional)

I had a cat,
And the cat pleased me.
Fed my cat
Under yonder tree.
Cat went fiddle-i-fee.

I had a hen,
And the hen pleased me.
Fed my hen
Under yonder tree.
Hen went chimmey-chuck, chimmey-chuck.
Cat went fiddle-i-fee.

I had a dog,
And the dog pleased me.
Fed my dog
Under yonder tree.
Dog went bow-wow, bow-wow.
Hen went chimmey-chuck, chimmey-chuck.
Cat went fiddle-i-fee.
Cat went fiddle-i-fee.

Five Flying Frogs by Pam Schiller

Tune: "Bumping Up and Down in My Little Red Wagon"
Five flying frogs,
Five flying frogs,
See them up high
Float in the sky.
They look so cute on a lily pad.
It certainly is the latest fad.
Have you ever seen such a sight in the night
As five flying frogs,
Five flying frogs?

Five Little Ducks (Traditional)

Five little ducks went out one day,
Over the hills and far away,
Papa duck called with a "quack, quack, quack."
Four little ducks came swimming back.

Repeat, losing one more duck each time, until you are left with one duck. In the last verse, the momma duck calls and the song ends with "five little ducks came swimming back."

Head, Shoulders, Knees, and Toes
(Traditional)
Touch the parts of the body as they are mentioned in the song.

Head and shoulders, knees and toes,
Knees and toes, knees and toes.
Head and shoulders, knees and toes,
Eyes and ears and mouth and nose.

I Met a Bear (Traditional, adapted by Pam Schiller)
Tune: "Sippin' Cider Through a Straw"
The children echo each line after you sing it. The chorus is each verse repeated and sung in unison.

The other day,
I met a bear,
A great big bear,
oh way out there.
(Chorus: Above lines in unison)

He looked at me,
I looked at him,
He sized up me,
I sized up him.
(Chorus: Above lines in unison)

He said to me,
"Why don't you run?
It's time to
Have some fun."
(Chorus: Above lines in unison)

I said to him,
"That's a good idea.
Now legs get going,
get me out of here!"
(Chorus: Above lines in unison)

And so I ran,
Away from there,
But right behind me,
Was that bear.
(Chorus: Above lines in unison)

In front of me,
There was a tree,
A great big tree,
Oh glory be!
(Chorus: Above lines in unison)

The lowest branch,
Was ten feet up,
So I thought I'd jump,
And trust my luck.
(Chorus: Above lines in unison)

And so I jumped,
Into the air,
But I missed that branch,
A way up there.
(Chorus: Above lines in unison)

Now don't you fret,
And don't you frown,
I caught that branch,
On the way back down!
(Chorus: Above lines in unison)

This is the end,
There ain't no more,
Unless I see,
That bear once more.

If You're Happy and You Know It (Traditional, adapted by Pam Schiller)
Tune: "If You're Happy and You Know It"
If you're happy and you know it,
Point to the letter B. Hello B!
If you're happy and you know it,
Point to the letter B. Hello B!
If you're happy and you know it,
Let the letters you know show it.
If you're happy and you know it,
Point to the letter B. Bye B!

Itsy Bitsy Spider (Traditional)

The itsy bitsy spider
Went up the waterspout.
Down came the rain
And washed the spider out.
Up came the sun
And dried up all the rain,
And the itsy bitsy spider
Went up the spout again.

Little Hunk of Tin (Traditional)

Tune: "I'm a Little Acorn Brown"

I'm a little hunk of tin. (cup hand as if holding
   something)
Nobody knows what shape I'm in. (hold hands to side
   palm up and shrug)
Got four wheels and a running board. (hold up four
   fingers)
I'm a four-door. (shake head yes)
I'm a Ford.

Chorus:
Honk, honk (pull ear)
Rattle, rattle. (shake head)
Crash, crash. (push chin)
Beep, beep. (push nose)
(Repeat chorus twice.)

Little Red Caboose (Traditional)

Little red caboose, chug, chug, chug.
Little red caboose, chug, chug, chug.
Little red caboose, behind the train, train, train, train.
Smokestack on his back, back, back, back.
Chugging down the track, track, track, track.
Little red caboose behind the train.

The Little Red Hen by Pam Schiller

Tune: "Itsy Bitsy Spider"

The clever barnyard hen found some grains of wheat.
She thought making bread would be a tasty treat.
She asked her friends to help but everyone said, "no."
So she planted the seeds and helped them all to grow.

When the wheat was ready she turned it into dough.
The friends were asked to help but everyone said, "no."

The clever barnyard hen baked the bread alone
And when the bread was ready she ate it all alone.

Old MacDonald Had a Farm (Traditional)

Old MacDonald had a farm,
E-I-E-I-O
And on this farm she had a cow,
E-I-E-I-O
With a moo, moo here,
And a moo, moo there,
Here a moo, there a moo,
Everywhere a moo, moo.
Old MacDonald had a farm,
E-I-E-I-O!

Additional verses:
Pig—oink, oink
Cat—meow, meow
Dog—bow-wow
Horse—neigh, neigh

One Flea Fly Flew (Traditional)

Tune: "The Battle Hymn of the Republic"

One flea fly flew up the flue and
The other flea fly flew down.
Oh, one flea fly flew up the flu
And the other flea fly flew down.
Oh, one flea fly flew up the flue
And the other flea fly flew down.
Oh, one flea fly flew up the flue
And the other flea fly flew down.
They were only playing flu fly,
They were only playing flu fly,
They were only playing flu fly
In the springtime and the fall.

Reader's Wiggle (author unknown)

Tune: "Hokey Pokey"

When I read a book, (hold hands out palms up as if
   reading)
I start from left to right. (shake left hand and turn the
   right hand palm up)
And I do the very same thing, (shake finger as if
   saying I told you so)

When I want to write. (shake left hand and turn the
   right hand palm up)
I do the Reader Wiggle, (put hand over head and
   shake, wiggle hips)
And I turn myself about, (turn around)
That's how I read and write! (shake finger as if saying
   I told you so)

Chorus:
I do the R-e-a-d-e-r Wiggle, (hold hands overhead,
   wiggle fingers, and turn around)
I do the R-e-a-d-e-r Wiggle, (hold hands overhead,
   wiggle fingers, and turn around)
I do the R-e-a-d-e-r Wiggle, (hold hands overhead,
   wiggle fingers, and turn around)
That's how I read and write! (shake finger as if saying
   I told you so)

When I read "The Three Bears" (hold hands out
   palms up as if reading)
I move from left to right. (shake left hand and turn
   the right hand palm up)
I go from word to word (point finger as if moving
   word to word)
And I know I've got it right. (point to self—shake
   your head yes)
I do the Reader Wiggle, (put hand over head and
   shake, wiggle hips)
And I turn my self about, (turn around)
That's how I read and write! (shake finger as if saying
   I told you so)

Rhyme Time (author unknown)
Chorus:
Tap, tap... Rhyme time, tap, tap... Rhyme time,
Tap. tap... Rhyme time, tap, tap...Rhyme time

Tap can...tap pan.
Tap fan...tap ran.
Tap man...tap tan.
Tap "an"
The "an" family.
(Chorus—say between each verse)

Additional verses:
Pet, jet, vet, net, let, set...et

Like, hike, bike, mike, trike, pike...ike
Pot, dot, hot, not, lot, got...ot
Ball, call, hall, fall, tall, mall...all
Book, look, cook, hook, took, gook...ook

A Sailor Went to Sea (Traditional)
A sailor went to sea, sea, sea,
To see what he could see, see, see.
But all that he could see, see, see,
Was the bottom of the deep blue sea, sea, sea.

Say and Rhyme by Pam Schiller
Tune: "Mary Had a Little Lamb"
Rhyming words are lots of fun,
Lots of fun, lots of fun.
Rhyming words are easy to do
Join in and try a few.
When you say bread, I touch my head.
Touch my head, touch my head.
When you say bread, I touch my head,
Rhyming words—bread and ___!

Additional verses:
go—toe, bee—knee, dear—ear

Rhyming words are lots of fun,
Lots of fun, lots of fun.
Rhyming words are easy to do,
And now we know a few.

Sing a Song of Opposites by Pam Schiller
Tune: "Mary Had a Little Lamb"
This is big and this is small.
This is big; this is small,
This is big and this is small,
Sing along with me.

Additional verses:
This is tall and this is short....
This is up and this is down....
This is in and this is out....
This is happy and this is sad....
This is soft and this is hard....
This is fast and this is slow....
This is here and this is there....

Six White Ducks (Traditional)

Six white ducks that I once knew,
Fat ducks, skinny ducks, they were, too.
But the one little duck with the feather on her back,
She ruled the others with a quack, quack, quack!
Down to the river they would go,
Wibble, wobble, wibble, wobble all in a row.
But the one little duck with the feather on her back,
She ruled the others with a quack, quack, quack!

S-M-I-L-E (Traditional)

Tune: "The Battle Hymn of the Republic"

It isn't any trouble
Just to S-M-I-L-E.
It isn't any trouble
Just to S-M-I-L-E.
So smile when you're in trouble,
It will vanish like a bubble,
If you'll only take the trouble
Just to S-M-I-L-E.

It isn't any trouble
Just to L-A-U-G-H. (or ha-ha-ha-ha laugh)
It isn't any trouble
Just to L-A-U-G-H. (or ha-ha-ha-ha laugh)
So laugh when you're in trouble,
It will vanish like a bubble,
If you'll only take the trouble
Just to L-A-U-G-H. (or ha-ha-ha-ha laugh)

It isn't any trouble
Just to G-R-I-N, grin.
It isn't any trouble
Just to G-R-I-N, grin.
So grin when you're in trouble,
It will vanish like a bubble,
If you'll only take the trouble
Just to G-R-I-N, grin!

Ha! Ha! Ha! Ha! Ha! Ha!
Ha! Ha! Ha! Ha! Ha! Ha! Ha!
Ha! Ha! Ha! Ha! Ha! Ha!
Ha! Ha! Ha! Ha! Ha! Ha! Ha!
Ha! Ha! Ha! Ha! Ha! Ha!
Ha! Ha! Ha! Ha! Ha! Ha! Ha!
Ha! Ha! Ha! Ha! Ha! Ha! Ha! Ha! Ha!

This Little Light of Mine (Traditional)

This little light of mine
I'm gonna let it shine.

This little light of mine
I'm gonna let it shine.

This little light of mine
I'm gonna let it shine.

Let it shine, let it shine, let it shine.

Twinkle, Twinkle, Little Star (Traditional)

Twinkle, twinkle, little star,
How I wonder what you are!
Up above the world so high,
Like a diamond in the sky,
Twinkle, twinkle, little star,
How I wonder what you are!

When the blazing sun is set,
And the grass with dew is wet,
Then you show your little light,
Twinkle, twinkle, all the night.

The Weather Song (Traditional)

Tune: "Clementine"

Sunny, sunny
Sunny, sunny,
It is sunny in the sky.
S-u-n-n-y, sunny,
It is sunny in the sky.

Cloudy, cloudy,
Cloudy, cloudy,
It is cloudy in the sky.
C-l-o-u-d-y, cloudy,
It is cloudy in the sky.

Rainy, rainy,
Rainy, rainy,
It is rainy in the sky.
R-a-i-n-y, rainy,
It is rainy in the sky.

Foggy, foggy,
Foggy, foggy,
It is foggy in the sky.
F-o-g-g-y, foggy,
It is foggy in the sky.

What Goes Together? by Pam Schiller

Tune: "Itsy Bitsy Spider"
What goes together?
A button and a coat.
What goes together?
Grass and a goat.
What goes together?
A dog and a flea.
Putting things together,
Good friends like you and me.
(Repeat)

The Wheels on the Bus (Traditional)

The wheels on the bus go round and round.
Round and round, round and round.
The wheels on the bus go round and round,
All around the town.
The windshield wipers go swish, swish, swish.
The baby on the bus goes, "Wah, wah, wah."
The horn on the bus goes beep, beep, beep.
The money on the bus goes clink, clink, clink.

Where Is Thumbkin? (Traditional)

Where is Thumbkin?
Where is Thumbkin?
Here I am.
Here I am.
How are you today, sir?
Very well, I thank you.
Come and play.
Come and play.

Y-O-U Spells You by Pam Schiller

Tune: "Row, Row, Row Your Boat"
Y-O-U spells you,
And you are my friend
Y-O-U, Y-O-U,
Y-O-U spells you.

Zzzz! Zzzz! Snort! Snort! by Pam Schiller

Tune: "The Wheels on the Bus"
The firefly at night goes zzzz, zzzz, zzzz,
Zzzz, zzzz, zzzz, zzzz, zzzz, zzzz.
The firefly at night goes zzzz, zzzz, zzzz,
All around my yard.

Other verses:
The bees in the flowers go buzz, buzz, buzz…
The birds in the trees go chirp, chirp, chirp…
The cat on the porch goes meow, meow, meow…
The dog by the gate goes bow-wow-wow…
The pig in the pen goes snort, snort, snort…

Games and Dances

Go In and Out the Windows (Traditional)

Go in and out the windows, (IT walks around circle,
    weaving in and out between children)
Go in and out the windows,
Go in and out the windows,
As we have done before.

Additional verses:
Stand and face you partner… (IT chooses a partner)
Now follow her/him to London… (IT and partner
    weave through circle)
Bow before you leave her/him… (IT leaves partner
    [new IT] and joins circle)

Say and Touch (Traditional)

Say, "red" and touch your head.
Say, "sky" and touch your eye.
Say, "bear" and touch your hair.
Say, "hear" and touch your ear.
Say, "south" and touch your mouth.
Say, "rose" and touch your nose.
Say, "in" and touch your chin.
Say, "rest" and touch your chest.
Say, "farm" and touch your arm.
Say, "yummy" and touch your tummy.
Say, "bee" and touch your knee.
Say, "neat" and touch your feet.

Who Took the Cookies from the Cookie Jar? (Traditional)

Who took the cookies from the cookie jar?
(Child's name) *took the cookies from the cookie jar.*
Who me?
Yes, you.
Couldn't be.
Then who?
(Continue the game by allowing the child named in
    the first round to name another child.)

Chants and Rhymes

Animal Cookie Jar Chant (Traditional, adapted by Pam Schiller)

Clap syllables in animals' names.

Who took the cookies from the cookie jar?
Giraffe took the cookies from the cookie jar.
Clap Gir–affe? (clap the syllables)
Clap again. Gir–affe. (clap syllables again)
Giraffe took the cookies from the cookie jar.
Who me?
Yes, you.
Not me.
Then who?

Tiger took the cookies from the cookie jar.
Clap Ti–ger? (clap syllables)
Clap again, Ti–ger? (clap syllables again)
Tiger took the cookies form the cookie jar.
Who me?
Yes, you.
Not me.
Then who?

Seal took the cookies from the cookie jar.
Clap Seal? (clap syllables)
Clap again, Seal? (clap syllables again)
Seal took the cookies from the cookie jar.
Who me?
Yes, you.
Not me.
Then who?

Continue with:
Elephant (el–e–phant)
Dinosaur (di–no–saur)
Hippopotamus (hip–po–pot–a–mus)

End with:
Cookie Monster!
Cookie Monster?

Bo-bo Ski Watten Totten (Traditional)

Bo-bo ski watten totten,
Ah-ah-ah, boom boom boom,
Itty bitty wotten totten,
Bo-bo ski watten tatten,
Bo-bo ski wotten tatten—BOOM.

Chim, Chimmy Chimpanzee by Pam Schiller

Provide rhythm sticks. Encourage children to tap the words in each sentence, as directed in the chant.

Chim, chimmy chimpanzee
Won't you tap along with me?
Tap–Chim (children repeat each of the following lines)
Tap–Chim chews
Tap–Chim chews cheese
Tap–Chim chews cheese chunks.
Tap–Silly, silly Chimpanzee!

Kate, Katie kangaroo
Will you help tap along too?
Tap–Kate (children repeat each of the following lines)
Tap–Kate wears
Tap–Kate wears pink
Tap–Kate wears pink pajamas!
Tap–Silly, silly kangaroo.

Buzz, buzzy bumblebee,
Won't you tap along with me?
Tap–Buzz (children repeat each of the following lines)
Tap–Buzz bathes
Tap–Buzz bathes in
Tap–Buzz bathes in bubbles.
Tap–Silly, silly bumblebee.

Invite the children to help make up additional sentences to tap.

The Elephant Goes (author unknown)

The elephant goes (move around slowly on all fours)
Like this, like that.
He's terribly big, (standing up, reach arms high)
And he's terribly fat. (stretch arms out to the sides to
    show how fat elephant is)
He has no fingers. (fisted hands, hiding fingers)
He has no toes. (wiggle toes)
But goodness gracious,
What a nose! (thumb to nose and wiggle fingers, as if
    extending trunk)

Five Little Sparrows by Pam Schiller

Five sparrows sitting on a limb
First one said, "The sun's growing dim."
Second one said, "There's a chill in the air."
The third one said, "We don't care."
The second one said, "Let's fly! Let's fly!"
The first one said, "Why, why, why?"
Then swoosh went the wind with a pitter-patter
    splash,
And the five little sparrows were gone in a flash.

Flea Fly Flow (Traditional)

Flea fly
Flea fly flow
Flea fly flow mosquito
Oh no-no, no more mosquitoes
Itchy itchy, scratchy scratchy, ooh I got one down my
    backy!
Eet biddly oatten boatten boe boe boe ditten dotten
Wye doan choo oo
Chase that
Big bad bug
Make it go away!
SHOO! SHOO!

The Fly and the Flea (Traditional)

A fly and a flea in a flue (clap, clap)
Were caught, so what could they do? (clap, clap)
"Let us fly," said the flea.
"Let us flee," said the fly.
So they flew through a flaw in the flue. (clap, clap)

Have You Ever? (Traditional)

Have you ever, ever, ever, in your long-legged life
Met a long-legged sailor with a long-legged wife?
No, I never, never, never, in my long-legged life
Met a long-legged sailor with a long-legged wife.

Additional verses:
Have you ever, ever, ever, in your short-legged life…
…pigeon-toed wife…
…bow-legged wife…

Hey, Diddle, Diddle (Traditional)

Hey diddle diddle,
The cat and the fiddle.
The cow jumped over the moon.
The little dog laughed to see such a sight.
And the dish ran away with the spoon.

Hickey Picky Bumblebee (Traditional)

Hickey, picky bumblebee,
Won't you say your name to me? (point to a child)
Evan (child says his name)
Evan (group repeats name)
Let's clap it.
Ev-an (clap syllables)
Let's snap it.
Ev-an (snap syllables)
Let's tap it
Ev-an (tap syllables)
Hickey, picky bumblebee, (repeat chant)
Won't you say your name to me?

Repeat with another child.

Hickory, Dickory, Dock (Traditional)

Hickory, dickory, dock,
The mouse ran up the clock.
The clock struck one,
The mouse ran down.
Hickory, dickory, dock.

Humpty Dumpty (Traditional)

Humpty Dumpty sat on a wall.
Humpty Dumpty had a great fall.
All the King's horses and all the King's men
Couldn't put Humpty together again.

I Had a Little Puppy (Traditional, adapted by Pam Schiller)

I had a little puppy; his name was Tiny Tim,
I put him in the bathtub to see if he could swim,
He drank all the water; he ate a bar of soap,
The next thing you know he had a bubble in his throat.
In came the doctor,
In came the nurse,
In came the lady with the alligator purse.
Out went the doctor,
Out went the nurse,
Out went the lady with the alligator purse.

I'm a Bouncing Ball (Traditional)

I'm bouncing, bouncing everywhere.
I bounce and bounce into the air.
I'm bouncing, bouncing like a ball.
I bounce and bounce until I fall.

I Took a Trip (author unknown)

I took a trip on a boat.
I packed myself a goat.
I took a trip in a car.
I packed myself a star.
I took a trip on a plane.
I packed myself a cane.

If you took a trip in a boat
What would you pack?
If you took a trip in a car
What would you pack?
If you took a trip on a plane
What would you pack?

Miss Mary Mack (Traditional)

Miss Mary Mack, Mack, Mack,
All dressed in black, black, black,
With silver buttons, buttons, buttons,
All down her back, back, back.

She asked her mother, mother, mother,
For fifteen cents, cents, cents
To see the elephants, elephants, elephants,
Jump the fence, fence, fence.
They jumped so high, high, high,
They touched the sky, sky, sky,
And they didn't come back, back, back
'Til the fourth of July, ly, ly.
And they didn't come down, down, down
'Til the fourth of July, ly, ly.

One Potato (Traditional)

One potato, two potato,
Three potato, four,
Five potato, six potato,
Seven potato, more.
Eight potato, nine potato,
Where is ten?
Now we must count over again.

Peas Porridge Hot (Traditional)

Peas porridge hot,
Peas porridge cold,
Peas porridge in the pot
Nine days old.
Some like it hot,
Some like it cold,
Some like it in the pot
Nine days old.

Saying Goodbye by Pam Schiller

First I kiss my mom goodbye, (blow a kiss)
And then I hug her tight. (hug self)
Then just before she's out of sight,
I wave goodbye with all my might. (wave
    enthusiastically)

Teddy Bear, Teddy Bear (Traditional)

Teddy bear, teddy bear,
Turn around.
Teddy bear, teddy bear,
Touch the ground.
Teddy bear, teddy bear,
Touch your shoe.
Teddy bear, teddy bear,
Say how-di-do.
Teddy bear, teddy bear,
Go up the stairs.
Teddy bear, teddy bear,
Say your prayers.
Turn out the light.
Say goodnight.

Who Is Traipsing on My Bridge?
   by Pam Schiller

Who is traipsing on my bridge?
Trip, trap, trip, trap! Get off my bridge!
No one should be traipsing there.
Get off! Get off! Don't you dare!

Words and Letters by Pam Schiller

Words and letters all around,
They're everywhere I look—
License plates and names on cars
And in my favorite book.
Words and letters all around,
Signs that tell us when to "Stop,"
Letters on my best T-shirt,
And breakfast cereal box.
Letters here and letters there,
I'm learning them one by one.
And when I know them A to Z
I'll have some reading fun.

Stories

Abby the Tabby by Pam Schiller

My cat Abby loves to be scratched behind her ears and under her chin. It makes her purr because she is happy (purr).

She also loves to play. I dangle a piece of yarn and she bats it with her paw. Playing makes her happy (purr).

Abby does not like it when our neighbor's puppy comes over to play. She hisses at him when he gets too rough. The sight of him makes Abby very unhappy (hiss).

On sunny days, Abby lies on the floor by the window and enjoys the warmth of the sun. Lying there, she is content and happy (purr).

When we take Abby to the vet, she is really unhappy (hiss). She does not like to ride in the car. Mommy says it makes her feel sick.

When Abby is happy (purr) she is so much fun. When she is unhappy (hiss) she is not so much fun. But it doesn't matter to me. I love my cat Abby, happy (purr) or unhappy (hiss). She is my best friend.

A Weather Story by Pam Schiller

Directions: Have the children sit on the floor. Give half of them sticks and the other half ribbons. Tell them that they are to listen for specific words in the story. Those with sticks should tap their sticks when they hear the words "walk," "run," and "thunder," and those with ribbons should shake their ribbons when they hear the words "wind," "rain," and "lightning." Here are specific directions for using the sticks and ribbons with specific words:

Raindrops: Ribbons shake slowly (swoosh— swoosh—swoosh)

Wind: Ribbons shake quickly (swoosh, swoosh, swoosh)

Lightning: Ribbons shake very quickly (swoosh- swoosh, swoosh-swoosh, swoosh-swoosh)

Walk: Sticks tap slowly (tap—tap—tap)

Run: Sticks tap faster (tap, tap, tap)

Thunder: Sticks tap together (tap-tap, tap-tap, tap-tap)

Narrator: *Everyone sit down on the floor and listen carefully. Sticks tap when you hear "walk," "run," or "thunder." Ribbons shake when you hear "wind," "rain," or "lightning."*

The children were excited. It was time to play outdoors. They walked (tap—tap—tap—tap) *to their lockers to put on their coats, mittens, and hats. Then, they ran* (tap, tap, tap).

The wind (swoosh, swoosh, swoosh) *was strong. It blew hard against them. The children had a difficult time walking* (tap—tap—tap—tap).

The wind (swoosh, swoosh, swoosh) *blew the swings crooked. The children decided to try the slide instead. They climbed up the ladder. When they went down the slide, the wind* (swoosh, swoosh, swoosh) *pushed them faster.*

Some of the children rode on the tricycles. Other children ran (tap, tap, tap) *after the ball. The wind* (swoosh, swoosh, swoosh) *pushed them as they rode and as they ran* (tap, tap, tap).

Suddenly the children began to feel raindrops (swoosh—swoosh—swoosh). *The children ran* (tap, tap, tap) *inside. Just in time. Because, just when they closed the door and looked out the window, they saw lightning* (swoosh-swoosh, swoosh-swoosh, swoosh-swoosh) *streak across the sky and they heard a big clap of thunder* (TAP-TAP, TAP-TAP, TAP-TAP!).

Patterns and Teacher-Made Materials

Graph for Name Comparisons in Chapter 4

Child's Name	1	2	3	4	5	6	7	8	9	10	11	12	

Alphabet Tally Sheet for Letter Walk in Chapter 4

Make several copies of the recording sheet. Place one of the recording sheets on a clip board.

A												
B												
C												
D												
E												
F												
G												
H												
I												
J												
K												
L												
M												
N												
O												
P												
Q												
R												
S												
T												
U												
V												
W												
X												
Y												
Z												

Head, Shoulders, Knees, and Toes Rebus

The publisher grants permission for this page to be photocopied for teachers' classroom use only.
© Gryphon House, Inc. 800-638-0928. www.gryphonhouse.com

Trail Mix

Count 5 marshmallows,

5 pretzels,

5 pieces of cereal

and 5 peanuts.

Put into a plastic cup.

Enjoy!

What Am I? Game Cards

Directions: To make What Am I? game cards, cut six or eight sheets of white poster board in half. Cut an oval the size of a child's face on one half of each half-sheet of poster board. Glue a simple photo of a butterfly, a cow, a dog, a book, or any other object on the other half of each sheet of poster board. Place the cards face down. Ask a volunteer to draw a card and, without looking at the photo side, put the card in front of her face. Encourage the volunteer to ask her classmates questions that will help her know what is pictured on the cards. All questions must have only a yes-or-no response.

Letter Finder

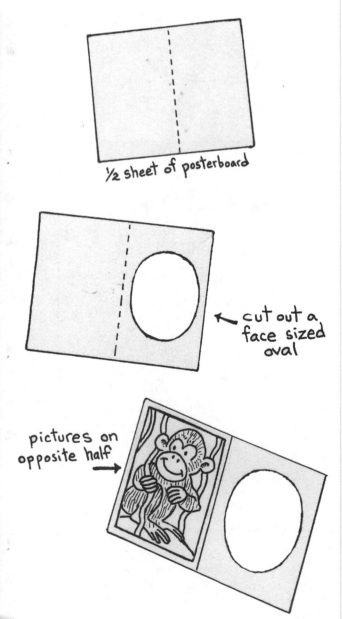

½ sheet of posterboard

← cut out a face sized oval

pictures on opposite half →

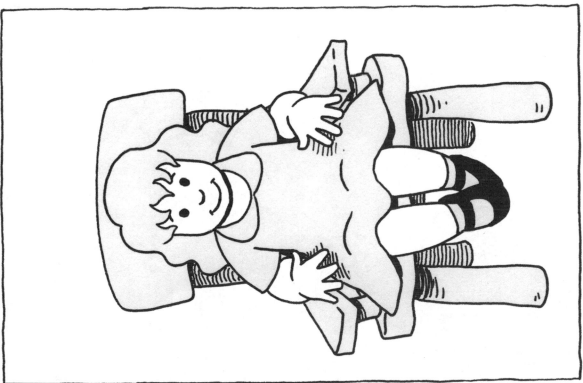

Three Billy Goats Gruff Stick Puppet Patterns

Prop Boxes

Baby: baby dolls and clothes, blankets, baby bottles, rattles, pacifiers, teethers, diapers, diaper bag, empty baby powder container, bibs, towels, washcloths

Beach: towels, sunglasses, hats, radio, swimsuits, beach ball, cooler/ice chest, buckets, pails, sand tools/scoops, beach chairs, empty suntan lotion bottles, tapes with ocean sounds, beach bags, swim fins, face mask, snorkel tubes, seashells

Beauty Salon or Barber Shop: telephone, appointment book, pencils, combs, brushes, mirrors, hair clips, towels, cape, play scissors (that don't cut), empty shampoo, conditioner and hairspray bottles, curlers, barrettes, no-pull ponytail fasteners, dolls with hair, broom, dustpan, chair, plastic tub for washing hair, hair dryer (remove the cord), magazines, cash register, money

Camping: sleeping bags, pillows, logs, wood, backpacks, flashlights, tent, cooking utensils, canteen, binoculars, plastic picnic set, small cooler

Firefighters: hats, yellow raincoats, black boots, oxygen tanks*, goggles, hose

Grocery Store: bags, cart, empty food containers, plastic fruits and vegetables, baskets, money, cash register, money, pretend credit cards, checkbook, signs, coupons, telephone

Hospital: white doctors' coats (cut arms off an adult-size white shirt), stethoscope, medical bag, tongue depressors, shower caps (for surgeon caps), bandages, gauze, medicine bottles, toy medical kit

Magician: magic wand, hat, gloves, cape, stuffed rabbit and birds, flowers, scarves, cards, boxes, table

Office Worker: writing pads, pencils, phone, phonebook, phone message pads, keyboard, folders, stapler, paper clips, envelopes, stamps, stamp pads, table for a desk, briefcase

Restaurant: hats, aprons, cups, straws, napkins, menus, order pads and pencils, play dishes from house area, serving tray, plastic food, cash register, money

School: chalkboard, chalk and erasers, report cards, calendar, clock, stickers, workbooks, notebooks, paper, pencils, crayons, stapler, books, table and chairs

Space: helmet, costume, moon rocks, spaceship (painted boxes), flag, dried food packets (granola), oxygen tanks*, hose

Western: straw hats, bandanas, boots, vest, ropes, cowboy shirts, chaps, saddle, stick horses, campfire logs, metal pots and pans, blanket, sleeping bag

* Oxygen tanks for divers, firefighters, and astronauts can be created using two-liter plastic pop bottles taped or glued together. Add clear plastic tubing. Attach loops of ribbon to create a backpack.

Letter Cards

Preparation

Make Letter Cards—print one letter of the alphabet onto each sheet of 4" x 8" tag board using uppercase letters only. Make Sandpaper Letter Cards—using upper- and lowercase magnetic letters as templates, trace each letter onto a piece of sandpaper. Cut out each letter to create sandpaper letters. Make Tactile Letter Cards—make a second set of sandpaper letters and glue them onto small index cards. Make Tactile Playdough—mix two teaspoons of sand into a traditional playdough recipe.

KWL Chart

What We Know	What We Want to Know	What We Learned

© Gryphon House, Inc. 800-638-0928. www.gryphonhouse.com

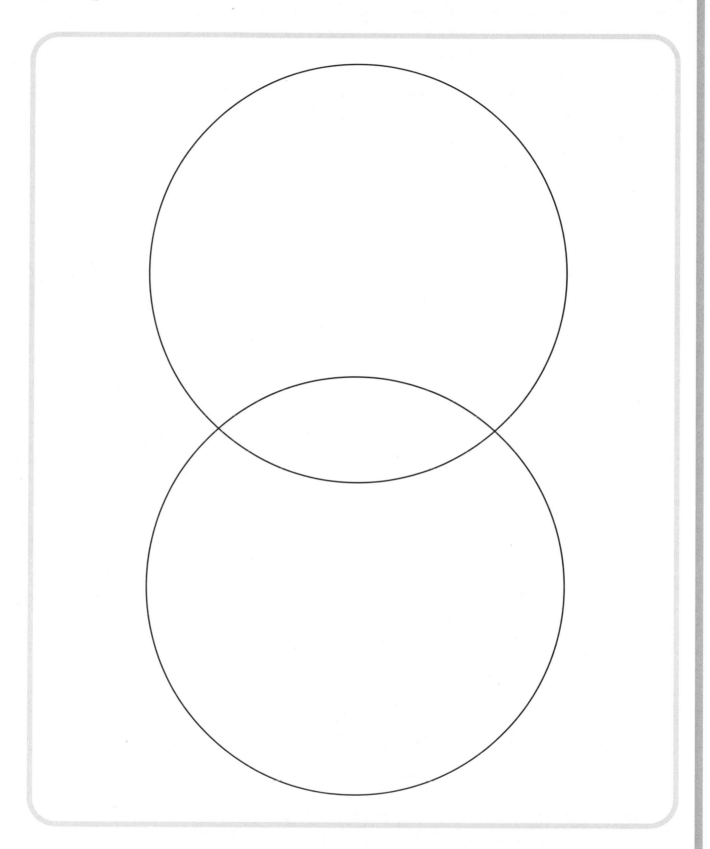

Story Maps

Story maps help children understand the organization and structure of a story. In narrative text, there is a setting, one or more characters, a sequence of events, and usually some type of problem the character or characters solve. There is a plot and a theme. Story maps help children see how the parts of a story make up the whole story. Children need many experiences with story maps. On the following two pages are three different styles of story maps you may want to use, or you can develop your own.

Story Map #1

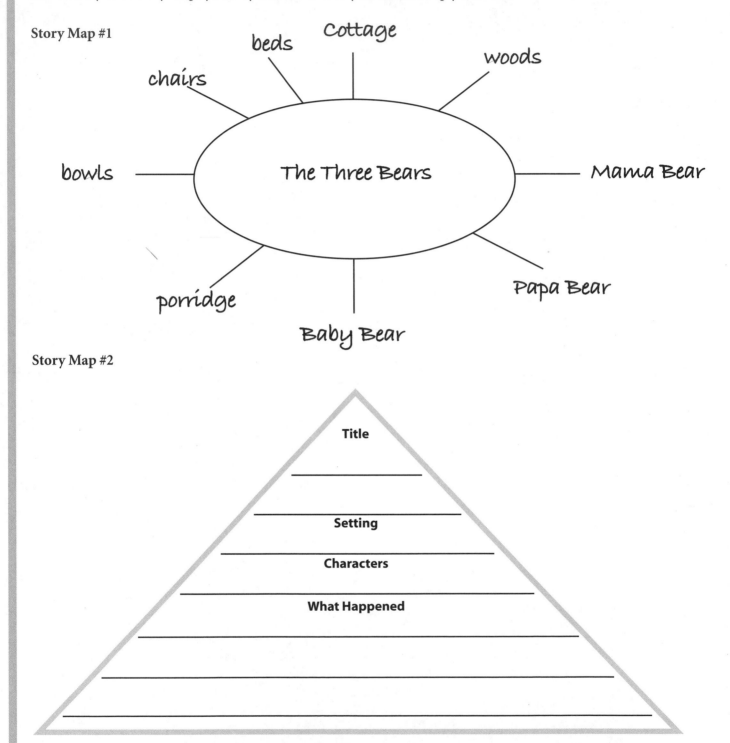

Story Map #2

Story Maps

Title: _____

Author: _____

Theme: _____

Plot
_____

Characters
_____

Setting
_____

Conflict
_____

Resolution
_____

Writing Continuum

As children begin to form letters, use this guide to determine where they are on the writing continuum. Place a copy of this form in each child's observation folder. Use the models when assigning numerical labels to work samples.

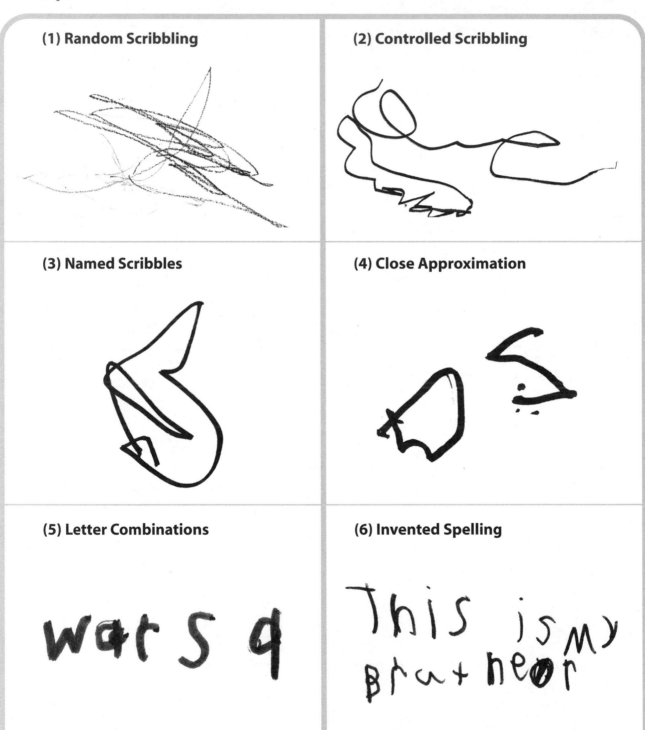

(1) Random Scribbling

(2) Controlled Scribbling

(3) Named Scribbles

(4) Close Approximation

(5) Letter Combinations

(6) Invented Spelling

Literacy Checklist

Child's Name: _____

Date of Birth: _____

Classroom: _____

School: _____

Observation Dates

1. _____ to _____
2. _____ to _____
3. _____ to _____
4. _____ to _____

Key

N: Not currently performing

O: Occasionally performing

C: Consistently performing

Objectives/Head Start Outcomes		Recording Periods			
Listening		1	2	3	4
1. Listens with increasing attention.	Demonstrates increasing ability to attend to and understand conversations, stories, songs, and poems.				
2. Listens for different purposes.					
3. Responds accurately to questions following a story.					
4. Follows simple oral directions.	Shows progress in understanding and following simple and multiple-step directions.				
Oral Language/Speaking and Communicating		1	2	3	4
5. Engages in conversation.					
6. Experiments with the sounds of language.					
7. Shows a steady increase in listening and speaking vocabulary.	Understands an increasingly complex and varied vocabulary.				
8. Refines and extends understanding of known words.	Uses an increasingly complex and varied spoken vocabulary.				
9. Attempts to use communication beyond current vocabulary.					
10. Uses new vocabulary, when introduced.					

Literacy Checklist (continued)

Objectives/Head Start Outcomes		Recording Periods			
Oral Language/Speaking and Communicating		1	2	3	4
11. Uses language for a variety of purposes.	Develops increasing abilities to understand and use language to communicate information, experiences, ideas, feelings, opinions, needs, and questions and for other varied purposes.				
12. Uses sentences of increasing length.	Progresses in clarity of pronunciation and toward speaking in sentences of increasing length and grammatical complexity.				
13. Tells a simple personal narrative.					
14. Uses language for familiar routines.					
15. Asks questions and makes comments during class discussions.	Progresses in abilities to initiate and respond appropriately to conversation and discussion with peers and adults.				
16. Engages in conversation following conversational rules.					
17. Retells the sequence of a story.					
Segmentation		1	2	3	4
18. Breaks sentences into words using claps, taps, and snaps.					
19. Breaks words into syllables, using claps, taps, and snaps for syllable breaks.	Shows growing ability to hear and discriminate separate syllables in words.				
Phonological Awareness		1	2	3	4
20. Recognizes differences between similar sounding words.	Progresses in recognizing matching sounds and rhymes in familiar words, games, songs, stories, and poems.				
21. Shows sensitivity to the sounds of spoken words.	Shows increasing ability to discriminate and identify sounds in spoken language.				
22. Recognizes and uses onomatopoeic words.					
23. Begins to identify rhymes and rhyming words.					

Literacy Checklist (continued)

Objectives/Head Start Outcomes		Recording Periods			
Phonological Awareness		1	2	3	4
24. Begins to attend to beginning sounds of familiar words (for example, alliteration and onset of rhyme).	Associates sounds with written words, such as awareness that different words begin with the same sound.				
Book Knowledge and Appreciation		1	2	3	4
25. Understands that reading and writing are ways to obtain and communicate thoughts.	Shows growing interest and involvement in listening to and discussing a variety of fiction and nonfiction books and poetry.				
26. Demonstrates an interest in books; asks to have a favorite book reread; engages in pretend reading; demonstrates delight in story time; imitates the special language of books.	Shows growing interest in reading-related activities, such as asking to have a favorite book read, choosing to look at books, drawing pictures based on stories, asking to take books home, going to the library, and engaging in pretend reading with other children.				
27. Enjoys listening to and discussing stories.					
28. Begins to predict what will happen next.					
29. Chimes in with predictable text.					
30. Asks questions pertaining to the story.					
Comprehension		1	2	3	4
31. Retells stories in own words. Acts stories out.	Demonstrates progress in abilities to retell and dictate stories from books and experiences, to act out stories in dramatic play, and to predict what will happen next in a story.				
32. Understands the difference between letters and numbers.					
33. Responds accurately to thinking questions following a story.					

Literacy Checklist (continued)

Objectives/Head Start Outcomes		Recording Periods					
34. Understands that illustrations carry meaning but cannot be read.	Demonstrates increasing awareness of concepts of print, such as that reading in English moves from top to bottom and from left to right, that speech can be written down, and that print conveys a message.						
35. Understands that print carries a message (for example, labels, lists, signs).							
36. Understands that print moves from top to bottom and left to right.							
37. Handles books appropriately (for example, holds books correctly, turns pages in correct sequence).	Progresses in learning how to handle and care for books—knowing to view one page at a time in sequence from front to back, and understanding that a book has a title, author, and illustrator.						
38. Understands that books have a title, author, and illustrator.							
39. Follows print when it is read.	Shows progress in recognizing the association between spoken and written words by following print as it is read aloud.						
40. Understands conventions of print (for example, groups of letters make up words, words are separated by spaces).	Recognizes a word as a unit of print, or awareness that letters are grouped to form words, and that words are separated by spaces.						
41. Understands the function of print, (for example, text, lists, labels, and so on).	Develops growing understanding of different function or forms of print, such as signs, letters, newspapers, lists, messages, and menus.						
	Shows increasing awareness of print in classroom, home, and community settings.						
42. Begins to identify letters.	Knows that letters of the alphabet are a special category of visual graphics that can be individually named.						
43. Identifies 10 or more letters.	Identifies at least 10 letters of the alphabet, especially those in own name.						
44. Recognizes letters in words.	Increases in ability to notice the beginning letters in familiar words.						

Literacy Checklist (continued)

Objectives/Head Start Outcomes		Recording Periods			
Letter Knowledge		1	2	3	4
45. Begins to match letters and sounds.	Shows progress in associating the names of letters with their shapes and sounds.				
46. Recognizes some familiar words (for example, *Mommy, me, Daddy*).					
Early Writing		1	2	3	4
47. Attempts to write messages as part of play.	Develops understanding that writing is a way of communicating for a variety of purposes.				
48. Uses a variety of tools for writing.	Experiments with a growing variety of writing tools and materials, such as pencils, crayons, and computers.				
49. Uses letter approximations to communicate (for example, writes name on papers).	Progresses from using scribbles, shapes, or pictures to represent ideas to using letter-like symbols to copying or writing familiar words, such as own name.				
50. Dictates words, phrases, and sentences (for example, letter writing, labeling, storytelling).	Begins to represent stories and experiences through pictures, dictation, and play.				

Index of Children's Books

Index

A

Adapted crayons, 207
Adapted markers, 207
Adaptive handles, 54, 73, 93, 127, 147
    making, 251
Adaptive pulls, 109
Adaptive sticks, 159
Adaptive switches, 23, 49
    purchasing, 250
Adaptive walkers, 22, 45, 217
Adjectives. *See* Descriptive language
Advertisements, 86, 180, 194, 222
Alliteration, 10–12, 105, 130, 132, 134, 136
    books that support, 154
    defined, 245
Alphabet posters, 84
Alphabet wall cards, 158, 162
Analysis, 230, 240
Animals
    plastic, 114, 122, 140
    stuffed, 39, 65, 68, 143, 157, 200, 237, 280
    toy, 143
Appointment books, 280
Art center, 38, 60, 208
    materials, 246
Articulation disorder, 24
    defined, 245
Assessment, 245
Astronaut costumes, 280
Attention span, 10, 13, 21, 33, 71, 135, 157, 161, 227
Attribute blocks, 62
Attributes, 62, 80, 243
    defined, 245
Audio recorders. *See* Recording devices
Autism spectrum disorder, 24–26, 45, 75, 83, 101, 103, 117, 125, 137, 165, 169, 179, 209, 213
    adaptations for, 26
    defined, 245
    sensory integration issues, 26

B

Baby talk, 23
Backpacks, 28, 280
Bags, 62, 114, 192
    beach, 280
    diaper, 280
    gift, 61
    lunch, 140
    medical, 280

    paper, 114, 122, 138, 166, 174, 180, 130, 280
    zippered plastic, 88, 98, 178
Balls, 70, 72, 96, 117–118, 152, 205
    beach, 280
    tennis, 57
    therapy, 26, 28–29, 109
Baskets, 44, 62, 64, 68, 72, 116, 118, 142, 144, 146, 152, 181, 186, 208, 232, 280
Beads, 136, 190, 198, 208
Beanbag chairs, 26, 28–29, 109, 119, 239
Beanbags, 36, 46, 76, 202
Behavioral/social-emotional issues, 25–26
Bells, 44, 46, 49, 107, 111, 113, 121, 129, 135, 171
Bilingual instruction, 245
Blindfolds, 40
Block center, 47, 126, 140, 234, 211
    materials, 246
Blocks, 76–77, 116–118, 130, 136, 146, 156, 160, 176, 190, 200, 208, 234
    attribute, 62
    letter building, 176
Bloodgood, J. W., 30
Book lights, 16, 225
Books, 34, 52, 77, 90, 98, 106, 142, 200, 202, 222, 224, 237, 280
    about dogs, 64
    large print, 250
    multilingual, 154
    on tape, 250
    picture dictionaries, 220
    wordless, 224
Bottles
    baby, 280
    hairspray, 280
    pill, 36, 118, 280
    plastic, 280
    shampoo, 280
Bowls, 134
Box lids, 49
Boxes, 52, 60, 76–77, 86, 92, 115, 128, 131, 146, 150, 172–173, 209–210, 280
    cardboard, 249
    prop, 92, 280
    shoe, 115
    word, 212
Braille, 15
Brain research, 9
    defined, 245
Buckets, 114, 280
Bulletin board paper, 204
Bullying, 14
Burgess, S. R., 30

  ■ **Inclusive Literacy Lessons for Early Childhood** ■